TCP/IP and
Related Protocols

Related Titles

To order or receive additional information on these or any other McGraw-Hill titles, in the United States please call 1-800-822-8158. In other countries, contact your local McGraw-Hill representative.

TCP/IP and Related Protocols

Uyless Black

Second Edition

McGraw-Hill, Inc.
New York San Francisco Washington, D.C. Auckland Bogotá
Caracas Lisbon London Madrid Mexico City Milan
Montreal New Delhi San Juan Singapore
Sydney Tokyo Toronto

Library of Congress Cataloging-in-Publication Data

Black, Uyless.
  TCP/IP & related protocols / by Uyless Black. — 2nd ed.
    p. cm.
  Includes index.
  ISBN 0-07-005560-2
  1. TCP/IP (Computer network protocol) 2. Computer network
protocols. I. Title. II. Title: TCP/IP and related protocols.
TK5105.55.B53 1994
004.6'2—dc20   94-37669
                                                                    CIP

hc 1 2 3 4 5 6 7 8 9 0 DOC/DOC 9 8 7 6 5 4

ISBN 0-07-005560-2

*The sponsoring editor of this book was Brad J. Schepp, the supervising
editor was Lori Flaherty, the book editor was Theresa Burke, and the
production supervisor was Katherine G. Brown. It was set in ITC
Century Light. It was composed by TAB Books, Blue Ridge Summit, Pa.*

Printed and bound by Donnelley & Sons Company.

To Ross Black, my brother and role model

Contents

Chapter 3. Naming, Addressing, and Routing in an Internet   39

Preface

I became involved with TCP/IP a few years ago when a client asked me to examine the feasibility of operating X.25 with the TCP/IP protocols. At about the same time, another client of mine had received an IP-like protocol in a LAN package and asked me to evaluate its performance capabilities.

At that time, I had experience in several aspects of data communications networks. My background was principally in SNA, X.25, X.75, SDLC, LAPB, the V Series specifications, and the design of packet switching topologies to support connection-oriented network interfaces.

As I began to unravel the TCP/IP operations, I was struck by: (1) how fast TCP/IP operated (in comparison to X.25) and (2) how little it did. Yet, TCP/IP served the basic needs of my clients.

As I learned more about the operations of TCP/IP, I was also struck by the wealth of related standards that I could not find in the Open Systems Interconnection (OSI) suite. As examples, address mapping and route discovery were well established in TCP/IP but simply were not available in the CCITT and ISO standards. I was very pleasantly surprised to find many of these related protocols readily available in the marketplace.

I also found the documentation the TCP/IP protocols easy to read and assimilate, but in some instances, incomplete and incorrect. This gap in the TCP/IP specifications made my introduction to TCP/IP an interesting one to say the least.

In one respect, I have found the use of the TCP/IP protocols (and their rapid growth) has made my life easier because of the ability of my clients to work with common communications protocols. Ironically, in another respect, the success of TCP/IP has made my life (and the lives of many of my clients) more difficult because of the problems TCP/IP presents to the migration to the OSI Model. I have more to say about this issue later in the book.

In the past few years, my clients have asked me to evaluate the TCP/IP suite for use on numerous other systems: the OSI suite, ISDN, frame relay,

SMDS, etc. I provide you with my TCP/IP background because you should know that I consider myself a user of TCP/IP and not a developer. This book reflects this user-oriented view. It also reflects the fact that most of my experience with TCP/IP is with its use on private networks.

Intended Audience

This book is written for the reader who is a newcomer to the TCP/IP suite of protocols, or a person who is interested in filling in some gaps about these protocols. For the more advanced reader, I highly recommend Volume II of *Internetworking with TCP/IP* by Douglas E. Comer (Prentice Hall, Inc.).

Some of the protocols associated with TCP/IP are not communications protocols and reside in a conventional applications layer of a layered protocol model. The emphasis of this book is on the lower communications layers of the TCP/IP standards with an overview of the applications layer.

Insofar as possible, the book is designed to be modular in that the reader can skip around the chapters without loss of continuity. It should also be emphasized that this book assumes the reader has a basic understanding of data communications systems and computer networks. Therefore, the book does not spend time discussing aspects of modems, why communications systems are used or needed, the rationale for layered protocols, and so on.

I believe I am correct in stating that I was the second author to write a text on TCP/IP. Douglas Comer's fine text was the first. My emphasis was (and remains the same in this second edition) on the lower layer protocols of the Internet suite of protocols, and secondarily on the Internet. My day-to-day work is with clients who are designing and developing software for private and commercial products that use TCP/IP and related protocols. This edition reflects my experience.

How times change. I visited a bookstore not too long ago and found more than 15 books on the Internet. However, the books focus on just how to use the Internet; my focus is on how to use TCP/IP.

Uyless Black
The Shenandoah Valley area, Virginia

Acknowledgments

The many individuals who participated in the development and nurturing of the TCP/IP suite of protocols deserve a medal. The pioneering efforts of the these individuals have paved the way for the acceptance of standardized communications protocols and the sharing of valuable information about internetworking. Their efforts have solved many problems that heretofore were not being addressed in the data communications network industry. Their efforts have also paved the way for numerous international standards.

On a personal note, I owe thanks to many programmers, designers, and engineers who have listened to my ideas about how network and transport protocols should operate. I also owe them many thanks for their input that led to the creation of this book.

Acronyms

ABM	asynchronous balanced mode
ACK	positive acknowledgment
ACSE	association control service element
AFI	authority format identifier
ARP	address resolution protocol
AS	autonomous system
ASN.1	Abstract Syntax Notation One
ATM	asynchronous transfer mode
AUI	attachment unit interface
BER	basic encoding rules
BGP	border gateway protocol
BISDN	broadband ISDN
BIU	bus interface unit
BOOTP	bootstrap protocol
CATV	coaxial cable TV
CLNP	connectionless network protocol
CMIP	common management information protocol
CMOT	common management information services and protocol over TCP/IP
CR	carriage return
CRC	cyclic redundancy check
CSMA/CD	carrier sense, multiple access collision detection
DA	destination address
DBUR	designated backup routers
DNIC	data network identification code
DNS	domain name system
DPA	destination physical address
DQDB	distributed-queue-dual-bus
DSAP	destination service access point

DSP	domain-specific part
DSU	digital service unit
DTE	data terminal equipment
DTP	data transfer protocol
EGP	external gateway protocol
EOT	end of transmission
FCS	frame-check sequence
FDDI	fiber distributed data interface
FF	form feed
FNC	Federal Networking Council
FTAM	file transfer and access management
FTP	file transfer protocol
GGP	gateway-to-gateway protocol
GOES	geosynchronous orbiting environmental satellite
GOSIP	U.S. Government OSI Profile
HDLC	high-level data link control
HF	high frequency
HMP	host monitoring protocol
I	information (field)
I/G	individual/group (address bit)
IAB	Internet Advisory Board
IAC	interpret as command
ICMP	internet control message protocol
IDI	initial domain identifier
IDP	initial domain part
IEEE	Institute of Electrical & Electronics Engineers
IETF	Internet Engineering Task Force
IGMP	Internet group management protocol
IGP	internal gateway protocol
IMP	interface message processor
INOC	Internet Network Operations Center
IP	internet protocol
IPDU	internetwork PDU
IPX	Internet packet exchange protocol
IRTF	Internet Research Task Force
ISDN	integrated services digital network
ISO	International Standards Organization
ISS	initial send sequence
ITU-T	International Telecommunication Union— Telecommunication Standardization Sector
IWU	internetworking unit
IVD	integrated voice/data
LAN	local area network
LAPB	link access protocol, balanced

LCP	link control protocol
LF	line feed
LF	low frequency
LLC	logical link control
LPP	lightweight presentation protocol
LSAP	link service access point
LSDU	link service data unit
MAC	media access control
MAN	metropolitan area network
MAU	medium attachment unit
MCF	MAC convergence function
MDI	medium dependent interface
MIB	Management Information Base
MTU	maximum transmission unit
MX	mail exchange
NAK	negative acknowledgment
NCC	network control center
NFS	network file system
NIC	Network Information Center
NIST	National Institute of Standards and Technology
NN	national number
NS	name server
NSAP	network service access point
NTN	network terminal number
NTP	network time protocol
NVT	network virtual terminal
OSI	Open Systems Interconnection
OSPF	open shortest path first
OUI	organization unique identifier
PA	prearbitrated (access)
PAD	packet assembly and disassembly
PARC	Palo Alto Research Center
PCI	protocol control information
PDN	public data networks
PDU	protocol data unit
PL	physical layer
PLP	packet layer procedures
PMA	physical medium attachment
PT	processing time
QA	queued-arbitrated (access)
QOS	quality of service
RARP	reverse address resolution protocol
RD	receive delay
RDN	relative distinguished name

RER	residual error rate
RFCs	Request for Comments
RIP	routing information protocol
RN	relative name
RNR	receive not ready
ROSE	remote operations service element
RPC	remote procedure call
RR	resource record
RRQ	read request or receive not ready
RTT	round-trip time
SABM	set asynchronous balanced mode
SAP	service application point
SDH	synchronous digital hierarchy
SD	send delay
SDLC	synchronous data link control
SEQ	sequence (field)
SFD	start frame delimiter
SGMP	simple gateway monitoring protocol
SIP	simple internet protocol
SMDS	Switched Multimegabit Data Service
SMI	Structure for Management Information
SNAP	subnetwork access protocol
SNMP	simple network management protocol
SOA	zone authority format
SRI	Stanford Research Institute
SRTT	smoothed round trip time
SSAP	source service access point
STDM	statistical time division multiplexing
TCB	transmission control block
TCP	transmission control protocol
TID	transfer identifier
TLV	type, length, and value
TOS	type-of-service (field)
TP4	transport protocol class 4
TP0	transport Protocol Class 0
TTL	time-to-live
TUBA	TCP & UDP with bigger addresses
U/L	universal/local (bit)
UDP	user datagram protocol
UI	unnumbered frame
ULP	upper layer protocol
UT	Universal Time
VT	vertical tab
WAIS	wide area information servers

WAN	wide area network
WEB	worldwide web
WRQ	write request
XDR	external data representation
XID	exchange identification
XNS	Xerox network system

Recent Development

Shortly after this book was written, the Internet authorities decided upon the "next generation" Internet Protocol (IP). It is called IPng or simply IP, version 6. Its major aspect is the agreement on a 16-byte address. The final specification is slated for publication in late 1994 or early 1995. Some of the issues surrounding this topic can be found in the last part of Chapter 5.

TCP/IP and the Internet

Overview

Data communications networks were developed to allow users to share computer and information resources, as well as a common communications system. As organizations have brought the computer into almost every facet of business, it has become obvious that a single network, while very useful, is inadequate to meet the information needs of businesses and individuals. A user of one network, for example, often needs to access and share the resources of computers and databases that belong to another network. Merging all resources into one network is prohibitively complex and expensive.

In the late 1960s and early 1970s, networks were not designed to allow resource sharing between users residing on different networks. Network administrators also were reluctant to allow outside users to tap into their resources because of concerns about security and the excessive utilization of their network resources. As a result, it was difficult for a user to extend the use of an information system to another user across networks. The networks were either incompatible with each other or could not communicate because of administrative problems.

During this time, it became increasingly accepted that sharing resources among user applications made sense. To do so, however, network administrators had to agree upon a set of common technologies and standards so that the networks could communicate with each other. Applications, such as electronic mail and file transfer, also needed to be standardized to permit interconnections of end-user applications and not just the networks.

In the early 1970s, several groups around the world began to address network and application compatibility. At that time, the term *internetworking*, which means the interconnecting of computers and networks, was coined. The concepts of internetworking were pioneered by the International Telecommunication Union—Telecommunications Standardization Sector (ITU-T), the International Standards organization (ISO), and especially the original designers of the ARPANET. *ARPA* refers to the Advanced Research Projects Agency, which is a U.S. Department of Defense (DOD) organization.

In fairness to the pioneers of internetworking concepts (and layered protocols, discussed shortly), the ARPA protocols were well in existence before the ISO and the ITU-T took an interest in this important subject. The procurement for ARPANET occurred in 1968. The machines selected were Honeywell 316 interface message processors (IMPs). The initial effort was contracted through Bolt, Bernak & Newman (BBN), and the ARPANET nodes were initially installed at UCLA, University of California at San Bernardino, the Stanford Research Institute (SRI), and the University of Utah. The well-known Requests for Comments (RFCs) resulted from this early work.

After the pioneer work of Vinton Care and Robert E. Kahn, these initial efforts were organized through the ARPANET Network Working Group. The group was disbanded in 1971, and the Defense Advanced Project Research Agency (DARPA) assumed the work of the earlier organization. DARPA's work in the early 1970s had led to the development of an earlier protocol, the network control program, and later, the Transmission Control Protocol and the Internet Protocol (TCP/IP). Two years later, the first significant parts of the Internet were placed into operation. At about this time, DARPA started converting some of its computers to the TCP/IP suite of protocols. DARPA stated that by January 1, 1983 all computers connected to ARPANET must use TCP/IP.

Initially TCP/IP was used to connect ARPANET, the Packet Radio Net (PRNET), and the Packet Satellite Net (SATNET). Most user computers were large mainframes with terminals attached through terminal access servers. As ARPANET grew, the Department of Defense decided to split it into two networks. The other network was named MILNET and was set up for military purposes. ARPANET continued to be used for its original intent: A network to support R&D (research and development) applications. By the mid-1980s, the "ARPA Internet" was now called "the Internet." In 1990, the last original ARPANET node was taken out of commission.

Perhaps one of the most significant developments in TCP/IP was DARPA's decision to implement TCP/IP around the UNIX operating system. Of equal importance, the University of California at Berkeley was selected to distribute the TCP/IP code. Some implementors have said that releasing such complex and functionally rich code was a "license to steal." Whatever one's view on the matter, it was a very significant and positive move in the industry. Because the TCP/IP code was nonproprietary, it spread rapidly among universities, private companies, and research centers. Indeed, TCP/IP has become the standard suite of data communications protocols for UNIX-based computers.

During this period, other networks were coming into existence using TCP/IP based on funding from the U.S. government and other research agencies. The NSFnet was established as a high-capacity network by the National Science Foundation and is still in existence. NSF has played a key role in the development of the Internet, both in funding and strategic guidance. It provides a communications backbone principally for scientific and research centers, initially in the United States and now in other parts of the world. Its high-capacity lines are designed to support supercomputer transmissions. The supercomputer centers serve as backbones from which lower-speed networks are attached. Today, NSFnet has evolved from the 56-kbit/s carrier lines to DS3 speeds of 45 Mbit/s. MCI has now installed optical fiber connections over the NSF backbone network.

Organization of the Internet

As the Internet grew, its organization and management were delegated to the Internet Advisory Board (IAB)(see Figure 1.1). Originally, the IAB consisted of a number of subsidiary organizations but their main function was to coordinate the Internet task forces. In 1989, the task forces were placed

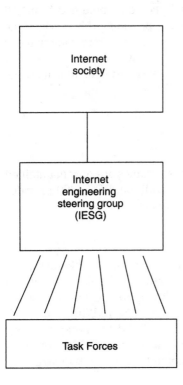

Figure 1.1 The Internet Organization.

into two major groups within the IAB: the Internet Research Task Force (IRTF) and the Internet Engineering Task force (IETF). The IRTF is responsible for ongoing research activities. The IETF concerns itself with tactical issues (implementation and engineering problems).

Requests for comments (RFCs)

A brief reference was made earlier to RFCs. The RFCs are technical notes on an Internet protocol and represent the documentation of the Internet. An RFC is submitted to the RFC Editor in Chief. Anyone can submit an RFC by using the instructions for authors of RFCs found in the file RFC: AUTHOR-IN-STRUCT.TXT.

Some RFCs are de facto standards for the TCP/IP; others are published for informational purposes, and still others are the result of research and might eventually become future standards. Presently, over 1000 RFCs are in existence, although quite a number of these specifications have been superseded.

Obtaining Internet Information

The intent of this book is to provide a general understanding of TCP/IP. There is no substitute, however, for the actual source documents (the RFCs). They can be obtained from a wide variety of sources on the Internet if one has electronic access. Previously, RFCs could be obtained from SRI International, but this organization is no longer providing this service. The reader can obtain the RFCs from a number of sources through anonymous FTP or E-mail (check with your Internet access provider).

You can also send an E-mail message to rfc-info@ isi.edu. Your message should appear as:

```
Retrieve: RFC
DOC-IO: RFCxxxx
```

where xxxx is the RFC number.

All Internet IP Network numbers and domain names are now maintained at the Internet name: RS.INTERNIC.NET. In addition, RFC 1400 provides more details on how to obtain Internet information.

TCP/IP and the OSI

Before we move into tutorial discussions of networking architectures, you should know that the use of TCP/IP and related protocols continues to grow, raising some interesting points in relation to the Open Systems Interconnection (OSI) Model. Many people believe that TCP/IP is a more viable approach for a number of reasons. First, TCP/IP is here; it works. Second, a wealth of products are available that use the TCP/IP protocol suites. Third, it has a well-founded, functioning administrative structure through the IAB. Fourth, it provides easy access to documentation. Fifth, it is used in many UNIX products.

Notwithstanding the preceding reasons, it is the intent of the original Internet sponsor, the Department of Defense, to move away from the TCP/IP protocol suites. (We discuss these issues in detail in Chapter 14.) The Internet approach, however, is to stay with existing standards and protocols and write new specifications only if necessary. This approach also includes international standards, if available. Lastly, the Internet approach is to remain vendor-independent as far as possible.

Internetworking Architecture

To grasp the operations of TCP/IP, several terms and concepts must first be understood. Once these concepts are explained, we can discuss the architecture more fully.

Terms and concepts

The Internet uses the term *gateway* or *router* to describe a machine that performs relaying functions between networks. The preferred term today is router; this book uses both terms in deference to past practice. Figure 1.2 shows a gateway placed between networks A, B, and C. (*Router* and *gateway* are defined further in Chapter 2.)

Networks A, B, and C are often called *subnetworks*. The term does not mean that they provide fewer functions than a conventional network. Rather, the three networks consist of a full logical network, and the subnet-

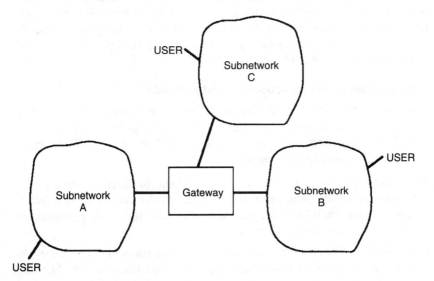

Figure 1.2 Gateway and Subnetworks.

works contribute to the overall operations for internetworking. Stated another way, the subnetworks compose an internetwork or an internet.

An internetworking gateway is transparent to the end-user application. Indeed, the end-user application resides in the host machines connected to the networks; rarely are user applications placed in the gateway. This approach is attractive from several standpoints. First, the gateway need not burden itself with application layer protocols. Because these protocols are not invoked at the gateway, the gateway can dedicate itself to fewer tasks, such as managing the traffic between networks. It is not concerned with application-level functions, such as database access, electronic mail, and file management. Second, this approach allows the gateway to support any type of data application because the gateway considers the application message nothing more than a transparent protocol data unit (PDU).

In addition to application-layer transparency, most designers attempt to keep the gateway transparent to the subnetworks and vice versa. That is, the gateway does not care which type of network is attached to it. The principal purpose of the gateway is to receive a PDU that contains adequate addressing information to enable the gateway to route the PDU to its final destination or to the next gateway. Transparency is also attractive because it makes the gateway somewhat modular; the gateway can be used in different types of networks.

It should be emphasized, however, that this transparency is not achieved magically. Software must be written to enable communications to take place between the subnetwork protocol and the gateway. These procedures are usually proprietary, and standards do not describe this interface between the gateway and the subnetwork. The exception to this statement is the publication of the Institute of Electrical and Electronics Engineers (IEEE), OSI, and Internet service definitions that describe procedures (abstractly) between the host and gateway protocols (layers). These service definitions are examined later in this book.

Connectionless and connection-oriented protocols

The concept of connectionless and connection-oriented operations is fundamental to any communications protocol, and the Internet standards use both. It is essential that you clearly understand their features. Their principal characteristics are as follows:

- *Connection-oriented operations*: A user and network set up a logical connection before transfer of data occurs. Usually, some type of relationship is maintained between the successive data units being transferred through the user/network connection.

- *Connectionless-mode operations*: No logical connection between the user and the network is established prior to data transmission. The data units are transmitted as independent units.

The connection-oriented service requires a three-way agreement between the two end users and the service provider (for instance, the network). It also allows the communicating parties to negotiate certain options and quality-of-service (QOS) functions. During connection establishment, all three parties store information about each other, such as addresses and QOS features. Once data transfer begins, the PDUs do not need to carry much overhead protocol control information (PCI). This approach usually entails fixed routing within the network because the data packets do not contain sufficient addresses to permit dynamic (on-the-spot) routing decisions. All that is needed is an abbreviated identifier to allow the parties to access the tables and look up the full addresses and QOS features. Because the session can be negotiated, the communicating parties do not need to have prior knowledge of all the characteristics of each other. If a requested service cannot be provided, any of the parties can negotiate the service to a lower level or reject the connection request.

In the past, a connection-oriented service provided for the acknowledgment of all data units (with a few exceptions). If problems occurred during transmission, a connection-oriented protocol provided mechanisms for retransmission of the errored units. In addition, most connection-oriented protocols ensured that the data arrived in the proper order at the final destination. These services (sequencing and traffic accountability) can no longer be assumed in a connection-oriented protocol. In more recent systems (for example, frame relay), traffic management is not provided by the system, and must therefore be provided by another entity, such as a user program, residing in the end-user workstation. Figure 1.3 summarizes the characteristics of connection-oriented networks.

Connectionless service manages user PDUs as independent and separate entities. No relationship is maintained between successive data transfers, and few records are kept of the ongoing user-to-user communications process through the network(s). Options are not negotiated, nor are tables created or maintained about the data transfer. In a few systems, the communicating entities must have a prior agreement on how to communicate, and the QOS features must be prearranged. More often, QOS is provided for each PDU transmitted, and each PDU contains fields that identify types and levels of service.

---

* Connection mapped through network

* Abbreviated addressing

* Usually fixed routing between networks

* Accountability may or may not be provided

Figure 1.3 Connection-Oriented Networks.

- Limited end-to-end mapping

- Full addressing with data unit

- Use of alternate routing

- Limited accountability

Figure 1.4 Connectionless Service.

In theory, connectionless networks can perform data integrity support functions such as positive and negative acknowledgments (ACKs and NAKs, respectively) and sequencing. In practice, most connectionless systems do not provide these services.

By its very nature, connectionless service can achieve the following:

- a high degree of independence from specific protocols within a subnetwork

- considerable independence of the subnetworks from each other

- a high degree of independence of the subnetwork(s) from the user-specific protocol.

A connectionless network is likely more robust than its connection-oriented counterpart because each PDU is handled as an independent entity. Therefore, data units can take different routes to avoid failed nodes or congestion at a point in the network(s). Connectionless protocols do, however, consume more overhead in relation to the length of the headers and in proportion to the amount of user data in the PDU than their connection-oriented counterparts. The characteristics of connectionless networks are summarized in Figure 1.4.

Before leaving the subject of connectionless and connection-oriented protocols, note that the practical network manager realizes the benefits of both connection-oriented and connectionless layers within a system. The choice depends on the type of service needed by the end user, and the cost and overhead to obtain that service. Because most vendors provide for a variety of connection-oriented and connectionless products, it becomes a matter of deciding in which layer one wants the options of the various services. But let there be no mistake, if you care for your data, you must have a protocol residing somewhere in the system that accounts for the proper reception of all traffic.

Evolution of connectionless and connection-oriented systems

Many internets are connectionless, with little or no support for sequencing and acknowledgment. Most local area networks fit into this category, as does IP. In contrast, TCP is connection-oriented and provides several data integrity support functions. (We examine the rationale for these combinations later in this book.) For now, it is useful to note that some newer technologies are using connection-oriented techniques, such as frame relay and asynchronous transfer mode (ATM). One of the main reasons for this evolution is the ability to use short headers, such as the abbreviated identifier (a virtual circuit ID), in the protocol data unit. Thus, overhead bits are few, which translates into more efficient operations.

The Internet Layers

Both software and hardware operating on TCP/IP networks typically consist of a wide range of functions to support the communications activities. The network designer is faced with an enormous task in dealing with the number and complexity of these functions. To address these problems, an internet is structured by layering the functions.

Although modern networks are described by dividing them into seven conceptual layers, the Internet architecture is based on only four layers. Figure 1.5 depicts the Internet layer architecture. The bottom layer of the Internet contains the subnetworks and the subnetwork interfaces. These subnetworks allow data to be delivered within each network. Examples of subnetworks are WilTel, Transpac, and an Ethernet local area network (LAN). Although this layer does include a subnetwork, in actual implementations, the data link and physical layers are required in all machines communicating with a subnet or gateway; therefore, Figure 1.5 is quite abstract because this layer must also include the data link and physical layers. Later figures show this lower layer in more detail.

The next layer is the *internetwork* layer. This layer provides the functions necessary for connecting networks and gateways into one coherent system. This layer is responsible for delivering data from the source to the final destination. It contains the IP and the Internet control message protocol (ICMP). As discussed later, other supporting protocols for route discovery and addressing mapping also reside with the IP at this layer.

The third layer is known as the *service provider protocol layer*. This layer is responsible for end-to-end communications. If connection-oriented,

Applications Service
Service Provider Protocol
Internetwork
Subnetworks

Figure 1.5 The Internet Layers.

it provides reliability measures and has mechanisms that account for all traffic flowing through an internet. This layer contains the TCP and the user datagram protocol (UDP).

Finally, the upper layer is the *applications service layer*. This layer supports the direct interfaces to an end user application. The Internet applications are responsible for functions such as file transfer, remote terminal access, remote job execution, electronic mail, etc. This layer contains several widely used protocols, such as the file transfer protocol (FTP).

Example of the Layer Operations

Figure 1.6 shows the relationship of subnetworks and gateways to layered protocols. The layers depicted earlier in Figure 1.5 have been changed to show the lower data link and physical layers, and the upper layers have been renamed with terms more widely used in the industry.

In this figure, assume the user application in host A sends an application PDU to an application layer protocol in host B, such as a file transfer system. The file transfer software performs a variety of functions and sends file records to the user data. In many systems, the operations at host B are known as *server* operations and the operations at host A are known as *client* operations.

As indicated by the downward arrows in the protocol stack at host A, this unit is passed to the transport layer protocol. This layer performs a variety of operations (discussed in later chapters) and adds a header to the PDU passed to it. The unit of data is now called a *segment.* The PDU from the upper layer is considered data to the transport layer.

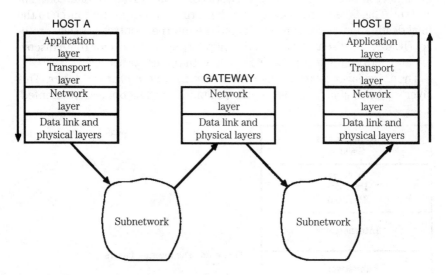

Figure 1.6 Example of Internet Layer Operations.

Next, the transport layer passes the segment to the network layer, also called the *IP layer*, which again performs specific services and appends a header. This unit (now called a *datagram* in Internet terms) is passed down to the lower layers. Here, the data link layer adds its header as well as a trailer, and the data unit (now called a *frame*) is launched into the network by the physical layer. Of course, if host B sends data to host A, the process is reversed and the direction of the arrows is changed.

The Internet protocols are unaware of what goes on inside the network. The network manager is free to manipulate and manage the PDU in any manner necessary. In some instances, however, the Internet PDU (data and headers) remains unchanged as it is transmitted through the subnet. In Figure 1.6, we see its emergence at the gateway where it is processed through the lower layers and passed to the IP (network) layer. Here, routing decisions are made based on the addresses provided by the host computer.

After the routing decisions are made, the PDU is passed to the communications link connected to the appropriate subnetwork (consisting of the lower layers). The PDU is reencapsulated into the data link layer frame and passed to the next subnetwork. As before, this unit is passed through the subnetwork transparently (usually), where it finally arrives at the destination host.

The destination (host B) receives the traffic through its lower layers and reverses the process that transpired at host A; it decapsulates the headers by stripping them off in the appropriate layer. The header is used by the layer to determine the actions the layer must take; the header therefore governs the layer's operations.

The PDU created by the file transfer application in the applications layer is passed to the file transfer application residing at host B. If hosts A and B are large mainframe computers, this application is likely an exact duplicate of the software at the transmitting host. The application might, however, perform a variety of functions, depending on the header it receives. It is conceivable that the data could be passed to another end-user application at host B, but in many instances, the user at host A merely wants to obtain the services of a server protocol, such as a file transfer or electronic mail. If this is the case, it is not necessary for an end-user application process to be invoked at host B.

To return the retrieved data from the server at host B to the client at host A, the process is reversed. The data is transferred down through the layers in the host B machine, through the network, through the gateway, to the next network, and up the layers of host A to the end user.

The TCP/IP Model: A Closer Look

Figure 1.7 depicts an architectural model of TCP/IP and several of the major related protocols. The stacking of the layers of this model vary, depend-

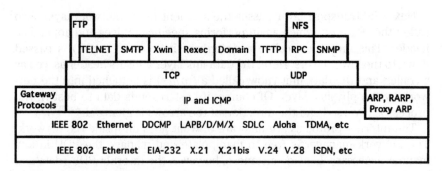

Figure 1.7 The IP Suite.

ing on the needs of the network users and the decisions made by the network designers. For now, we see some of the protocols explained in the previous material, specifically, IP and TCP. The protocols above TCP (and UDP) are examples of the application-layer protocols, also labeled *applications service* in Figure 1.5. The lower two layers represent the data link and physical layers and, as the figure depicts, are implemented with a wide choice of standards and protocols. This figure is used later in the book to explain the operations of the layers in more detail.

Ports and Sockets: An Introduction

Each application layer process using the TCP/IP protocols must identify itself by a *port* number. This number is used between the two host computers to identify which application program is to receive the incoming traffic. The use of port numbers also provides a multiplexing capability by allowing multiple user programs to communicate concurrently with one application program, such as the FTP. The port numbers identify these application entries. The concept is quite similar to a service access point (SAP) in the OSI Model.

In addition to the use of ports, TCP/IP-based protocols use an abstract identifier called a *socket*. The socket was derived from the network input/output operations of the 4.3 BSD UNIX system. It is quite similar to UNIX file access procedures in that it identifies an endpoint communications process.

In the Internet, some port numbers are preassigned. These are called *well-known ports* and are used to identify widely used applications, called *well-known services*. The well-known port numbers occupy values ranging from 0 to 255. Organizations should not use the numbers within these ranges because they are reserved; if you need to assign a port number to a specific application, you should use a number above 255. Later discussions examine ports and sockets in more detail.

Challenges of Internetworking

Armed with this background information, we can examine several difficult issues and problems a network administrator encounters in providing internetworking services. Regarding TCP/IP specifically, these issues are discussed throughout the book. For now, however, we keep the discussion general.

Different networks can use different length sizes for PDUs. If different-length sizes are used, the networks or gateways must provide for fragmentation of the data units. And in so doing, the identity of the data units cannot be lost. The varying length sizes of the data units do not eliminate the requirement to maintain a sequence number relationship on an end-to-end basis, either. In Chapter 5, we learn that an IP gateway can fragment data units, and the receiving host computer can reassemble the fragments into the full PDU.

The timers, timeouts, and retry values often differ between subnetworks. For example, assume network A sets a wait-for-acknowledgment timer when a data unit is forwarded. The timer ensures that an end-to-end acknowledgment occurs within a specified period. The data unit is passed to network B, but this network does not have an end-to-end timer. Thus, we have a dilemma. Should network A return an acknowledgment to the transmitting user upon passing the data unit to network B and assume the second network does indeed deliver the data unit? A false sense of security would result for the user in network A because the data unit might not have arrived at the end destination. TCP/IP provides for end-to-end timing support, but the function is not invoked during the data unit's traversal through the subnetworks, only at the host computers. Therefore, a network is free to devise any type of timer it needs.

Subnetworks can use different addressing conventions. For example, one could use logical names and another could use physical names. In such a case, address resolution and mapping might differ between the two subnetworks. Indeed, most networks use network-specific addresses. For example, an SNA address simply does not equate to a DECnet address. Fortunately, the Internet provides standards to support several types of addresses. In addition, Internet systems are available to support address mapping from network-layer-to-physical-layer addresses. Other systems can be invoked that derive network addresses from user-friendly names.

Subnetworks can exhibit different levels of performance. For example, one subnetwork might be slower and experience more delay and less throughput than another network. The Internet protocols do not concern themselves to any significant extent about these issues. As we learned earlier in this chapter, the protocols are designed to operate transparently on different types of networks. Of course, the network manager must be concerned with these problems and can use some of the Internet software as tools to help solve these problems (as discussed later, TCP is a valuable tool in this regard).

Subnetworks can employ different routing methods. For example, one might use a fixed routing directory and another might use an adaptive routing directory. In the former case, the network logic for resequencing is sparse. In the latter, resequencing logic is extensive. The TCP/IP suite contains many protocols to support gateway routing but does not become involved in intranetworking routing, although many organizations use these protocols within their networks.

Subnetworks can require different types of user interfaces. For example, a subnetwork might employ a connection-oriented, user-to-subnetwork interface and another might use a connectionless, datagram protocol. The interface type influences error recovery and flow control. As we see in several of the chapters of this book, the internetworking of connectionless and connection-oriented protocols poses several very challenging problems (and opportunities) for the network manager.

Subnetworks can require different levels of security. For example, one network could require encryption and another might only support clear-text transmissions. TCP/IP does not concern itself with security, other than allowing a user to specify a level of security desired for the transmission of the data. The security designation is then used by the network to be implemented in any way the network chooses.

Troubleshooting, diagnostics, and network maintenance can differ between the subnetworks, or they might not be used across more than one network. A problem created in one subnetwork can affect another subnetwork, yet the affected subnetwork could have no control in error analysis and correction. Any exchange of network management information between networks is carried transparently by the Internet protocols. The Internet network management standards, discussed later, however, are intended to provide considerable support for network management.

Clearly, the internetworking task is not simple, and it requires considerable analysis and forethought before it is implemented. Yet the task is not insurmountable. As we see in this book, the TCP/IP product vendors and standards organizations have already developed and implemented many effective internetworking techniques.

Typical Internet Topologies

During the discussions of TCP/IP and related protocols, several figures are used to illustrate points. Figure 1.8a shows two networks connected by a gateway (labeled G). The networks are identified with network addresses (network ID). The network on the left of the figure is identified as network 11.4 and the other network is 128.1. (The scheme for creating these numbers is described in Chapter 3.) The term *network cloud* is used in this figure because the topology and operations of the networks are not shown. The topologies of the networks are depicted in subsequent figures.

In some instances, the network cloud figure is used as depicted in Figure 1.8*a* when the explanations do not require a discussion of the operations

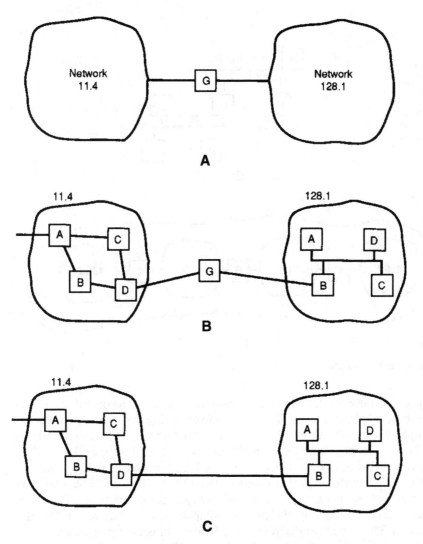

Figure 1.8 Typical Internet Topologies: (*a*) Network Clouds and Gateways (*b*) Gateway Connecting Networks (*c*) Packet Switches or Hosts as Gateways (*d*) LAN Gateways (*e*) Common Gateways between LANs (*f*) Multiple Gateways in an Internet.

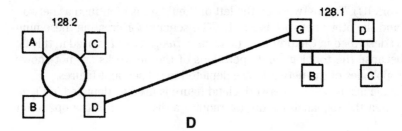

D

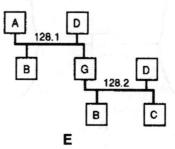

E

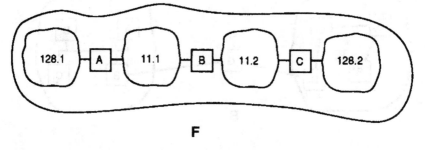

F

Figure 1.8 *(Continued)*

within the network. Other instances require examining the operations within the network, in which case the other networks in Figure 1.8 are used. For example, Figure 1.8*b* shows the topologies of a conventional packet-switched network (network 11.4) and an Ethernet-type LAN (network 128.1). The boxes labeled A, B, C, and D inside network 11.4 symbolize packet switches, which are connected with communications links. They could also be computers that serve the dual function of hosts and packet switches. The boxes inside network 128.1 symbolize host computers, workstations, or file/print servers. The two networks in Figure 1.8*b* are connected by a gateway.

Figure 1.8*c* shows that host B in network 128.1 is acting as a gateway to packet switch D in network 11.4. In the case of the packet switch serving as a gateway, this arrangement is quite common. In the case of the host serving as a gateway, the arrangement is less common because the host might not have the resources to run user applications and gateway functions.

Figure 1.8d is also used to explain LAN configurations. Notice that two interconnected gateways are attached to an Ethernet-type topology (network 128.1) and a token ring topology (network 128.2). This configuration is common within office buildings that have a number of interconnected LANs. Figure 1.8e shows one gateway (G) connecting two Ethernet-type networks together. This approach is also quite common. Note that Figures 1.8d and 1.8e are drawn without the network cloud.

Finally, Figure 1.8f shows several network clouds. From the perspective of an internet user, the outer cloud represents the user's virtual network. The user is not concerned with the fact that user data might traverse four networks (128.1, 11.1, 11.2, and 128.2) and three gateways (A, B, and C) to reach its final destination.

This discussion has used the term *gateway* to describe all internetworking functions. Chapter 3 expands this description to examine and contrast gateways, bridges, and routers.

Summary

The Internet protocols are designed to permit and facilitate sharing computer resources across different networks. Because these protocols were sponsored by the U.S. Government, and their operations are simple yet effective, they have become one of the most widely used set of data networking protocols in existence. Although the Internet protocols are called TCP/IP, these two standards represent only a small part of a wealth of standardized data network standards.

Introduction to Networks, Bridges, Gateways, and Routers

TCP/IP has been implemented on both wide area and local area networks (WANs/LANs). This chapter describes several prominent types of WANs/LANs and explains their primary operating characteristics. We also examine routing schemes used to relay traffic between networks (internetworking) and examine bridges, routers, and gateways in the chapter. We finish with an introduction to source routing and spanning tree protocols and their relationship to TCP/IP. This chapter introduces the Internet routing and gateway discovery protocols, which are further discussed in Chapter 8, and the IP routing algorithm, further discussed in Chapters 3 and 5.

A General Taxonomy

Communications systems on many WANs employ switches to route traffic from multiple users on a limited number of links. The stations attached to the network use the switch to share the links. Without the switch, each station would need multiple lines to communicate with the other stations. Indeed, a fully meshed network requires many lines—clearly an impossible task if many stations are involved. An alternative to a switched network for sharing links is the broadcast network in which only one link is used. The multiple stations copy all the data units and discard those that are not addressed to a particular station. Most LANs use some type of broadcast protocol.

Figure 2.1 depicts the layers of WANs and LANs from the context of the seven-layer OSI Model. As the figure reveals, WANs reside in the lower

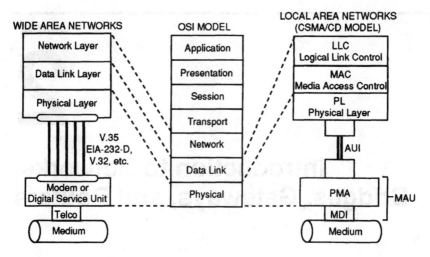

Figure 2.1 Layers of Local and Wide Area Networks.

three layers and LANs in the lower two layers of the OSI Model. Does this mean that we need not be concerned with the upper layers of the model when dealing with TCP/IP? Indeed not; the TCP/IP model also encompasses the transport layer and the application layer. These layers are highlighted during this discussion as well.

The left side of Figure 2.1 shows the layers for a WAN. As mentioned above, these layers encompass the physical, data link, and network layers of the OSI Model. The physical layer (PL) typically consists of modems for analog lines and data service units (DSUs) for digital lines. As the figure shows, the modem or DSUs are connected to a telephone company (telco) medium, such as a twisted wire pair. The connection between the user device and the modem or DSU is usually effected through an EIA 232-E connector and one of the appropriate ITU-T V-Series modem standards.

Resting above the physical layer is the data link layer. Its principal function is to provide for error detection and the retransmission of damaged data; that is, data that have encountered problems on the communications link (media). Today, most vendors support the data link layer with high-level data link control (HDLC) protocols, such as link access protocol balanced (LAPB) or synchronous data link control (SDLC). HDLC is a widely used data link standard. The network layer switches and routes traffic through the network. In addition, standards such as X.25 define the interface procedures for the user device and the network.

The right side of Figure 2.1 shows the layers for a LAN. The physical layer performs the same functions as a WAN. The parts of the physical layer are labeled in this figure as *attachment unit interface* (AUI), *medium at-*

tachment unit (MAU), *physical medium attachment* (PMA), and *medium dependent interface* (MDI).

The AUI provides the attachment between the physical layer of the unit device and the LAN medium. It contains connectors quite similar to EIA 232-E or to telephone jacks, such as RJ-45. The MAU actually consists of both the PMA and MDI. Its principal function is to manage the connection of the data terminal equipment (DTE) to the cable (LAN media) and provide services for transmitting and receiving data, detecting problems, testing operations, and checking signal quality. The PMA contains the circuitry to support the functions of the MAU. The MDI provides the mechanical and electrical interfaces between the medium and the PMA.

The *media access control (MAC)* layer is responsible for managing the traffic on the LAN. It determines when the LAN media is free to transmit data, detects collisions of data on certain types of LANs, and determines when retransmissions should occur. It is media independent but specific to a particular protocol, such as token bus or token ring.

The *logical link control (LLC)* layer provides the interface between the LAN and the user layers. LLC can be configured to provide a very basic service (connectionless) or a very elaborate service (connection-oriented). It is based on the *HDLC*; thus it can be configured to provide data link service with the unnumbered information (UI) frame or connection-oriented service with the asynchronous balanced mode (ABM) frame. The choice of how to configure LLC for operations with TCP/IP is an important one and is discussed in several parts of this book.

You might wonder why a LAN does not contain the network layer. Indeed, the very idea seems anomalous because a LAN is a network. The reason is simple. The network layer (as originally conceived through the OSI Model) serves to support routing and interface operations. The routing aspect of the network layer is not found in the vast majority of LANs because they are broadcast networks and do not utilize switching techniques. Second, network interfaces were conceived to define the interface between the user and the network and to negotiate quality of service (QOS) features for the user/network connection. These needs do not exist in most LANs because the interfaces are quite simple, and QOS options are usually not available. Consequently, the network layer in a LAN is either nonexistent or very lean. If it exists, it is usually implemented with a simple protocol, such as the Internet protocol (IP).

Wide Area Networks

Now that you understand the layers of WANs and LANs, we turn our attention to more detailed aspects. For WANs, four switching techniques are explained: circuit switching, message switching, packet switching, and cell relay. Packet switching is emphasized because it has become the prevalent approach for switched data networks and for control networks in telephone systems. Cell relay, however, is a new technology and is seen by many as an eventual replacement to packet switching.

Circuit switching

Circuit switching provides a direct connection between two components. The direct connection of a circuit switch serves as an open pipeline, permitting the two end users to use the facility as they see fit—within bandwidth and tariff limitations. Many telephone networks use circuit switching systems.

Circuit switching is arranged in one or a combination of three architectures: concentration (more input lines than output lines), expansion (more output lines than input lines), or connection (an equal number of input and output lines). In its simplest form, a circuit switch is an $N×M$ array of lines that connect to each other at crosspoints. In a large switching office, the N lines are input from the subscriber (terminals, computers, etc.) and the M lines are output to other switching offices.

Circuit switching simply provides a path for the sessions between data communications components. Error checking, session establishment, frame flow control, frame formatting, and selecting codes and protocols are the responsibility of the users. Little or no care of the data traffic is provided in a pure circuit switching arrangement. Consequently, the telephone network is often used as the basic foundation for a data communications network, and additional facilities are added by the value-added carrier, network vendor, or user organization. Other switching technologies (e.g., message and packet) often use circuit switching as the basic transmission media and then provide additional value-added functions and facilities, such as store-and-forward services and protocol conversion.

Message switching

In the 1960s and 1970s, the pervasive method for switching data communications traffic was message switching. The message switch is typically a specialized computer responsible for accepting traffic from attached terminals and computers (through dial-up or leased lines). It examines the address in the header of the message and switches (routes) the traffic to the receiving station or the next switch in the route. Unlike circuit switching in telephone networks, message switching is a store-and-forward technology; the messages are stored temporarily on disk units at the switches.

Because the data are usually stored, the traffic is not considered interactive or real-time. Selected traffic can, however, be sent through a message switch at very high speeds by establishing levels of priority for different types of traffic, and this approach could support interactive applications. High-priority traffic is queued for a shorter period than low-priority traffic.

Storing the messages temporarily on disk also helps smooth traffic by queuing the lower-priority traffic during peak periods. Queuing also decreases the chances of traffic being blocked because of network congestion. For example, traffic can be stored temporarily and later routed to stations when the stations are available to accept the traffic.

The message-switching technology may operate in a master/slave relationship. Typically, the switch performs polling and selection functions to manage the incoming and outgoing traffic. For example, assume user A has data for user D. The switch performs a polling cycle of the attached computers on which the users are operating. Upon polling A, the data are transmitted to the switch. Based on the priority assigned to the message, it is stored in one of several disk queues. The switch eventually dequeues the message and sends a select command to D, depending on overall traffic conditions and priority-level. At site D, an acknowledgment can be sent to the switch, after which the message is transmitted to D.

Message switching has served the industry well, but it suffers from three deficiencies. First, because message switching is inherently a master/slave structure, the entire network can be lost if the switch fails because all traffic must go through the switch. Consequently, many organizations install a duplicate (duplexed) switch, which assumes the role of the primary switch in the event of a failure. The second major deficiency stems from the hub arrangement of a message switch. Because all traffic must go through one switch, the switch itself is a potential bottleneck. Degraded response time and decreased throughput can result from such an arrangement. Third, message switching does not use the communications lines as efficiently as other techniques discussed in the next section. For these reasons, modern data networks no longer employ message switching.

Packet switching

Because of the problems associated with message switching, the industry began to move toward a different WAN switching technique in the 1970s: packet switching. Packet switching distributes the risk to more than one switch, reduces vulnerability to network failure, and provides better utilization of the lines than does message switching. Packet switching is so named because user data (for example, messages) are divided into smaller pieces. These pieces, or *packets*, have protocol control information (PCI) headers placed around them and are routed through the network as independent entities.

A packet-switching network contains multiple switches that allow the network load to be distributed to multiple switching sites (see Figure 2.2). Additional communications lines are also attached to the switches. The arrangement allows alternate routing, avoiding failed or busy nodes and channels. For example, in Figure 2.2, a packet switch can route the packets of one message to more than one packet switch.

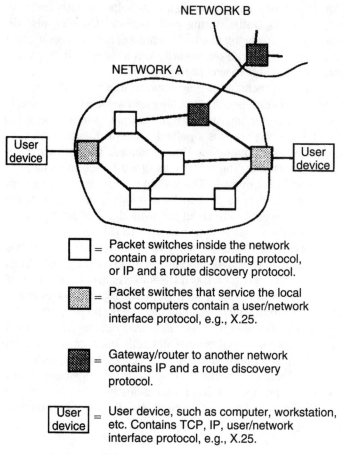

Figure 2.2 Packet Switching.

Packet switching works well with data communications traffic because many devices, such as keyboard terminals, transmit traffic in bursts. The data is sent on the channel, which is then idle while a terminal user inputs more data into the terminal or pauses to think about a problem. The idle channel time could be wasted line capacity, but a packet switch interleaves multiple transmissions from several terminals onto one channel. In effect, packet switching achieves statistical time division multiplexing (STDM) across the communications line. This approach thus provides better use of the expensive communications channel.

Packet switching goes one step further than the simple multiplexing of communications lines. It can also multiplex multiple user sessions onto a single communications port on the computer. Instead of dedicating one port to one user, the system interleaves the bursts of traffic from multiple users across one port.

Packet switching also provides an attractive feature for connecting the terminals and computers together for a session. In a circuit-switched telephone structure, connect time is often slow. A switched telephone call requires that a number be dialed and all resources be set up before the call can be routed to the destination. With a packet-switching system, however, dedicated leased lines are available for multiple users to transmit and receive their data traffic. The lines do not require any circuit setups because they are permanently connected through the system. This technique can improve the slow connect time associated with multiple telephone circuit switches. Of course, leased lines are very expensive and are used only for applications that cannot tolerate dialing delays.

Figure 2.2 also shows the relationship of some of the TCP/IP protocols to the packet-switching components. Note that it shows only one of several configurations that exist in the industry; it is not meant to be all inclusive. Typically, the user device (host) interfaces into a packet-switched network with a user/network interface protocol. The most widely used network interface protocol in the industry today is the ITU-T's X.25 standard. It provides several interface options for connecting the user to the network, including reverse charge, call forwarding, and QOS features such as throughput and delay negotiations. IP is also stored at the host machine because the gateways rely on the IP header to be created by the host computer. Additionally, the transmission control protocol (TCP) resides at the host machine to provide end-to-end integrity for the transmission between the two end-user devices. Inside the network, the packet switches might contain a vendor's proprietary routing protocol, or, in some instances, IP is employed with a companion route discovery protocol. (Remember that IP is a routing protocol but not a route discovery protocol.)

The gateways in this figure could be configured with IP as in the case with an internet. In a large number of public packet networks, the gateway protocol is often X.75. The X.75 protocol, although a gateway protocol, is quite different from IP because it is connection-oriented.

Choosing the packet route. Packet-switched networks route user traffic based on a variety of criteria, generally referred to as *least-cost routing* (also called the cost metric), which is examined in Chapter 8. The name does not mean that routing is based solely on obtaining the least-cost route in the literal sense. Other factors are often part of the routing algorithm, including the following:

- capacity of the link
- number of packets waiting for transmission onto the link

- load leveling through the network
- security requirements for the link
- type of traffic in relation to type of link
- number of intermediate links between the transmitting and receiving stations
- ability to reach (connect to) intermediate nodes as well as the final receiving station.

Whatever the least-cost criteria may be, the network designer's goal is to determine the best least-cost, end-to-end path between any two communicating stations.

Although networks vary in least-cost criteria, three constraints must be considered: delay, throughput, and connectivity. If delay is excessive or throughput too little, the network does not meet the needs of the user community. The third constraint is obvious: the communications devices must be able to reach each other; otherwise, all other least-cost criteria are irrelevant.

The algorithms used to route the packets through the network vary. A few algorithms are set up at a central site but most are executed at each individual packet switch. They might provide a static, end-to-end path between the two users of the network, or they might route the traffic through different packet switches. Algorithms vary in how they adapt to changing network conditions. Some algorithms adapt only to failures, while others adapt as traffic conditions change.

Within many WANs, the TCP/IP protocols are not invoked. Typically, a vendor uses a proprietary product to manage packets within the network and then uses a gateway protocol such as IP or X.75 to manage the data between networks. This approach, however, is changing. Because the TCP/IP suite has several protocols to support powerful routing operations, some networks have adopted the philosophy of "Why reinvent the wheel?" and have adapted TCP/IP standards.

Before leaving the subject of routing, it should be emphasized that IP routes datagrams by using a routing table (directory). It does not, however, create this table. The table is created by a *route discovery protocol*, which is examined in Chapter 8. IP is therefore of little use unless a route discovery protocol has created the IP routing table for use by IP.

Cell switching (cell relay)

An emerging technology called *cell relay* is seen by many as an eventual replacement to packet-based networks. In contrast to packet relay, cell relay uses a fixed length PDU, which is called a cell. The cell consists of a 48-octet payload with a 5-octet header. This cell (with slight variations) is being used on asynchronous transfer mode (ATM) and the IEEE 802.6 standards, more commonly known as the metropolitan area network (MAN) specification. The switched multimegabit data service (SMDS) is based on 802.6. Cell relay takes advantage of small headers and short labels to provide a fast relay service. Its technology is appropriate for both local or wide area networks.

Local Area Networks

TCP/IP is now found in many LANs. Indeed, many LAN vendors offer TCP/IP as part of their overall LAN package and use TCP/IP as an integral part of their product. Therefore, a brief description of LANs is in order. Definitions of LANs are plentiful. While one definition has not gained prominence, most definitions include the following information:

- The connections between the user devices are usually within a few hundred to several thousand meters.

- Most LANs transmit data (a few support voice and video) between user stations and computers.

- The LAN transmission capacity is usually greater than that of a WAN. Typical bit rates range from 1 to 20 Mbit/s, with higher speed LANs operating in the 100 Mbit/s range.

- The LAN channel is typically owned by the organization using the facility. The telephone company is usually not involved in channel ownership or management.

- The error rate on a LAN is considerably better than a WAN-oriented telephone channel—for instance, error rates of 1 in 10^9 bits transmitted are not uncommon.

LAN components

A LAN contains four major components to support the transmission of data between end users:

- the channel
- the physical interface
- a protocol
- the user station

LAN *channels* (media) consist of a coaxial cable, coaxial baseband cables, twisted pair cable, or optical fiber. Coaxial cable TV (CATV) is used on many networks because it has a large transmission capacity, a good signal-to-noise ratio, low signal radiation, and low error rates. Twisted pair cable and microwave are also found in many LANs. Coaxial baseband is perhaps the most widely used transmission path, offering high capacity as well as low error rates and low noise distortion. Thus far, optical fiber paths have seen limited application, but their positive attributes ensure their continued use.

The *physical interface* between the path and the user station can take several forms. It could be a single CATV tap, infrared diodes, microwave antennas, or laser-emitting semiconductors for optical fibers. Some LANs provide regenerative repeaters at the interface; others use the interface as buffers for data flow.

The *protocol control logic component* controls the LAN and provides for the end user's access onto the network. The LAN protocols employ methods and techniques discussed later in this chapter. The last major component is the *user workstation*. It can be anything from a word processor to a mainframe computer. Several LAN vendors provide support for other vendors' products, and several layers of the OSI Model are supported by some LANs.

Types of LANs

These types of LANs are preeminent today:

- carrier sense-collision detection, with CSMD/CD and IEEE 802.3
- token ring
- token bus

In the following subsections, broadcast technology implemented in Ethernet and token networks is emphasized for each type of LAN, as it is the prevalent approach to switching in LANs.

Carrier sense-collision detection

Carrier sense-collision detection is widely used in LANs. Many vendors use this technique with Ethernet and the IEEE 802.3 specification. A carrier sense LAN considers all stations as peers; the stations contend for the use of the channel on an equal basis. Before transmitting, the stations monitor the channel to determine if the channel is active (that is, if another station is sending data on the channel). If the channel is idle, any station with data to transmit can send its traffic onto the channel. If the channel is occupied, the stations must defer to the station using the channel.

Figure 2.3 depicts a carrier sense-collision detection LAN. Stations A, B, C, and D are attached to a channel (such as coaxial cable) by bus interface units (BIU). Assume stations A and B want to transmit traffic. Station D, however, is currently using the channel, so the BIUs at stations A and B "listen" and defer to the signal from station D, which is occupying the channel. When the line goes idle, A and B then attempt to acquire the channel.

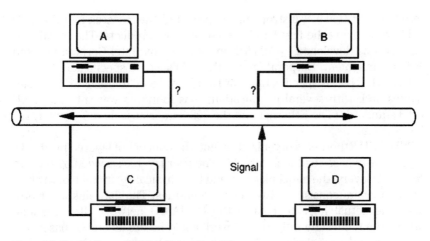

Figure 2.3 Carrier Sense-Collision Detection LAN.

Because A's transmission requires time to propagate to other stations, these other stations might be unaware that A's signal is on the channel. In this situation, A could transmit its traffic even if another station seized the channel when it detected the channel to be idle. This problem is called the *collision window*. The collision window is a factor of the propagation delay of the signal and the distance between two competing stations (propagation delay is the delay that occurs before the stations know another one is transmitting).

Carrier sense networks are usually implemented on short-distance LANs because the collision window lengthens as the channel gets longer. Longer channels provide opportunity for more collisions and can reduce throughput in the network. Generally, a long propagation delay coupled with short frames and high data transfer rates give rise to a greater incidence of collisions. Longer frames can mitigate the effect of long delay, but they reduce the opportunity for competing stations to acquire the channel.

Each station is capable of transmitting and listening to the channel simultaneously. When two signals collide, they create voltage irregularities on the channel, which are sensed by the colliding stations. The stations then turn off their transmission and, through an individually randomized wait period, attempt to seize the channel again. Randomized waiting decreases the chances of another collision because it is unlikely that the competing stations generate the same wait time.

CSMA/CD and IEEE 802.3

The best-known scheme for controlling a LAN on a bus structure is carrier sense-multiple access with collision detection (CSMA/CD). The most widely used implementation of CSMA/CD is found in the Ethernet specification.

Xerox Corporation was instrumental in providing the research for CSMA/CD and in developing the first baseband commercial products. The broadband network was developed by MITRE. In 1980, Xerox, Intel Corporation, and Digital Equipment Corporation jointly published a specification for an Ethernet LAN. This specification was later introduced to the IEEE 802 committees and, with several modifications, has found its way into the IEEE 802.3 standard. (The Ethernet and the 802.3 interfaces do differ in formatting conventions.)

CSMA/CD Ethernet is organized around the concept of layered protocols, as previously described in Figure 2.1. The user layer is serviced by the two CSMA/CD layers, the data link layer, and the physical layer. Each of the bottom two layers consists of two separate entities. The data link layer provides the actual logic to control the CSMA/CD network. It is medium independent; consequently, the network could be broadband or baseband. The 802 standard includes both broadband and baseband options.

The MAC sublayer consists of the following sublayers:

Transmit data encapsulation

- accepts data from LLC
- calculates the CRC value and places it in the FCS field

Transmit media access management

- presents a serial bit stream to the physical layer
- defers transmission when a medium is busy
- halts transmission when a collision is detected
- reschedules a retransmission after a collision is detected
- inserts the packet assembly and disassembly (PAD) field for frames with an LLC length less than a minimum value
- enforces a collision by sending a jam message

Receive data decapsulation

- performs a cyclic redundancy check (CRC) check
- recognizes and accepts any frame whose destination address (D/A) field is an address of a station
- presents data to LLC

Receive media access management

- receives a serial bit stream from the physical layer
- discards frames that are less than the minimum length

The physical layer is medium dependent. It is responsible for such services as introducing the electrical signals onto the channel, providing the timing on the channel, and data encoding and decoding. The physical layer comprises two major entities: data encoding/decoding and transmit/receive channel access (although the IEEE 802.3 standard combines these entities in its documents). The major functions of these entities are as follows:

Data encoding/decoding

- provides the signals that synchronize the stations on the channel (this synchronization signal is called the *preamble*)
- encodes the binary data stream to a self-clocking code at the transmitting site
- decodes the Manchester code back to binary code at the receiver

Channel access

- introduces the physical signal onto the channel on the transmit side and receives the signal on the receive side of the interface
- senses a carrier on the channel (indicating the channel is occupied) on both the transmit and the receive side
- detects a collision on the channel on the transmit side (indicating two signals have interfered with each other).

In a CSMA/CD network, each station has both a transmit and receive side to provide the incoming and outgoing flow of data. The transmit side is invoked when a user wants to transmit data to another DTE on the network; conversely, the receive side is invoked when data is transmitted to the stations on the network.

Token ring

The token ring topology is another LAN protocol offered by a number of vendors and is published as IEEE 802.5. IBM has based many of its LAN products around the token ring, illustrated in Figure 2.4. The stations are connected to a concentric ring through a ring interface unit (RIU). Each RIU is responsible for monitoring the data passing through it, as well as regenerating the signal and passing it to the next station. If the address in the header of the transmission indicates the data are destined for a station, the RIU copies the data and passes the information to the user device.

If the ring is idle (that is, no user data occupies the ring), a "free" token is passed around the ring from node to node. This token indicates that the ring is available, and any station with data to transmit can use the token to transmit traffic. The control of the ring is passed sequentially from node to node around the ring.

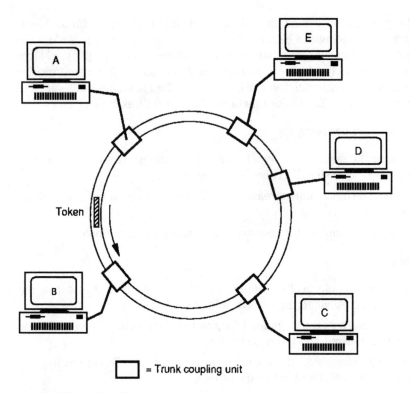

= Trunk coupling unit

Figure 2.4 Token Ring LAN.

When a station has the token, it controls the ring. Upon acquiring the token (i.e., marking the token as busy), the transmitting station inserts data behind the token and passes the data through the ring. As each RIU monitors the data, it regenerates the transmission, checks the address in the header of the data, and passes the data to the next station. When the data arrives at the transmitting station, this station frees the token and passes it to the next station on the ring, preventing one station from monopolizing the ring. If the token passes completely around the ring without being used back to the station that just transmitted, that station can once again use the token and transmit data.

Many token ring networks use priority schemes. The object of the priority scheme is to allow each station an opportunity to reserve the use of the ring for the next transmission. As the token and data circle the ring, each node examines the token, which contains a reservation field. If a node's priority is higher than the priority number in the reservation field, it raises the reservation field number to its level, thus reserving the token on the next round. If another node does not make the reservation field higher, the station uses the token and channel on the next pass around the ring.

The station with the token must store the previous reservation value in a temporary storage area. Upon releasing the token, the station restores the network to its previous lowest priority request. In this manner, once the token is freed for the next round, the station with the highest reservation can seize the token.

Token bus

Token bus LANs (IEEE 802.4) use a bus topology yet provide access to the channel as if it were a ring. The protocol eliminates the collisions found in the carrier sense-collision detection systems but allows the use of a bus-type channel. The token bus requires no physical ordering of the stations on the channel, allowing the stations to be logically configured to pass the token in any order.

The protocol uses a control frame called an *access token* or *access right*. This token gives a station the exclusive use of the bus. The token-holding station uses the bus for a period of time to send data. It then passes the token to a designated station called the *successor station*. In bus topology, all stations listen to the channel and receive the access token, but the only station allowed to use the channel is the successor station. All other stations must wait their turn to receive the token. The stations receive the token through a cyclic sequence, which forms a logical ring on the physical bus.

The LLC Sublayer

Figure 2.1 introduced the LLC protocol. This section examines it in more detail because many LANs use it to interface with the network layer (including the IP). The IEEE 802 standards split the data link layer into two sublayers: MAC and LLC. As discussed earlier in this chapter and illustrated in Figure 2.1, MAC encompasses 802.3, 802.4, and 802.5. LLC includes 802.2. This sublayer was implemented to make the LLC sublayer independent of specific LAN access methods. The LLC sublayer is also used to provide an interface into or out of the specific MAC protocol.

The MAC/LLC split provides several attractive features. First, it controls access to the shared channel among the autonomous user devices. Second, it provides for a decentralized (peer-to-peer) scheme that reduces the LAN's susceptibility to errors. Third, LLC is independent of specific access methods, while MAC is protocol specific, giving an 802 network a flexible interface with upper layer protocols (ULPs) such as IP or the OSI's connectionless network protocol (CLNP) discussed in Chapter 5.

Classes of service

The 802 LAN standards include four types of service for LLC users:

Type 1: unacknowledged connectionless service

Type 2: connection-oriented service

Type 3:   acknowledged connectionless service

Type 4:   all of the above services

All 802 networks must provide unacknowledged connectionless service (Type 1). Optionally, connection-oriented service can be provided (Type 2). Type 1 networks provide no acknowledgments (ACKs), flow control, or error recovery. Type 2 networks provide connection management, ACKs, flow control, and error recovery. Type 3 networks provide no connection setup or disconnect, but they do provide for acknowledgment of data units.

Most Type 1 networks use a higher-level protocol (i.e., TCP in the transport layer) to provide connection management functions. IP can reside over LLC as well. Therefore, a LAN-layered model could be as follows: Physical, MAC, LLC, IP, TCP, and an application layer. Chapter 5 discusses the relationship of TCP/IP and LLC in more detail.

Repeaters, Bridges, Routers, Brouters, and Gateways

Networks were originally conceived to be fairly small systems consisting of relatively few machines. As the need for data communication services has grown, networks must be connected together to share resources and distribute functions and administrative control. In addition, some LANs, by virtue of their restricted distance, often need to be connected together through other devices. These devices have numerous names in the industry; in this section we explain and define each.

Figure 2.5 shows the relationships of these devices using a layered model. A *repeater* is used to connect the media on a LAN, typically called media segments. The repeater has no upper layer functions; its principal job is to terminate the signal on one LAN segment and regenerate it on another. So, a reporter has no internetworking capabilities.

The term *bridge* is usually associated with an internetworking unit (IWU). It operates at the data link layer (always at the MAC sublayer and sometimes at the LLC sublayer). Typically, it uses MAC physical addresses to perform its relaying functions. As a general rule, it is a fairly low-function device and connects homogeneous networks (for example, IEEE-based networks).

A *router* operates at the network layer using network layer addresses (for example, IP, X.121, E.164). It usually contains more capabilities than a bridge and can offer flow control mechanisms as well as source routing or nonsource routing features, which are discussed in the next section.

Gateway describes a machine or software module that not only performs routing capabilities but can also act as a protocol conversion or mapping facility (also called a *convergence function*). For example, such a gateway could relay traffic and also provide conversion between two different types of mail transfer applications. Unfortunately, the term gateway is used in many

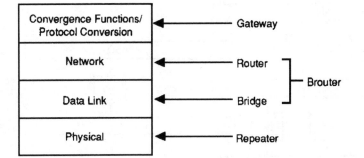

Figure 2.5   Placement of Internetworking Operations.

ways in the data communications industry. Some people use it to describe any internetworking device. I use the term gateway and router interchangeably.

Yet another term is *brouter* (as if there were not enough terms). *Brouter* describes a machine that combines the features of a router and a bridge. At first glance, this machine seems redundant, but the brouter is a powerful and flexible addition to internetworking products. Most high-end routers can perform bridging or routing operations.

To avoid any confusion among these terms, some people use the term *internetworking unit*. An IWU is a generic term used to describe a router, gateway, bridge, or anything else that performs relaying functions between networks.

Source routing and spanning tree bridges

How internetworking PDUs, or datagrams or packets, are routed between networks is sometimes a source of confusion. The two major methods to perform routing are *source routing* and *nonsource routing*. Source routing derives its name from the fact that the transmitting device (the source) dictates the route of the PDU through an internet. The source (host) machine places the addresses of the "hops" (the intermediate networks or IWUs) in the PDU. Such an approach means that the internetworking units need not perform address maintenance but simply use an address in the routing field to determine where to route the frame.

In contrast, nonsource routing makes decisions about the route and does not rely on the PDU to contain routing information. Spanning tree routing is usually associated with nonsource routing and bridges and is quite prevalent in LANs.

An example of source routing on a LAN is illustrated in Figure 2.6. The routing information field contains the LAN and bridge identifiers for each intermediate hop through the LAN network. Routing is accomplished by each bridge, which examines successive LAN and bridge numbers in the routing information field and makes a routing decision accordingly. As an

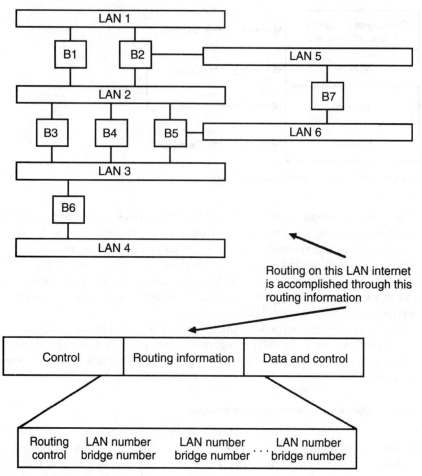

Figure 2.6 Source Routing.

example, bridge 5 might receive a frame from LAN 3. Based on the routing information in the routing field, LAN 5 might need to route the frame out of its port to LAN 6 or out of another port to LAN 2. Again, under these conditions, the bridge has no control over how the frame is routed.

Figure 2.7 depicts the operations of a spanning tree bridge. The bridge processor forwards frames based on an examination of the destination address. The bridge processor compares this address to its bridge and routing information database. If the destination address is found in the forwarding table in its database, it determines the direction of the frame. If the frame is not intended for the port from which it came, it is forwarded on the correct port to the address indicated in the database. Otherwise, it is discarded. If the source address in the frame is not contained in the database, this address is then added with the appropriate port on which it was received and a timer started. The purpose of the timer is to keep the forwarding database updated in as timely a manner as possible.

As an example, assume that a frame is received at port A on the LAN in Figure 2.7. The source MAC address in this frame is 1234. The bridge checks if this address is in the forwarding database. If not, it stores address 1234 with a notation that it can be found at port A. Later, assume that a frame arrives at port B at destination address 1234 in the frame. The bridge processor examines its forwarding table and determines that station 1234 can be found at port A; consequently, it forwards this frame to the network attached to port A.

The IP is not aware of the spanning tree operations on the LAN because the IP PDU resides in the I (information) field of the LAN frame. The bridge does not process the I field, but treats it transparently. Consequently, the bridge is only concerned with MAC source and destination addresses. Any higher-level addresses (such as a network address) that reside in the IP PDU are not acted on by the spanning tree bridge. As we see in later chapters, however, these network addresses become vital for processing PDUs across WANs because the MAC addresses are stripped away before the frame is sent through a wide area internet.

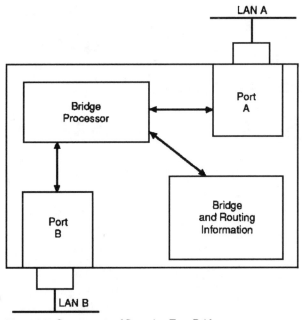

Figure 2.7 Components of Spanning Tree Bridge.

The relationships of IP and LAN addresses can be summarized as follows:

- Bridges make routing decisions on a layer 2 MAC address. Therefore, a layer 3 IP address is not processed by a bridge.

- Routers make routing decisions on a layer 3 IP address. Thus, a layer 2 MAC address of an incoming frame is examined by a router to determine if this frame (the I field) is to be processed by the router. If so, the IP address that resides in the I field of the frame is examined to determine where the IP traffic is to be routed—either to another LAN attached to the router or to a WAN through a wide area network link, also attached to the router.

Summary

TCP/IP runs on both LANs and WANs. Indeed, the TCP/IP logic is unaware of the type of network because it is isolated from the LAN physical and data link layers and any wide area subnetwork logic, such as packet routing. The IP module of TCP/IP can support both source routing and nonsource routing. Any type of spanning tree bridging on a LAN remains transparent to IP. The addresses used in IP remain transparent to the LAN bridges.

Naming, Addressing, and Routing in an Internet

A newcomer to data networks is often perplexed when the subject of naming and addressing arises. Addresses in data networks are similar to postal addresses and telephone numbering schemes. Indeed, many of the networks that exist today have derived their addressing structures from the concepts of the telephone numbering plan.

Let us clarify the meaning of names, addresses, and routes. A *name* is an identification of an entity (independent of its physical location), such as a person, an applications program, or even a computer. An *address* is also an identification, but it reveals additional information about the entity; principally, information about its physical or logical placement in a network. A *route* is information on how to relay traffic to a physical location (or address).

A network usually allows a network user to furnish the network with the name of something (another user, an application, etc.) that is to receive traffic. A network *name server* then uses this name to determine the address of the receiving entity. This address is then used by the routing protocol to determine the physical route to the receiver.

Using this approach, a network user does not become involved nor is aware of the physical address or physical location of other users and network resources. This practice allows the network administrator to relocate and reconfigure network resources without affecting end users. Likewise, users can move to other physical locations while their names remain the same; the network then simply changes its naming/routing tables to reflect the user's relocation.

This chapter introduces the issues surrounding naming and addressing, as well as the concepts of physical and network address resolution (mapping). Chapter 4 then continues with naming and describes the domain name system (DNS). We also introduce Internet protocol (IP) routing in this chapter when we discuss the relationship of addresses and routing. IP is explained further in Chapter 8.

Upper Layer, Network, Data Link, and Physical Names and Addresses

Communication between users through a data network requires several forms of addressing. Typically, two or three addresses are required: a physical address, a data link address, and a network address are used on some systems. A more common approach is the use of only the physical and network address. With this approach, the physical and data link address are the same. Practically speaking, other addresses are needed for unambiguous end-to-end communications between two users, such as upper layer names and port numbers.

Physical addresses

Each device (such as a computer or workstation) on a communications link or network is identified with a physical address. This address is often called the *hardware address*. Many manufacturers place the physical address on a logic board within the device or in an interface unit connected directly to the device. Two physical addresses are employed in a communications dialogue: one address identifies the sender (source), and the other address identifies the receiver (destination). The length of the physical address varies; most systems use two 48-bit addresses, but other address sizes are also used. The 48-bit address structure is considered too long by some designers, but both the Ethernet and IEEE protocols use it, so it is widespread. This address is called the media access control (MAC) address, which was briefly discussed in the previous chapter.

From the context of a layered data communications model, the physical address is used at the physical or data link layers. The receiving device examines the destination address of an incoming PDU. If the address matches the physical address of the device, it is passed to the next upper layer. If the address does not match the device's address, it is ignored. Thus, address detection at a lower layer prevents the data from being passed needlessly to upper layers.

Physical address detection on a LAN is illustrated in Figure 3.1. Device A transmits a frame onto the channel, which is broadcast to all other stations attached to the channel—stations B, C, and D. Assume that the destination physical address (DPA) contains the value C. Consequently, stations B and D ignore the frame. Station C accepts it and passes the PDU to the next upper layer.

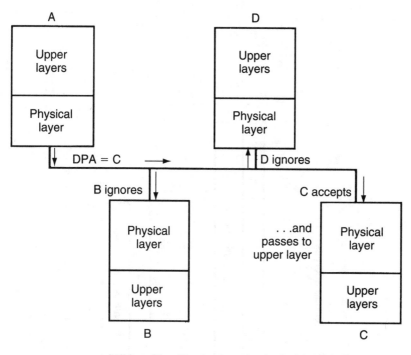

(DPA = C) = Destination physical address is C.

Figure 3.1 Physical Address Detection.

Universal physical addresses and protocol identifiers

IEEE has assumed the task of assigning universal LAN physical addresses and protocol identifiers. Previously, this work was performed by the Xerox Corporation, who administered what were known as block identifiers (Block IDs) for Ethernet addresses. The Xerox Ethernet Administration Office assigned these values, which were three octets (24 bits) in length. The organization who received this address could use the remaining 24 bits of the Ethernet address any way it chose.

Based on the progress of the IEEE 802 project, IEEE assumed the task of assigning these universal identifiers for all LANs, not just carrier sense-multiple access with collision detection (CSMA/CD) networks. IEEE, however, continues to honor the assignments made by the Ethernet administration office, although it now calls the block ID an *organization unique identifier* (*OUI*).

Each OUI provides an organization the 24-bit address space, although the true address space is actually 22 bits because the first two bits are used for control purposes (described shortly). Thus, the address space is 2^{22}.

The format for the OUI is shown in Figure 3.2. The least significant bit of the address space corresponds to the individual/group (I/G) address bit.

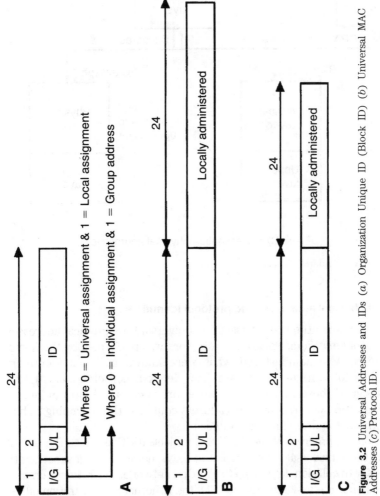

Where 0 = Universal assignment & 1 = Local assignment

Where 0 = Individual assignment & 1 = Group address

Figure 3.2 Universal Addresses and IDs (*a*) Organization Unique ID (Block ID) (*b*) Universal MAC Addresses (*c*) Protocol ID.

The I/G address bit, if set to 0, means that the address field identifies an individual address. If the value is set to 1, the address field identifies a group address used to identify more than one station connected to the LAN. If the entire OUI is set to all 1s, it signifies a broadcast address, which identifies all stations on the network.

The second bit of the address space is known as the universal or local bit (U/L). When this bit is set to 0, it has universal assignment significance—for example, from IEEE. If it is set to 1, it is a locally assigned address. Bit position two must always be set to 0 if administered by IEEE.

The OUI is extended to include a 48-bit universal LAN address (designated as the *MAC* address), also shown in Figure 3.2. The 24 bits of the address space are the same as the OUI assigned by IEEE. The second part of the address space, consisting of the remaining 24 bits, is locally administered and can be set to any value an organization chooses.

The locally administered 24 bits allow an organization to develop approximately 16 million unique and unambiguous addresses. If this address space is exhausted, IEEE assigns an additional OUI, but it does not assign additional OUIs until an organization uses all the values in the original 24-bit address space. Is the 48-bit address space sufficient for the future? Forty-eight bits provide for a 2^{48} value, which can identify approximately 281.475 trillion unique addresses, so it should be sufficient for a while.

The IEEE 802 project also administers a *protocol identifier*. This value is not a physical address but is discussed here because of its relationship with the other IEEE addressing schemes. The format for the identifier is shown in Figure 3.2c. The first 24 bits are for the OUI discussed earlier. The remaining 16 bits are locally administered by an organization; however, in some instances, these values are reserved for well-known protocols. The idea of the protocol ID is discussed further in the next sections of this chapter.

If you are interested in obtaining more information about any of these formats, contact the IEEE Standards Office, 445 Hoes Lane, Piscataway, NJ 08855-1331.

The CSMA/CD frame and MAC physical addresses

The MAC level CSMA/CD frame for 802.3 is shown in Figure 3.3. The *preamble* is transmitted first to achieve medium stabilization and synchronization. The *start frame delimiter (SFD)* follows the preamble and indicates the start of the frame. The 16- or 48-bit physical address fields contain the MAC addresses of the *destination* and *source stations.* The destination address identifies an individual workstation on the network or a group of stations. The *data length* field indicates the length of the logical link control (LLC) and data fields. If the *data* field is less than the maximum length, the packet assembly and deassembly (PAD) field is added to make up the

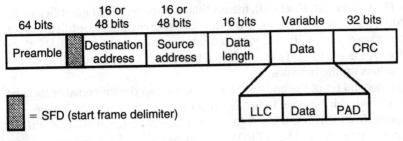

Figure 3.3 802.3 Frame.

difference. The *cyclic redundancy check (CRC)* value is contained in the frame-check sequence (FCS) field.

The Ethernet frame is shown in Figure 3.4. The formats of the Ethernet and 802.3 frames differ. First, the 802.3 frame contains an SFD, which, in actual practice, becomes part of the 64-bit preamble. The 802.3 standard allows 16- or 48-bit length addresses. The next 16 bits are used differently by the two protocols. The *type* field in Ethernet is used to identify different protocols running on the network; the same set of bits is used in the 802.3 frame to determine the length of the data field.

The issue of compatibility naturally arises when one looks at the formats. The older versions of Ethernet (version 1.0) are not compatible with the 802 standard. Newer releases of Ethernet have made these two standards compatible at the physical layer; however, they remain incompatible at the data link (LLC) layer. LAN vendors should be questioned to determine how their LAN products support the IEEE 802.3 and the Ethernet frame formats.

Link layer addresses (LSAPs)

The IEEE 802 standards use yet another address called the LSAP. Its purpose is to identify the specific protocol (or a specific instance of a protocol invocation) being used above the MAC layer. Table 3.1 lists some IEEE LSAP assignments and provides a description of the protocol. An 802 protocol must carry both a source and destination LSAP.

64 bits	48 bits	48 bits	16 bits	Variable	32 bits
Preamble	Destination address	Source address	Type	Data	CRC

Figure 3.4 Ethernet Frame.

TABLE 3.1 The Link Service Access Point (LSAP)

IEEE binary	Internet decimal	Description
00000000	0	Null LSAP
01000000	2	Individual LLC sublayer management
11000000	3	Group LLC sublayer management
00100000	4	SNA path control
01100000	6	DOD Internet protocol
01110000	14	Proway-LAN
01110010	78	EIA-RS511
01110001	142	Proway-LAN
01010101	170	Subnetwork access protocol (SNAP)
01111111	254	ISO DIS 8473
11111111	255	Global DSAP

It is possible to use only one address at the physical and data link layers. When only one address is used, it identifies the station (computer, workstation, etc.) on the link (channel), but nothing else. The practice of using one address is found on some WANs but is less common on LANs. As an example, the link access protocol balanced (LAPB) link-layer protocol uses the value A to identify a user device and B to identify the network switch on a point-to-point X.25 link. The value that is placed in the frame (A or B) depends on the type of frame being transmitted.

IEEE also specifies a code to identify the EtherType assignments. These codes are shown in Table 3.2. They identify the upper layer protocol (ULP) running on the LAN.

TABLE 3.2 EtherType Assignments (Examples)

Ethernet decimal	Hex	Description
512	0200	XEROX PUP
513	0201	PUP address translation
1536	0600	XEROX NS IDP
2048	0800	DOD Internet protocol (IP)
2049	0801	X.75 Internet
2050	0802	NBS Internet
2051	0803	ECMA Internet
2052	0804	Chaosnet
2053	0805	X.25 level 3
2054	0806	Address resolution protocol (ARP)
2055	0807	XNS compatibility
4096	1000	Berkeley trailer
21000	5208	BBN Simnet
24577	6001	DEC MOP dump/load
24578	6002	DEC MOP remote console
24579	6003	DEC DECnet Phase IV

TABLE 3.2   EtherType Assignments (Examples) (Continued)

Ethernet decimal	Hex	Description
24580	6004	DEC LAT
24582	6005	DEC
24583	6006	DEC
32773	8005	HP probe
32784	8010	Excelan
32821	8035	Reverse ARP
32824	8038	DEC LANBridge
32823	8098	Appletalk

Extension to the LSAP header (SNAP)

Because of the separate evolution of the Ethernet, TCP/IP, and IEEE LAN standards, additional requests for comments (RFCs) had to be defined to provide guidance on using IP datagrams over Ethernet and IEEE networks. Figure 3.5 shows the approach recommended by the Internet's RFC 1042, which is a standard for transmitting IP datagrams over IEEE 802 networks. The LLC destination and source service access points (DSAP and SSAP, respectively) are each set to a decimal value of 170. (The LLC control field is not affected by this standard.) The SNAP control field can identify a specific protocol ID, but it is normally set to an organization code of 0. Thereafter, the EtherType field is used to describe the type of protocol running on the LAN. The EtherType field is coded in accordance with the conventions shown in Table 3.2. Note that Table 3.1 shows the conventions for coding the SAP values (i.e., 170) for SNAP.

Network addresses

The easiest way to define a network address is that it identifies a network. Part of the network address can also designate a computer, terminal, or anything a private network administrator wants to identify as attached to a network. The Internet standards do, however, place very strict rules on what an IP address can identify.

A network address is at a higher layer than the physical or data link addresses. Higher-layer addresses are not concerned with lower-layer addresses. *Therefore, the components in a network or an internet that deal with network addresses do not need to be concerned with the final destination physical addresses until the data has arrived at the network link to which the physical device is attached.*

This important concept is illustrated in Figure 3.6. Assume that a user (a host computer) in Los Angeles transmits packets to a packet network to relay to a workstation on a LAN in London. The network in London has a network address of 128.1 (this address scheme is explained shortly). The packets are passed through the packet network (using the network's inter-

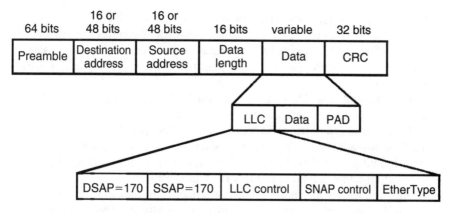

Figure 3.5 Subnetwork Access Protocol Format.

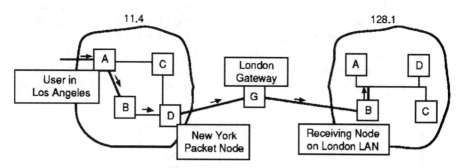

Figure 3.6 Network-Level Addressing.

nal routing mechanisms discussed in Chapter 2) to the packet switch in New York. The packet switch in New York routes the packet to the gateway located in London. This gateway examines the destination network address in the packet and determines that the packet is to be routed to network 128.1. It then transmits the packet onto the appropriate communications channel (or link) to the node on the LAN that communicates with the London gateway. In Figure 3.6, this node is labeled B in network 128.1.

Notice that this operation did not use the destination physical addresses in these routing operations. The packet switches and gateway were only concerned with the destination network address. Physical addresses are still being used, but they identify the next machine to receive the traffic and not the final destination machine.

Physical and network address resolution

You might question how the London LAN can pass the packet to the correct device (host). As we learned earlier, a physical address prevents every

packet from being processed by the upper-layer network-level protocols residing in every machine attached to the network. Therefore, the answer is
that the final destination network (or gateway) must be able to translate a
higher-layer network destination address to a lower-layer physical destination address.

In explaining how this task is accomplished, refer to Figure 3.7. Node B
on the LAN is tasked with address resolution. Assume that the destination
address contains a network address, such as 128.1, *and* a host address, say
3.2. The two addresses could therefore be joined (or concatenated) to create a full internet network address, which would appear as 128.1.3.2 in the
destination address field of the IP PDU (datagram).

Once the LAN node receives the datagram from the gateway, it must examine the host address and either look up the address in the table that contains the local physical address for the network address or query the station
for its physical address. Upon obtaining the correct physical address, the
node then encapsulates the user data into the physical layer frame, places
the appropriate physical layer address in the destination address of the
frame, and transmits the frame onto the LAN channel. All devices on the
network examine the physical address. If this address matches the device's
address, the PDU is passed to the next upper layer; otherwise, it is ignored.

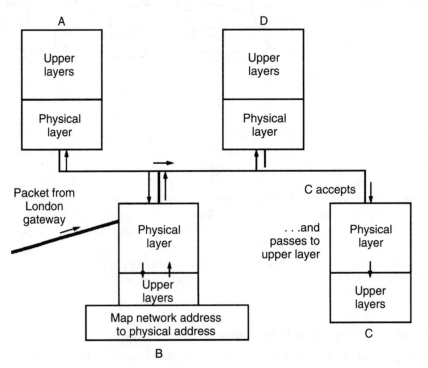

Figure 3.7 Mapping Network Addresses to Physical Addresses.

It is conceivable that the host address 3.2 also could be the actual physical address, but it is more common to assign different address values to a host address and its hardware physical address. For example, the value of 128.1.3.2 could be mapped into an IEEE MAC 48-bit physical address.

Are all these addresses necessary?

A number of my clients have complained about using both physical- and network-level addresses. After all, an address space for a MAC address of 2^{48} provides over 281 trillion unique identifiers. From my clients' perspective, it seems reasonable that this address space is sufficient to provide unique addressing without using additional address fields. Several reasons do exist for different levels of addressing schemes in any network.

Historically, the address spaces for LANs and internet networks were developed by separate groups. First, each group recognized the need for unique identifiers and devised them. The evolution of LANs and the Internet was such that the identifiers remained separate. Second, link capacity is still important in networks and will be for many years (notwithstanding optical fiber capacity). The use of a large address identifier, such as a 48-bit versus a slightly smaller 32-bit network address, is a savings of 50 percent of addressing bits transmitted. Third, under the present scheme, if the hardware interface (the board) of a computer station on a LAN becomes faulty, the board is replaced. If these addresses were used for network routing, each board replacement would require changing the network routing tables. Finally, designers believe it efficacious to hide lower layer physical addresses from upper layer software. It provides for cleaner interfaces and gives network administrators more flexibility in configuring network resources in various parts of the network.

All these arguments have merit. On a more general level, I think I speak for many people who would like a common-sense application of the multiplication principle. For example, a nine-digit number such as a social security number is more than adequate to distinguish any entity in the United States (10^9 = 1 billion). As another example, if we wish to identify something with, say, a more user-friendly six-letter sequence in the English alphabet, we could still obtain unique identifiers of more than 300 million things with a 26^6 notation. It is quite easy to lose patience with different companies, department stores, etc., who construct long and complex identifiers for passwords, account numbers, etc.

Upper layer addresses and names

Physical, data link, and network layer addresses are insufficient to move the packet to its final "destination" inside the host machine; other higher-layer addresses are needed. For example, a packet might be destined for a specific software application, such as an electronic mail or a file transfer system. Because both applications reside in the same upper layer (the application layer), some means must identify the application that is to process the packet. A ULP name or address is therefore used by the host machine to determine which application receives the data.

The upper layer identifiers are identified by a variety of terms. The Internet convention is to use the terms *protocol ID*, *port*, and *socket*. The Open Systems Interconnection (OSI) Model convention is to use the term *service access point (SAP)*. These Internet terms are explained in the next section.

A complete naming and addressing operation

Figure 3.8 shows an example of the names and addresses used in the Internet layers, both at a sending and receiving computer. The left part of the figure shows that a sending computer creates various names and addresses at different layers, that are used by the peer layer of the receiving computer (the right part of the figure) to identify the destination, the protocols to invoke, and the functions to perform.

The user application at the sending computer (such as a COBOL, C, or Fortran application) is responsible for creating its own user name. Typically, user names are created in accordance with the organization's specific protocols, or, in some instances, standards define user names. The user name is then passed along with data to the internet application layer.

The specific internet application (such as file transfer or electronic mail) is identified with a port number. Frequently used applications have reserved port numbers and are called *well-known ports*. Consequently, if the sending computer wants to invoke the internet application concerning file transfer, for example, it would code a port number of 20 in the destination port field.

The user name created by the user application might actually be identified with the port number. A source port number could be used in lieu of a user name to identify the end-user application. You should check with the specific installation to find out how specific upper-layer conventions are handled.

Next, the traffic is passed to the transport layer entity, which is typically either the transmission control protocol (TCP) or the user data protocol (UDP). In either case, this transport entity is identified by a *protocol ID*. At the receiving machine, the protocol number identifies the transport entity that is to receive the traffic. Consequently, the transport protocol ID identifies UDP, TCP, OSI's TP4, etc. After the transport layer entity, the traffic is passed down to the network layer, which handles the network addresses, also called *IP addresses*. These addresses are used in the network layer to determine where the traffic is to be routed through an internet.

After processing at the IP module, the traffic is passed to LLC. As discussed earlier, LLC works with destination and source SAPs. The concept of the SAP is quite similar to the concept of the port at the upper layer. The source SAP identifies that entity operating above LLC sending the traffic,

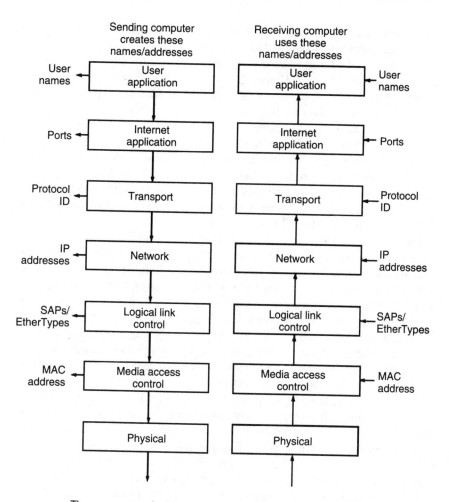

Sending computer creates these names/addresses

Receiving computer uses these names/addresses

Figure 3.8 Relationship of Names and Addresses to the Internet Layers.

and the destination SAP identifies the entity operating above LLC that is to receive the traffic. Ordinarily, this entity would be the IP residing at the network layer, but as we have learned from Table 3.1, the destination SAP could identify other entities, such as SNA's path control or the ISO's IP equivalent (DIS 8473). It is important to emphasize that for Ethernets, the EtherType field is used instead of the destination LSAP.

The last set of addresses used is the IEEE 48-bit MAC addresses. MAC receives the traffic from LLC and then creates the destination and source MAC addresses. As shown at the bottom of Figure 3.8, these names and addresses are sent to the receiving computer if it is on the same LAN or LAN segment as the sending machine. If the PDU is sent across a WAN, the addresses are stripped off before the unit is transmitted.

At the receiving end, the destination MAC address is used by MAC to determine if the traffic is to be received at this station. If so, MAC accepts the traffic and passes it (after stripping off the MAC fields) to LLC. LLC, in turn, uses the destination SAP to determine the proper protocol at the network layer. Ethernet uses the EtherType field.

Once the traffic is passed to the network layer, the IP address is used by gateways or routers to determine a route through the network. If the traffic has arrived at the receiving host computer, the IP address is used in conjunction with the port number to provide a unique and unambiguous connection between the two machines, known as the *socket*. We examine the socket in more detail in Chapter 7, which discusses TCP. The protocol identifier (ID) is then used to determine which transport layer protocol is to receive the traffic, which is then passed up to an internet application. The destination port number is then examined to determine which internet application entity is to receive the traffic.

Finally, the traffic might be passed to an end-user application at the receiving machine, although in many scenarios today, the end-user application resides only at the originating computer. This approach means that the internet application (such as the file transfer example) receives the data, services it, and perhaps returns a reply. This approach is quite common in a client-server relationship, where the sending computer contains the client and the receiving computer contains the server but not an actual end-user application.

The process can of course be reversed. In Figure 3.8, the direction of the arrows would be changed and data would be sent from the computer on the right side of the figure to the computer on the left.

The actual PDU transmitted on the channel contains considerable overhead just in names and addresses. The situation suggested at the bottom part of the figure, however, is not quite as onerous as it might appear because the destination and source MAC addresses are not transported across a WAN. As discussed earlier, these are inserted at the receiving network or computer using a process called *address mapping*. This topic is discussed shortly.

In summary, the Internet standards (used in conjunction with IEEE LANs) use the names and addresses at each layer, as shown in Table 3.3.

TABLE 3.3 Names and Addresses of Internet Standard Layers

Layer	Name/address used at this layer
User application	End-user IDs
Internet application	Port numbers
Transport	Protocol names
Network	IP addresses
Logical link control (LCC)	LSAP numbers*
Media access control (MAC)	MAC addresses
Physical	None

* For Ethernets, EtherType field used in place of destination LSAP

The IP Address Structure

This section describes the original format for the IP address, which is still in use. It also introduces some changes made in 1993 (under various stages of implementation) to improve the IP address. These changes are described in more detail in Chapter 5.

TCP/IP networks use a 32-bit address to identify a host computer and the network to which the host is attached. The structure of the <IP address is depicted in Figure 3.9. Its format is **IP Address = Network Address + Host Address**.

Class A

0	Network (7 bits)	Local address (24 bits)

Class B

10	Network (14 bits)	Local address (16 bits)

Class C

110	Network (21 bits)	Local address (8 bits)

Class D (Multicast format)

1110	Multicast address (28 bits)

Future format

11110	Future use

Figure 3.9 IP Address Formats.

Note that the IP address does not identify a host per se, but a host's connection to its network. Consequently, if a host machine is moved to another network, its address space must be changed.

IP addresses are classified by their formats. Four formats are permitted: class A, class B, class C, and class D. As illustrated in Figure 3.9, the first bits of the address specify the format of the remainder of the address field in relation to the network and host subfields. The host address can be called the local address or the REST field. We will see later that these classes are being replaced by a "classless" scheme.

The *class A* addresses provide for networks that have a large number of hosts. The host ID field is 24 bits. Therefore, 2^{24} hosts can be identified. Seven bits are devoted to the network ID, which supports an identification scheme for as many as 127 networks (bit values of 1 to 127). *Class B* addresses are used for networks of intermediate size. Fourteen bits are assigned for the network ID, and 16 bits are assigned for the host ID. *Class C* networks contain fewer than 256 hosts (2^8), and 21 bits are assigned to the network ID. Finally, *class D* addresses are reserved for multicasting, which is a form of broadcasting but within a limited area. Multicasting is described in later chapters.

In summary, the IP address space can take the forms shown in Table 3.4.

The maximum network and host addresses available for class A, B, and C addresses are as shown in Table 3.5.

For convenience, the Internet addresses are depicted with decimal notations. As an example, a Class B Internet address of binary 1000000 00000011 00001001 00000001 is written as 128.3.9.1. This address translates to network ID = 128.3 and host ID = 9.1. These notations might seem somewhat strange to humans, but the scheme works quite well with computers. Chapter 4 examines how user-friendly names can be used and translated into IP format.

TABLE 3.4 IP Address Formats

Class	Network address space values
A	0_127*
B	128_191
C	192_223
D	224_254

* Numbers 0 and 127 are reserved.

TABLE 3.5 Maximum Network and Host Addresses

Class	Maximum network numbers	Maximum host numbers
A	126*	16,777,124
B	16,384	65,534
C	2,097,152	254

* Numbers 0 and 127 are reserved.

TABLE 3.6 Decimal Notations for IP Address Spaces

A	network.host.host.host
B	network.network.host.host
C	network.network.network.host
D	(not applicable)

In summary, the decimal notations for the IP address space can take the forms shown in Table 3.6.

Some gateways and hosts can have multiple connections to other networks throughout an internet. These machines have two or more physical connections and are called *multihomed* hosts. Multihomed hosts must have a unique IP address for each of their physical connections. The multihomed hosts, while providing flexible routing, can also create problems in managing traffic.

The IP address structure depicted in Figure 3.9 can be coded with all 1s in the network or host ID fields. This coding identifies the datagram as a broadcast signal and can be used to send the datagram to all networks and hosts on a network. For example, the address of 128.2.255.255 means all hosts on network 128.2. Be aware that some TCP/IP software implementations do not support the broadcast option.

The IP address can also be coded with all 0s in the host ID, signifying that the address is identified as "this host." The network ID can also be coded with all 0s, referring to "this network." For example, 128.2.0.0 means this network; that is, network 128.2. The use of a network ID of 0 is helpful if a host does not know its IP address. It sends a datagram with 0s in the network ID field, and other hosts interpret this address as this network.

The capability to code either all 1s or all 0s in the internet address space can provide useful capabilities; however, the use of these features requires some thought. For example, as stated above, sending all 0s in the address space means "this host on this network." This coding should be used only when a host is trying to learn its own IP address. The same holds true for coding all 0s in the network address space with the host number in the host address space. As another example, consider coding all 1s in the entire IP address space. This coding simply means that the destination address is interpreted and received by every host on the connected network; however, it cannot be forwarded outside that one network. Other combinations can also be developed with these capabilities. You should check with the software vendor to see how these capabilities are implemented on specific software, as well as the implication of such capabilities on performance and operations.

Many users do not communicate through the Internet. Therefore, they can choose their own internet addressing structure. While users are free to select their own private internet addresses, considerable thought should be given to which class of address to use. Obviously, the ratio of networks to host machines is the principal consideration in choosing the address format. Additionally, the address format should be chosen based on an assessment of the future growth of the enterprise's computing resources, both in relation to networks and host computers.

Chapter 5, which discusses IP, examines the IP address specifically and some of the problems associated with it, namely the fact that the address space is not large enough to accommodate the continued growth of the Internet. In that chapter, several proposals for solving the problem are also examined. The interested reader can refer immediately to the section titled, "Classless Inter-domain Routing (CIDR)" in Chapter 5.

Destination Addresses and Routing

The following subsections discuss IP routing destinations, routing logic, and how multiple connections to networks are handled.

Direct and indirect destinations

IP uses the concepts of direct and indirect destinations in its routing logic. A *direct host* is a machine attached directly to the network and the network's gateway. An *indirect host*, meanwhile, is a destination host on a network other than that of the source host. Therefore, the datagram must be sent to an intermediate gateway before it is delivered to the destination host. Figure 3.10 demonstrates the concept of both types of destinations.

The way in which IP manages addresses and decides routing paths requires that a machine examine only the network address part of the destination IP address to determine if the destination host is directly or indirectly attached to the source host's network; that is, the machine compares if the network part of the destination and host address are the same.

If the destination host is indirectly attached to the source host, the IP module must then select the next IP module to process the datagram. The IP must therefore keep a set of mappings between destination networks and the relevant router to reach the network as well as the physical port to that router.

It is evident that routing tables do not need to contain a full address. Nonetheless, the awkward nature of the IP address structure becomes evident from an examination of Figure 3.10. Notice that router 8 has three IP addresses: 11.0.0.1, 13.0.0.4, and 10.0.0.1. While these addresses are certainly manageable, they do point out the need to carefully administer the IP addresses.

The problem stems from the fact that the IP address is an interface address. Therefore, every port on a machine must have an IP address. IP relies on a route discovery protocol to find the routes through an internet. For example, network 14.0.0.0 is reached from router 8 through a connection to network 13.0.0.0 out of the router's port 3 with an internet address of

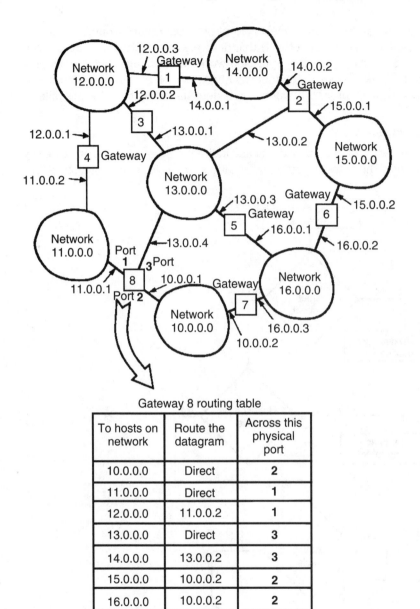

Gateway 8 routing table

To hosts on network	Route the datagram	Across this physical port
10.0.0.0	Direct	2
11.0.0.0	Direct	1
12.0.0.0	11.0.0.2	1
13.0.0.0	Direct	3
14.0.0.0	13.0.0.2	3
15.0.0.0	10.0.0.2	2
16.0.0.0	10.0.0.2	2

Figure 3.10 Direct and Indirect Destinations.

13.0.0.2. If the communications link at 13.0.0.4 fails, however, IP does not know that alternate routes are available on other interfaces.

Of course, most vendors' products today approach this problem in one of two ways. Some systems build secondary routes into the routing tables. In this example, the column labeled "Route the Datagram" would have a second dimension (or even a third) that describes alternate routes in case the first route fails. Again, this approach works well enough, but it does produce fairly complex routing tables. Other systems perform a spontaneous route discovery process as soon as it is determined that a route has failed.

IP routing logic

The preceding discussion of direct and indirect routing implies that a gateway needs only the network part of an IP address to perform routing. Figure 3.11

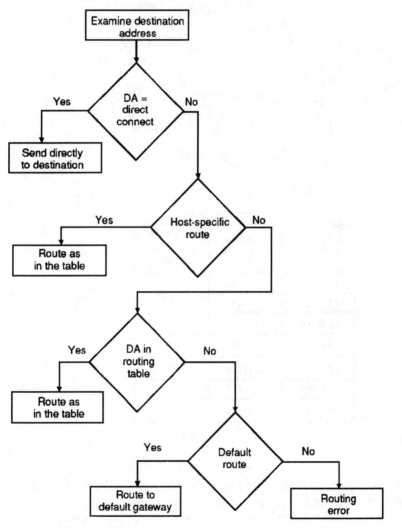

Figure 3.11 IP Routing Algorithm.

shows a logic flow chart of the IP algorithm for routing. Each machine maintains a routing table containing destination network addresses and the specified "next hop" machine. The table is used to perform three types of routing:

- direct routing to locally attached machines

- indirect routing for networks that must be reached via one or more routers

- default routing to the destination network if the first two types of routing are unsuccessful.

Multihomed hosts

Routers and hosts can have multiple connections to other networks throughout an internet. These machines have two or more physical connections and are called *multihomed hosts*. Multihomed hosts must have a unique IP address for each of their physical connections. As mentioned earlier, the multihomed hosts, while providing flexible routing, can create problems in managing traffic.

Multihomed hosts were originally intended to allow one physical interface to be identified by one IP address. In practice, however, some vendors allow combinations of multiple internet addresses across one physical interface. In addition, some interfaces are known as "logical hosts." Logical host interfaces occur when a host has more than one IP address, but the addresses have the same network number or the same subnetwork number. Such a logical host interface could share one or several physical interfaces.

As a practical matter, keep the host out of the routing business. If the host routing table has no information for the destination IP address, it simply chooses a default routing by selecting an entry in the routing table. The router should forward the datagram based on its routing table and return a message to the host stating that this event has indeed occurred. As we shall see, this message should entail a redirect message issued through the Internet control message protocol (ICMP). The host computer should then update its default entry to the appropriate designation returned by the router.

Address Resolution Issues

As we learned earlier, each device attached to a single physical LAN is identified by a physical hardware address. Other identifiers are also assigned, including network addresses. The vast majority of physical addresses are assigned by the manufacturer before the product is shipped to the customer or when the product is installed at the customer's site.

We now find ourselves with an interesting problem, which we have begun to address: how can we relate the physical address to a network address, and vice versa? As an example, if host A wishes to send a datagram to host D, it might not know the physical address of host D. To compound the problem, the higher-layer network address might also be unknown to host A. Therefore, some method must be devised to relate different levels of addresses to each other.

The Address Resolution Protocol

The IP stack provides a protocol for resolving addresses. The address resolution protocol (ARP) handles the translation of IP addresses to physical addresses and hides these physical addresses from the upper layers.

Generally, ARP works with mapping tables, referred to as the *ARP cache*. The table provides the mapping between an IP address and a physical address. In a LAN (such as an Ethernet or IEEE 802 network), ARP takes the target IP address and searches for a corresponding target physical address in a mapping table. If ARP finds the address, it returns the physical address back to the requester, which could be a device driver, a server on a LAN, or, for that matter, any other station (such as a workstation).

If the needed address is not found in the ARP cache, the ARP module sends a broadcast onto the network. The broadcast is called the *ARP request*, which contains an IP target address. Consequently, if one of the machines receiving the broadcast recognizes its IP address in the ARP request, it returns an ARP reply back to the inquiring host. This frame contains the physical hardware address of the queried host. Upon receiving this frame, the inquiring host places the address into its ARP cache. Thereafter, datagrams sent to this particular IP address can be translated into the physical address by accessing the cache. The ARP system thus allows an inquiring host to find the physical address of another host by using the IP address.

The concepts of ARP requests and replies are shown in Figure 3.12. Host A wishes to determine C's physical address. It broadcasts datagrams to B, C, and D. Only C responds because it recognizes its IP address in the incoming ARP request datagram. Host C places its address into an IP datagram in the form of the ARP reply.

In addition to mapping IP addresses to physical addresses, ARP allows the designation of specific hardware types. Therefore, when an ARP datagram is received by the queried host, it can use a field in the datagram to determine if the machine is using a particular type of hardware, such as an Ethernet interface or packet radio.

The ARP packet format is shown in Figure 3.13. It is encapsulated into the physical layer PDU. As an example, the physical layer PDU could be an Ethernet frame, described in Chapter 2. The EtherType field is set to 8035_{16} (or 32821_{10}) to identify an ARP frame, which is part of the field labeled "physical layer header" in Figure 3.13. Table 3.2 provides the EtherType values.

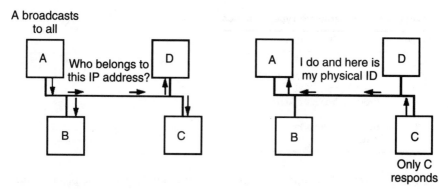

Figure 3.12 ARP Request and Reply.

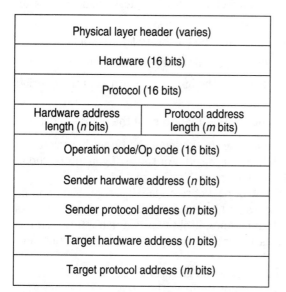

Figure 3.13 ARP Request and Reply Packet.

The following provides a brief description of each field:

Physical Layer Header: the header for the physical layer packet

Hardware: specifies the type of hardware interface in which the inquiring host seeks a response. Examples are Ethernet and packet ratio (Table 3.7 lists the assigned values).

Protocol: identifies the type of protocol the sender is using; typically the EtherType (see Table 3.2).

Hardware Address Length: specifies the length in bytes of each hardware address in the packet.

TABLE 3.7 ARP Hardware Type Examples

Type	Description
1	Ethernet (10 Mb)
2	Experimental Ethernet (3 Mb)
3	Amateur radio X.25
4	Proteon ProNET token ring
5	Chaos
6	IEEE 802 networks
7	ARCNET

Protocol Address Length: specifies the length in bytes of the protocol addresses in the packet (for example, the IP addresses).

Opcode: specifies whether the packet is an ARP request (value of 1) or an ARP reply (value of 2).

Sender Hardware Address: contains the hardware address of the sender.

Sender Protocol Address: contains the IP address of the sender.

Target Hardware Address: contains the hardware address of the queried host.

Target Protocol Address: contains the IP address of the queried host.

In the request packet, all fields are used except the target hardware address. In the reply packet, all fields are used. For those of you interested in further details, the logic of ARP is depicted in Figure 3.14.

Any ARP module can use an ARP packet to update its cache. The module examines the sending IP address and hardware address to determine if its cache has these entries. In this manner, it obtains as much information as possible from the traffic. This process is called "gleening"; it is not supported by all vendors.

You might wonder why a network would go through all this activity to determine addresses. After all, why not perform the broadcasting operation each time and allow the networks to simply discard traffic not destined for their hosts? Broadcast works well enough on a collision detection network, such as the Ethernet and the IEEE 802.3 network. Indeed, these networks are designed as broadcast networks. The practice of broadcasting all datagrams over other networks, however, could create unacceptable overhead because broadcast requires each station to pass the traffic up to a network layer to examine the network header for the proper destination IP address.

This capability proves useful to the user when addresses become invalid (thus preventing the sending of invalid addresses in frames). One example is the changing of Ethernet addresses in a LAN. As discussed in the next section, the use of an additional protocol, called *proxy ARP*, is another useful tool.

Check with your vendors on the frequency with which ARP broadcasts are transmitted. Some method should be available for controlling the num-

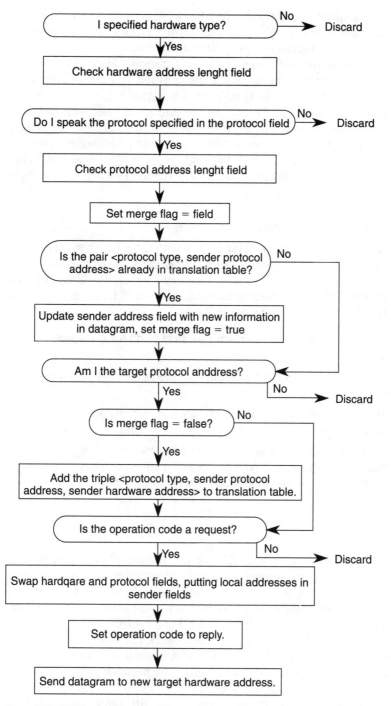

Figure 3.14 ARP Logic Flow Diagram.

ber of ARP requests for the same IP address. The simplest way to handle the broadcasting ARP problem is to establish a mechanism that prevents sending more than a given number within a set time.

It might also prove useful to save the first transmission of a PDU transmission. For example, imagine that a transmission was not delivered because of an invalid (unresolved) address. It is a good idea to save this first transmission and perhaps discard the remaining transmissions until the destination address issue has been resolved. In this manner, the system might not need to send out connection establishment messages created in a ULP (such as TCP or OSI's TP4) that might be using this initial PDU to determine round trip propagation time through the Internet. This retransmission delay would bias the results.

ARP address translation table

The Internet defines a mapping table used with the address mapping protocols, and this information is provided in RFC 1213. As depicted in Figure 3.15, the mapping table consists of a row entry for each IP address on each host gateway (machine). Four columns are provided for each row entry. The contents of these columns are as follows:

- The *ifIndex* contains the interface (physical port) for the specific interface for this address.

- The *physical address* entry contains the media dependent address (for example, a MAC address).

- The *IP address* entry contains the IP address, which corresponds to the physical address.

- The *mapping type* entry is set to one of four values: Other = 1 (none of the following), invalid = 2 (the mapping for this row entry is no longer valid), dynamic = 3 (the mapping could change), static = 4 (entry does not change).

Proxy ARP

Another protocol, called *proxy ARP* or *promiscuous ARP*, is used in a number of ways. One implementation allows an organization to use only one IP address (the network portion of an address) for multiple networks. In essence, proxy ARP maps a single IP network address into multiple physical addresses. The concept is illustrated in Figure 3.16.

Gateway 1 (G1) hides network X from network Y and vice versa. Thus, if host A wishes to send traffic to host D, host A might first form an ARP message to obtain the physical address of host D on network Y. The ARP message, however, does not reach host D. The gateway intercepts the message, performs the address resolution, and sends an ARP reply back to host A

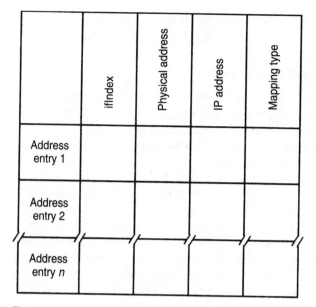

Figure 3.15 Address Translation Table.

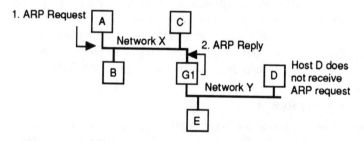

Figure 3.16 Proxy ARP.

with the gateway's physical address in the ARP target hardware address field. Host A then uses the ARP response to update its ARP table, and the ARP operation is complete. The example can also be reversed; the hosts on network X can be serviced by the gateway as discussed for host A.

Proxy ARP is quite flexible, and nothing precludes mapping different IP address prefixes to the same physical address. Some ARP implementations, however, have diagnostic procedures that display alarms to network control if multiple addresses are mapped to the same physical address. This problem is called *spoofing* and alerts network control of possible problems.

Proxy ARP works only if the organization has installed ARP. ARP is quite simple and does not work with complex topologies, such as where more than one gateway services more than one network. ARP can be used without changing routing tables in other parts of an internet. As mentioned at the start of this discussion, ARP hides physical networks through its mapping functions.

Reverse Address Resolution Protocol

The ARP protocol is a useful technique for determining physical addresses from network addresses. Some workstations, however, do not know their own IP address. For example, diskless (dataless) workstations do not have any IP address knowledge when booted to a system. The diskless workstations know only their hardware address.

The *reverse address resolution protocol (RARP)* works similarly to ARP except, as the name suggests, it works in reverse. The process is illustrated in Figure 3.17. The inquiring machine (for example, a diskless workstation) broadcasts an RARP request. This request specifies that machine A is the target machine, in contrast to the ARP protocol, which identifies the receiving machine as the target. The RARP datagram contains the physical address of the sending machine and sends the transmission out as a broadcast; therefore, all machines on this physical network receive this request. Only the RARP servers are allowed to reply, however.

The servers reply by filling in the target protocol address field. They also change the operation code in the RARP message from a request to a reply (3 signifies a request, and 4 signifies a reply). The packet is sent back to the inquiring station, which is then able to use the information in the frame to derive its IP address. The EtherType field in the frame is coded as 8035_{16} (32821_{10}) to identify the I (information) field as an RARP packet (see Table 3.2).

Primary and secondary RARPs

RARP is often used on LANs for booting the machines to the network. These networks experience low failure rates; the RARP messages are rarely lost, mishandled, or otherwise corrupted. In some networks, however, more than one RARP server is required because of workload conditions. Some

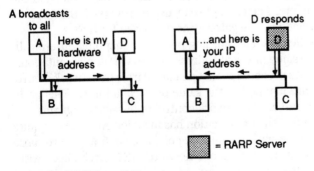

Figure 3.17 RARP Operations.

LANs use transmit timers and timeouts to ensure the user stations obtain expeditious service from the RARP server. They evoke retransmissions of the RARP messages upon a timeout.

Other systems, in addition to using timeouts and retransmissions, designate an RARP server as a primary or backup server. If the primary RARP server is down or unable to fulfill a request, the request can be serviced by a designated backup server. Of course, on the down side, if the request is sent to multiple servers, these servers could create redundant traffic when they respond. Indeed, for an Ethernet network, the replies from multiple servers increase the chance of collisions, which results in reduced throughput.

The solution to this problem is simple. In many networks, a secondary server cannot respond until it ascertains that the primary server has not responded. The secondary station thus monitors the channel to check for the reply from the primary RARP. If the reply is not detected within a set time, the secondary server times-out and assumes the role of the primary RARP. Another approach does not allow the secondary server to use the timeout function. Rather, if the requesting machine does not receive the reply from the primary server, it times-out and reissues the message. The secondary RARPs note this as a rebroadcast of the same request. At this time, a secondary RARP (or RARPs) services the message. Note that not all vendors implement RARP operations. You should check with your vendors to determine how or if RARP is used.

IP and X.121 Address Mapping

The ITU-T X.121 specification is widely used throughout the world, and the majority of public packet networks require X.121 as the network address. RFC 1236 provides guidance on the mapping of IP and X.121 addresses, as depicted through the DDN X.25/IP addressing conventions. Before discussing this standard, a brief tutorial on X.121 is provided.

International numbering plan for data networks (X.121)

X.121 uses a data network identification code (DNIC) based on the format *DCCN*, where DCC is a three-digit country code, and N is the network digit that identifies a specific network within a country. Figure 3.18 shows the structure for X.121. Some countries have more than 10 networks. In this situation, multiple DCCs are assigned to the country. For example, the United States is assigned the DCC values 310 through 316.

X.121 also defines a network terminal number (NTN). This value identifies the computer, terminal, etc., within the network and consists of a 10-digit identifier. Optionally, the NTN can be included as part of the terminal identifier. In this situation, the 11-digit field is called a *national number* (NN).

Figure 3.18 X.121 Address Format.

DDN IP addresses

The Internet DDN addresses consist of an ASCII text string of four decimal numbers separated by periods, which correspond to the four octet IP address. The four numbers are referred to as follows:

n = network

h = host

l = logical address

i = interface message processor or packet node

Thus, a class A address could be represented by n.h.l.i; a class B address by n.n.h.i; and a class C address by n.n.n.h.i. An example of a class A IP address is 16.9.0.122, where n = 16, h = 9, l = 0, and i = 122.

A user device can generate a 12- or 14-digit X.121 address. The last two digits of the 14-digit address are a subaddress and not used on DDN.

Mapping X.121 and IP Addresses

The X.121 and IP address mapping is shown in Figure 3.19. The DNIC is set to 0, and the flag digit identifies physical or logical addresses in the address space. The host ID is coded as values to represent h or i. The subaddress field is optional. The mapping rules depend on the class of address as well as the range of numbers used by the value h. Study RFC 1236 if you need more information.

Subnets, Subnet Addressing, and Address Masking

At first glance, it might appear that the IP addressing scheme is flexible enough to accommodate the identification of a sufficient number of net-

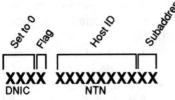

Figure 3.19 IP and X.121 Address Mappings.

Host ID = Combinations of *h* and *i*

works and hosts to service almost any user or organization. But this is not the case. The Internet designers were not shortsighted; they simply failed to account for the explosive growth of the Internet and the rapid growth of IPs in private networks.

The problem arises when a network administrator attempts to identify a large number of networks and computers (such as personal computers) attached to these networks. The problem becomes quite onerous because it is necessary to store and maintain the many network addresses, and these addresses must then be accessible using large routing tables. As we see in later chapters, using the gateway protocols to exchange routing information requires immense resources if the protocols need to access and maintain big addressing tables.

The problem is compounded when networks are added to an internet. This addition requires reorganizing routing tables and perhaps assigning additional addresses to identify the new networks. To solve this problem, the Internet establishes a scheme whereby multiple networks are identified by one internetwork address. Obviously, this approach reduces the number of network addresses needed in an internet. It also requires a slight modification to the routing algorithms, but the change is minor compared to the benefits derived.

Because one address is used to identify more than one network, the concept of a *subnet* was implemented in the Internet. A subnet is any network that operates transparently to a gateway, which understands only the IP part of the Internet address. For example, the host part of the IP address is transparent to the gateway. As illustrated in Figure 3.20, an internet address coming to gateway 1, an IP gateway, contains address 128.11.1.2. From the perspective of the networks attached to gateway 1, the Internet knows only about the gateway address of 128.11. Gateway G1 must resolve

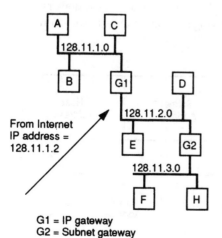

From Internet
IP address =
128.11.1.2

G1 = IP gateway
G2 = Subnet gateway

Figure 3.20 Subnet Addressing.

the local address values with either 1.0, 2.0, or 3.0, depending on which subnet is to receive the datagram.

Figure 3.20 also shows a subnet gateway labeled G2. This gateway is concerned with mapping the address 3.0 to the host address attached to the subnetwork. In this example, the gateway must establish the host addresses for hosts F and H. Ordinarily, this is done by accessing a look-up table in which the value of 3.0 is replaced with 3.n1, 3.n2, which identify hosts F and H, respectively.

Figure 3.21 shows the structure of the slightly modified Internet address. All that has occurred is the division of the local address, heretofore called the *host address*, into the subnet address (in this example, 1.0, 2.0, 3.0) and the host address (in this example, the addresses for hosts F and H). It is evident that both the initial internet address and the subnet address take advantage of hierarchical addressing and hierarchical routing. This concept fits well with the basic gateway functions inherent in the Internet. Referring once again to Figure 3.20 and taking it from the top down, we find that the internet is only concerned with the first half of the internet address. G1 is only concerned with the subnet address, and G2 is only concerned with what is now called the host address. Taking it from the bottom up, hosts F and H are not concerned with any of the higher-layer addresses. They can communicate with each other and their gateway, G2, with physical addresses or, if necessary, a ULP address.

Choosing the assignments of the "local address" is left to the individual network implementors. A prudent designer is careful to keep the numbering and identification consistent throughout the entire local subnetwork. Notwithstanding, the chosen values can vary. For example, one byte can be used as a subnet address; the second byte can be used as a host address. Alternately, the first 12 bits can be used for the subnet address and a half byte can be used as a host address. Many other choices exist in defining the local address. As mentioned before, it is a local matter, but it does require considerable thought. It requires following the same theme of the overall in-

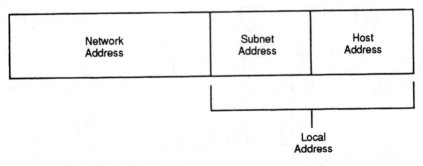

Figure 3.21 Subnet Address Structure.

ternet address of how many subnets must be identified in relation to how many hosts must be identified that reside on each subnet.

Subnet masks

To support subnet addressing, the IP routing algorithm was modified to support a subnet mask. The purpose of the mask is to determine which part of the IP address pertains to the subnetwork and which part pertains to the host. The convention used for subnet masking is a 32-bit field in addition to the IP address. The contents of the field (the mask) are set as follows:

Binary 1s: identify the network address portion of the IP address.

Binary 0s: identify the host address portion of the IP address. The example in Figure 3.20 would use the following mask for subnets 128.11.1, 128.11.2, and 128.11.3:

```
11111111  11111111  11111111  00000000
```

A *bitwise AND* function extracts the fields of the IP address as follows. A bitwise AND is performed on the IP address and the subnet mask. The results of this operation are matched against a destination address in a routing table. If the results are equal, the next hop IP address (relative to the destination address) is used to determine the next hop on the route. Therefore, the last octet of all 0s identifies the host on the subnet.

The mask becomes part of the routing algorithm's conditional statement: "If destination IP address and subnet mask equal my IP address and subnet mask, then send datagram to local network; otherwise, send datagram to gateway corresponding to destination address." Indeed, the use of masks handles routes to direct conventions, host-specified routes, and default routes.

An implementor should note the following guidelines for subnetting:

- The IP algorithm must be implemented on all machines in a subnet.
- Subnet masks should be the same for all machines.
- If one or more machines do not support masks, proxy ARP can be used to achieve subnetting.

Examples of the mask

Table 3.8 shows how the mask is interpreted on a bit-by-bit basis. To use this table, imagine that a mask is coded as 255.255.240.0. Table 3.8 reveals that the binary mask is 11111111 11110000 00000000. Thus, the lower-order 12 bits of the IP address are to be used for a host address. As another example, imagine that a mask is coded as 255.255.255.224. Table 3.8 reveals that the binary mask is 11111111 11111111 11111111 11100000, and the lower-order 5 bits of the IP address are to be used for a host address.

TABLE 3.8 Binary and Decimal
Equivalents in the Mask

00000000	0
10000000	128
11000000	192
11100000	224
11110000	240
11111000	248
11111100	252
11111110	254
11111111	255

As another example, assume a class B IP address of 128.1.17.1 with a mask of 255.255.240.0. To discover the subnet address value, the mask has a bitwise AND operation performed with the destination address as shown in Figure 3.22.

As this example shows, when the subnet mask is split across octets, the results can be a bit confusing. In this case, the actual value for the subnet address is 0001_2 or 1_{10}, even though the decimal address of the host space is 17.1. The software does not care about octet alignment; it is looking for a match of the destination address in the IP datagram to an address in a routing table. Therefore, each destination network and subnetwork address in the routing table is compared to the destination network and subnetwork address of 10000000 00000001 0001. If a match is found, the datagram is routed to the entry in the routing table designated as the next node for the destination address. Otherwise, the datagram is either discarded or sent to a default next node.

Summary of broadcast rules. Now that the subnet mask has been examined, the permissible formats for broadcast can be summarized.

Directed broadcast: This address allows broadcasts to a specified network. It is used only in the destination address, and its format is [network number, 255].

Limited broadcast: The destination IP address is formatted so that every host on a physical network receives the datagram. This format does not al-

IP address	10000000	00000001	0001	0001	00000001
Mask	11111111	11111111	1111	0000	00000000
Result	10000000	00000001	0001	don't care	
Logical address	128	1	1	don't care	
		network	sub net	host	

Figure 3.22 Destination Address for Mask with bitwise AND Performed.

low the datagram to be routed outside the one physical network. Its format is [255,255].

Subnet directed broadcast: With the use of the subnet address mask value, an internet can also direct a broadcast to a specified subnetwork. Again, this format should only be used in the destination address field, and its format is [network number, subnetwork number, 255].

All subnetworks directed broadcast: This address format (again only in the destination field) allows a datagram to be broadcast to all subnetworks on a specified subnetted network. Its format is [network number, 255, 255].

Vendors vary on how they support broadcasting in their products. Some machines have not been programmed to understand subnetting, which can cause problems if a subnet mask is used. Additionally, some machines do not understand the relationship of a link layer broadcast address and the IP broadcast address. The link layer and IP destination address should be complementary to each other. If one has a broadcast address, so should the other. At a minimum, if a link layer contains a broadcast address, the destination address field and the IP datagram should be an IP multicast address or an IP broadcast address.

It is also possible to build the address mask with noncontiguous 1s. For example, this option is permissible: 0100110001100000. Because the operation simply does bitwise AND functions, any combination of the 1s identifies the subnet. While this mask is possible, it is not a very good idea because it makes things unnecessarily complex.

Finally, before leaving subnet addresses, it should be emphasized that the selection of the address space is strictly up to the user. For example, using a class B address in which the host address space is 16 bits, the subnet address might be 8 bits, and the host address might be the other 8 bits, which allows the network administrator to configure 254 subnets with 254 hosts to each subnet (0 and 256 are not available). Or, as another alternative, using 6 bits for the subnet address space offers the capability of identifying 64 networks, $2^6 = 64$, which is equivalent to 10 bits for the host's identification attached to these networks, resulting in a maximum number of 10^{24} hosts for each network, $2^{10} = 1024$.

One scheme for assigning masks is to partition the subnet and host spaces (RFC 1219 provides further guidance). Assuming the use of a class C network with 8 bits available for the subnet and host addresses, assigning a number takes the following form: ssggghhh (where s = subnet, g = growth bits, and h = host bits). The mask for this address space is 11110000. If it becomes necessary to add hosts to the subnet and enlarge the hosts' address space, the address space could be changed to ssgghhh*h* and the mask is still 11110000. Suppose the Internet grows and needs more bits for subnet addresses. The address space could be changed to sssghhhh and the mask remains the same. Of course, if the hosts on this internet grew to the extent that the final g bit had to be used (ssshhhh*h*), at this time, the mask would be changed to 11100000.

Summary

Data networks need various types and levels of naming and addressing to unambiguously identify user and control traffic. The TCP/IP protocol suite provides a full array of these names and addresses as well as several protocols for mapping between physical and network addresses.

The IP address format has become a worldwide standard for network/ host identification. The subnet address space and the subnet masking operations considerably reduce the overhead associated with IP address maintenance.

4

The Domain Name System

This chapter continues the discussion of naming and addressing, concentrating on naming and internet name servers. You should be familiar with the material in Chapters 2 and 3 before reading this chapter.

The Internet Protocol (IP) address structure (consisting of 32 bits) is somewhat awkward to use. Indeed, instead of using the IP address, most organizations have adapted the use of acronyms and meaningful terms to identify a numeric address. This practice presents an interesting problem if a network user has adopted acronyms as an address but must internetwork with a network that uses the numeric IP addresses. How can the non-IP identifier be mapped to an IP address?

One could say that the user should conform and use the numeric IP addresses. Yet we cannot expect an end user to remember all the values for these addresses, much less to key in these addresses at the workstation. The solution instead is to devise a naming scheme wherein an end user can employ a friendly, easy-to-remember name to identify the sending and receiving entities. For this worthy idea to be implemented, procedures must first be established to provide both a framework for establishing user-friendly names and conventions for mapping the names to IP addresses.

In the Internet, the organization and managing of these names was provided originally by the SRI Network Information Center. It maintained a file called HOST.TXT that listed the names of networks, gateways, and hosts and their corresponding addresses. The original structure of *flat name* spaces worked well enough in the early days of the Internet. Flat names describes a form of a name consisting merely of characters identifying an object without any further meaning or structure. The Internet Network

Information Center administered name spaces and assigned them to new objects identified in the Internet.

The Domain Name System Architecture

As the Internet grew, the administration of HOST.TXT became a very big job. In recognition of this problem, the Internet administrators decided in 1983 to develop a system called the domain name system (DNS).

Similar to many addressing schemes (such as the ISO and ITU-T standards), DNS uses a hierarchical scheme for establishing names. Think of the hierarchies as similar to an organizational chart in a company. The Chief Executive Officer rests at the top of the tree hierarchy, with subordinates stacked in branches below. Another example of hierarchical naming is the telephone system, with country telephone codes at the top of the tree. Below country codes in the tree are area telephone codes, then local exchange codes, and finally, at the bottom of the hierarchy, a local telephone subscriber number.

One attractive aspect of hierarchical naming is that it allows naming administrators to manage their own names at the lower levels of the hierarchy (e.g., the naming domain) and only use upper-level names if they need to operate outside their internal operations and networks. This approach permits a high-level authority to assign the responsibility for administering a subdomain name space to a lower level in a *hierarchical name space*. Even though authority for naming passes from a higher level, these designated "agents" are permitted to cross the hierarchy to send information to each other regarding names. Partitioning can therefore be done in any manner deemed appropriate by an upper-level hierarchy, and the name space division can be small enough so the whole operation is manageable.

The concept of the DNS is shown in Figure 4.1. It is organized around a *root* and *tree* structure. A root is the highest entry and is also called a parent to the lower levels of the tree. The tree consists of *branches* which connect *nodes*. Each *label* of a node in the tree at the same node level must be completely unambiguous and distinct. That is, the label must be a relative distinguished name, which means distinguishable relative to that node level.

The hierarchical naming is established by tracing down through the tree, selecting the names attached to each label, and concatenating these labels together to form a distinguished name; that is, distinguishable at *all* levels in the tree. For example, the first node level under the root of the tree contains several names. We use COM as our example. Proceeding down the tree to the next level, several other names are listed, including ACME. Finally, below ACME, RD is found, which is the lowest level node in this tree. RD is called a *leaf* node because it has no dependent nodes (nodes underneath it). The concatenated name is shown at the bottom of the figure as RD.ACME.COM.

You might wonder about the notation in this example. The tree shows the hierarchy pursuing the route down to the bottom of the leaf; however, the ac-

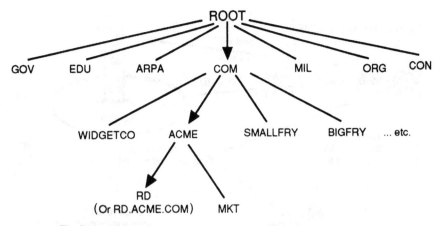

Figure 4.1 The Domain Name System (DNS).

tual name is written with the local label first and the top-most domain label last. This approach is different from the practice of other standards, and it does take some adjustment if you have been using other naming conventions.

Domain names are not intended to define addresses. Indeed, additional services are required to map names to addresses. As you will see shortly, these services are performed by name servers and name resolvers.

Internet names are no longer designated just for hosts. For example, an information class entitled *mail exchange* (MX information) is available that allows an organization to transmit mail, not just to individual workstations or computers per se, but to any machine designed as a mail server. In addition, the use of a domain name allows an MX machine to have domain names without being attached to the Internet. Organizations need only direct their mail to a mail server.

Figure 4.2 shows the typical operation of a name server. If an individual wishes to establish a connection (or send a message) to UBlack@RD.ACME .COM, the individual enters the name of the person to whom she wishes to establish a connection, and the person's enterprise (the domain name) into the workstation. To ascertain the network address of this name, a query is sent to a name server (or the query is matched against a table stored in the workstation). The response to the query contains the address for the name; in this hypothetical example, the address is 128.4.3.6. This address is placed into a datagram, which is then sent to a router. The router then uses this address to determine where the datagram is to be routed. The datagram is then routed to a next node, identified as 128.22.3.8 in this example.

Domain Names

Each domain is identified by an unambiguous *domain name*. Because of the hierarchical nature of the DNS, a domain can be a subdomain of another

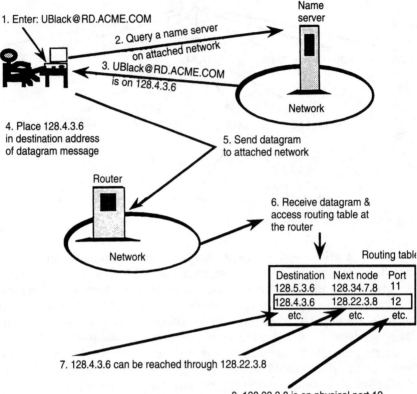

Figure 4.2 Typical Operation Using a Name Server.

domain. Subdomains are achieved by the naming structure, which allows encapsulation of naming relationships. In the example in Figure 4.1, the domain RD.ACME. is a subdomain of RD.ACME.COM.

The DNS provides two ways of viewing a name. One is called an *absolute name,* which consists of the complete name in the DNS. In the example in Figure 4.1, an absolute name is RD.ACME.COM. In contrast, a *relative name* consists of only a part of the name within a complete entry in the DNS. For example, in Figure 4.1, RD would be used to define a relative name. Absolute and relative names are quite similar to the OSI Model's description of a distinguished name (DN) and a relative distinguished name (RDN), respectively.

Top-Level Domains

Presently, the DNS contains seven top-level domain names. They are shown in Figure 4.1 and are as follows:

GOV: any government body

EDU: an educational institution

ARPA: ARPANET-Internet host identification

COM: any commercial enterprise

MIL: military organizations

ORG: any other organization not identified by previous descriptors

CON: countries using the ISO standard for naming their countries (ISO 3166)

Domain Name Resolution and Mapping Names to Addresses

To map user-friendly names to IP addresses, an Internet user must work with the concepts of domain name resolution. Request for Comments (RFC) 1035 defines the procedures for these operations.

Fortunately, the user's task is quite simple in resolving these names. The user need only provide a set of arguments to a local agent called a *name resolver*, which retrieves information based on a domain name or sends the request to a *name server*. The user also has a few other minor tasks, including forming the proper query to the name resolver and providing certain requirements for how the operation is performed. Figure 4.3 shows the structure for domain name resolution.

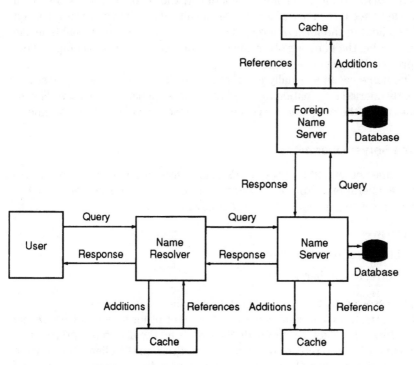

Figure 4.3 Domain Name Resolution.

The user sees the domain tree as a single name (a single information space). Conversely, the resolver assumes the task of resolving the name or sending the name to independent cooperative systems (the name servers) for name/address resolution. As the figure shows, the name server services a request from the name resolver. Thus, the resolver acts as a service provider to the user program. In turn, the resolver acts as a user to the name server.

The name servers can store some of the same information stored at the name resolvers for efficiency and backup. Regardless of how the information is stored at the name server, the name resolver must know the name of at least one name server to begin the query. The query is passed to the name server from the resolver. The server, in turn, then provides a response or makes a referral to yet another name server. With this approach, the resolver can learn more about the identities of other name servers and the information they hold.

Determining which name servers are to participate in the operation is based on the naming hierarchy tree shown in Figure 4.1. Each leaf entry of this tree can correspond to a name server. A server at a subdomain (leaf entry) knows which servers are under its domain and can choose the appropriate server to answer a query.

Figure 4.3 shows another component attached to the resolver, called the *name cache*. Upon receiving a user query, the resolver checks this local storage to see if the answer is available locally. If so, the answer is returned to the client in the form of a response. If the answer is not available in the name cache, the name resolver must then determine the best name servers to provide the response.

The name cache is usually incomplete, but it does provide the most frequently queried information to speed the process of name resolution. The information in the name cache is eventually erased through the use of timers.

Name Server Operations

The name server services the user's query with either recursive or nonrecursive operations. For *nonrecursive operations*, the response of the name server to a query is one of the following:

- an answer
- an identification of an error
- a referral to another server

The resolver must reissue a query to specific name servers.

In contrast, a local name server can contact other servers in *recursive operations*. In effect, this offloads the task from the user host and requires the name server to return the queried IP address to the client. If the name server does not return the IP address, it must send a negative response. The name server is not allowed to return a referral. The effect of the nonrecursive and recursive operations ensures that the user knows at least one server is at the address. It also ensures that a name server knows the IP address of at least one other name server.

The server is responsible for maintaining a portion of a subtree of a domain space, called a *zone*. It is a contiguous section of the domain space. Typically, a separate database exists for each zone. The name server is required to check periodically to ensure that its zone is correct and, if not, ensure that the zone is updated correctly. A zone can be updated only by the proper authority. The name server uses a *zone transfer protocol* to allow more than one name server to store data about a zone. If a name server for a domain name fails for any reason, redundant copies of the naming and addressing information are available at other name servers.

A name server is classified as either a *primary* name server or a *secondary* name server. As suggested by these terms, the function of the primary name server can be duplicated in other machines, which, in turn, are called secondary name servers. This approach provides reliability and efficiency in servicing the queries.

The query and reply messages transmitted between name servers can use either the transmission control protocol (TCP) or the user datagram protocol (UDP). Typically, the connectionless UDP is used for ongoing queries because it offers better performance. For activities that require database updates, such as zone refresh operations, however, TCP is preferable to obtain reliable transfer. Whatever the case, name servers can use either protocol.

As stated earlier, the Internet domain servers are arranged conceptually in tree structures such as the one shown in Figure 4.1. Each leaf in this hierarchical tree represents a name server, which is responsible for a single domain or subdomain. The entries in the conceptual tree in Figure 4.1 do not represent any actual physical connections. They simply show the name servers about which other name servers know and with whom they can communicate. To participate in the DNS, an organization must agree to operate and support a domain name server.

Resource Records

We learned earlier that a domain name is used to identify a node. Each node contains information about its resources. (If no resources are available, the node would have an empty resource.) The resource information associated with both a node and name is called a *resource record (RR)*. A resource record is contained in a database and is used to define domain zones. The RRs are also used for mapping between domain names and network objects.

An RR is identified by its mnemonic type and numerical code. These types and their values are listed in Table 4.1 and are explained in more de-

TABLE 4.1 Type Values of the DNS

Type	Value and meaning
A	1 = Host address
NS	2 = Authoritative name server
MD	3 = Mail destination (now obsolete; use MX)
MF	4 = Mail forwarder (now obsolete; use MX)
CNAME	5 = Canonical name for an alias
SOA	6 = Start of zone authority
MB	7 = Mailbox domain name
MG	8 = Mailbox member
MR	9 = Mail rename domain
NULL	10 = Null RR
WKS	11 = Well-known service
PTR	12 = Domain name pointer
HINFO	13 = Host information (experimental)
MINFO	14 = Mailbox or mail list information
MX	15 = Mail exchange
TXT	16 = Text strings
RP	17 = Responsible person (experimental)
AFSDB	18 = Authority format identifier-type services (experimental)
X.25	19 = X.25 address, X.121 (experimental)
ISDN	20 = ISDN address, E.163/E.164 (experimental)
RT	21 = Route through (experimental)
OSI NSAP	22 = OSI Network service access point address (experimental)

tail shortly. RRs are stored in a standard format. Figure 4.4 shows the format for the top-level part of an RR. The contents of an RR record have a standard format:

```
<<name>> <<TTL>> <<class>> <<type>> <<data>>
```

Some of these fields can be omitted in an RR. If the <<TTL>> field is blank, it defaults to a minimum time specified in another part of the database (explained later). If <<class>> is blank, it defaults to the last class specified in the database. The definitions of these fields are as follows:

name: contains the domain name (owner name) of the node for this RR. If blank, name defaults to the name of the previous RR.

TTL: The time-to-live parameter. It is optional and specifies the time (in seconds) that this RR definition is valid in the name server cache. If the value is 0, the RR should not be stored in cache (for example, if RR is volatile data). In practice, this value determines the time the resolver uses a server's data before it asks for an update.

class: contains the values of the RR class code (where IN = the Internet; CH = chaos system). If blank, class defaults to the last class specified.

type: contains a value to represent the RR type codes shown in Table 3.4.

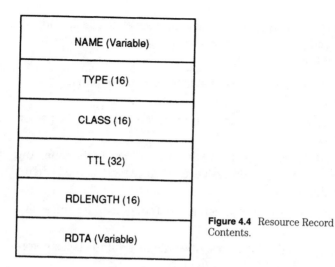

Figure 4.4 Resource Record Contents.

RD length: considered part of the data field; specifies the length, in octets, of the RDATA field.

data (RDATA): variable-length field describing the resource. The contents of RDATA vary depending on the type and class of RR. This field is examined in the next section of this chapter.

RDATA field

Figure 4.5 shows one of the more common RDATA formats, the start of zone authority format (SOA). Only one SOA record per zone should exist.

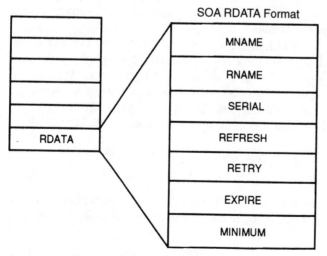

Figure 4.5 The Start of Zone Authority Format.

As the figure reveals, the SOA RDATA contains seven subfields. Most of these fields are used for administration and maintenance of the name server. Their contents are as follows:

MNAME: identifies the domain name that is the original or primary source of data for this zone.

RNAME: identifies a domain name to be used for the mailbox of the person responsible for this zone.

SERIAL: contains the version number of the original copy of the zone. Any transfers of zones must preserve this value. SERIAL is incremented when a change is made in the zone.

REFRESH: a count (in seconds) to determine the interval for refreshing the zone.

RETRY: a count (in seconds) that describes the interval to elapse before an unsuccessful refresh should be reattempted.

EXPIRE: a value (in seconds) that specifies when this zone is no longer authoritative.

MINIMUM: contains the minimum value for the TTL field that should be exported from any RR from the subject zone. It is a lower boundary for TTL for all RRs in a zone.

Explanation of DNS Types

Figure 4.6 shows the remainder of the fields for the RDATA formats. Each of these formats (actually, DNS types) is examined in the order they appear in this figure, from the top of the figure to the bottom. For purposes of simplicity, some of the optional entries in the formats are not discussed. Refer to Table 4.1 during this discussion.

The *name server (NS)* RDATA format contains the domain name and the host name that provides the DNS service. One NS record should exist per server. Also, a name server is not required to be within the domain name. The following entry shows how NS appears in a resource record (as well as on a hard-copy printout). Machines HOSTA.RD.ACME.COM. and HOSTC.MKT.COM. provide name service for the domain RD.ACME.COM.:

```
RD.ACME.COM. NS HOSTA.RD.ACME.COM.
                 HOSTC.MKT.COM
```

The *MG* RDATA format contains the name of a mailbox, which is a member of a mail group specified by name. In the figure, this value appears as MGNAME.

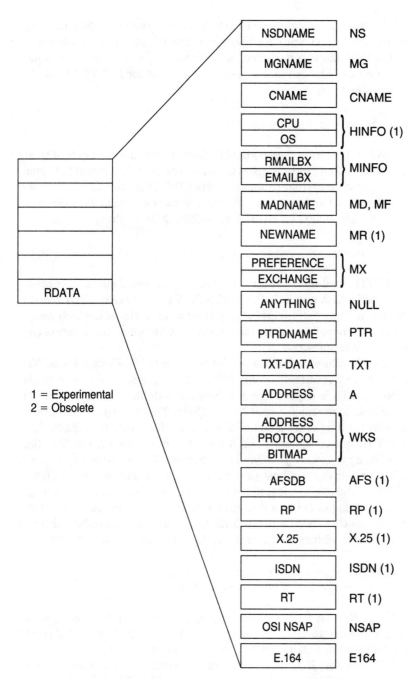

Figure 4.6 Other Contents for RDATA Field.

The *CNAME* (canonical name) RDATA format contains a domain name that is an alias (nickname) for another name (the proper, or canonical, name). CNAME allows a host to change its name (or use a shorter name) but also keep its older name. For example, an alias for HOSTA.RD.ACME. COM. might be ACME.:

```
ACME. CNAME HOSTA.RD.ACME.COM.
```

The *HINFO* (host information) RDATA format contains two fields of string information. The first field identifies the CPU type, and the second field identifies the operating system running on the CPU. This data format is quite useful in obtaining hardware and software information about a host machine. For example, the HINFO for HOSTA.RD.ACME.COM. might appear as

```
HOSTA.RD.ACME.COM. HINFO VAX-11 780 UNIX.
```

The MINFO (mail information) is in the experimental stage. It contains two fields, RMAILBX and EMAILBX. RMAILBX identifies a mailbox responsible for the mailing list. It can identify the owner of the RR, which means the owner is responsible for the mail. EMAILBX identifies the mailbox that is to receive error messages.

Several type values are obsolete. These are listed in Figure 4.6 as *MD*, *MF,* and *MB* RDATA formats. Study RFC 1035 for guidance on these fields.

The *MR* RDATA is experimental. It contains a domain name that identifies a mailbox. It renames a specified mailbox. This record is used principally as a forwarding entry if someone has moved to a different mailbox.

The *MX* (mail exchanger) RDATA format contains two fields. The first field is called a *preference field,* and its value specifies the precedence given to this RR for delivery to a host (low numbers are the highest priority). The second field is the *exchange field,* and it contains a domain name that identifies a host willing to act as a mail exchange for the owner name. The next example shows that HOSTA.RD.ACME.COM. wants its mail to be delivered to one of these machines, in the order indicated by the 10 and 20 values:

```
HOSTA.RD.ACME.COM. MX 10 HOSTC.MKT.COM.
                   MX 20 HOSTD.HQ.COM.
```

The *NULL* RDATA format allows anything to be placed in this field, as long as it does not exceed 65,535 octets. The RDATA fields, the *TXT* (text) RDATA field contains character strings for descriptive text.

The *PTR* (pointer) RDATA format contains a domain name that serves as a pointer to a location in the domain name space. This format is used for reverse mapping, in which Internet addresses are converted to names. To understand this important feature of the DNS, we must first examine the A (address format) and digress briefly to examine the IN-ADDR-ARPA domain. The *A* (address) RDATA format contains an Internet address for a name. For example, HOSTA has an Internet address of 128.11.1.1; its A record is

```
HOSTA.  IN A 128.11.1.1
```

IN-ADDR-ARPA

The structure depicted in Figure 4.1 facilitates name-to-address mapping by simply tracing down the domain tree and obtaining an address. Because the index is organized around a name, however, an address-to-name mapping is not so easy.

To solve this problem, an address mapping domain name called *IN-ADDR-ARPA* was created. It provides a reverse mapping from address to host name using the IN-ADDR-ARPA domain. The approach is to use the host address as an index to the host's RRs. Once the RRs are located, the name can be extracted. Within the IN-ADDR-ARPA domain are subdomains for each network with the proper network address.

As an example, consider that gateway 1 (GW1) needs to be located. (Gateways have the same PTR RRs as hosts and can be located solely by the network number, if necessary.) Assuming that the gateway connects two networks, the A records could appear as

```
GW1.RD.ACME.COM.  IN A 128.11.1.4.
                  IN A 129.12.1.3.
```

In each of the networks' zones, one of these *number-to-name* entries is found (notice that the Internet number octets are reversed for ease of use). With these entries stored in a database, the look-up for number-to-name resolution becomes a simple process using the PTR field.

```
4.1.11.128.IN-ADDR-ARPA.  PTR GW1.RD.ACME.COM.
3.1.12.129.IN-ADDR-ARPA.  PTR GW1.RD.ACME.COM.
```

Because gateways can be located by network number alone, each zone would have one of these number-to-name entries:

```
128.11.IN-ADDR-ARPA.  PTR   GW1.RD.ACME.COM.
129.12.IN-ADDR-ARPA.  PTR   GW1.RD.ACME.COM.
```

To continue with the other contents for the RDATA fields, the *WKS* (well-known services) RDATA format contains three fields. These fields describe services supported at a particular Internet address. The first field is a 32-bit address. The second field is called the *protocol field* and identifies an IP number. The third field is a bitmap. The bitmap works as follows. Each bit contains the identification of a specified protocol. For example, the first bit in this field corresponds to port 0, the second to port 1, and so on. The appropriate values for these ports and protocols can be found in RFC 1010. If the bits are set to 1, the particular protocols are supported at that host. Typically, the bits are established to identify protocols such as TCP, FTP, SMTP, etc. As an example of the WKS entry, HOSTA supports TCP, FTP, SMTP, and TELNET:

```
HOSTA.RD.ACME.COM. IN WKS 128.11.1.1.
                       TCP FTP SMTP TELNET
```

Several other experimental resource records have been added to the DNS. The *AFS* (originally called the Andrew file system) RR type maps from a domain name in the DNS to the name of an AFS database server. The record contains a host name, which must be a domain name for a host providing a service for an AFS cell database server.

The *RP* (responsible person) record RR is another experimental record. This record identifies the responsible person for a particular system or host. Typically, this would be a contact in the event a problem occurs at a computer. This record uses a new RR type with the mnemonic RP. An example of an RP record is as follows:

```
GW1.RD.ACME.COM. RP UDB.IEI.ACME.COM.
```

Because of the importance and prevalence of X.25-based networks and the emerging ISDN technology, the Internet has added resource records for X.25 and ISDN addresses.

The X.25 resource record is defined with a mnemonic *X25*. It allows the coding of an ITU-T X.121 address and the association of that address with a domain name. The value of this approach is that it takes only one more operation in a name-server database to relate the IP address to the domain name associated with the X.121 address in the record. An example of the X.25 RR is as follows:

```
ACME.COM. X25  3110.123456789.
```

The ISDN RDATA format works in a similar manner to the X.25 record (its mnemonic is *ISDN*). It allows a relationship to be established between an ISDN address coded typically with the E.164 format. As you might guess, it is a simple step to do an additional look-up in the file to relate an ISDN address to the IP counterpart address using the domain name (and assuming these relationships have been created by the network administrator). Additionally, the capability allows a mapping through the name server with the domain name as the pointer to all the relationships of the addresses; that is, X.25, ISDN, and IP. While experimental, these services hold enormous potential.

An experimental record added to the DNS by the Internet is the route-through (*RT*). The purpose of the RT record is to support a host that does not have its own WAN address. Its record identifies an intermediate host that can serve as the domain name for the host that does not have a WAN address. An example is: ACME.COM. E164 (an ISDN number). ISO 7498.3 and X.213 (Annex A) describe a hierarchical structure for the network service access point (NSAP) address, and ISO 8348/DAD 2 (Draft Addendum 2) specifies the structure for the NSAP address. The address consists of four parts:

initial domain part (IDP):   contains the authority format identifier (AFI) and the initial domain identifier (IDI).

authority format identifier (AFI):   contains a two-digit value between 0 and 99. It is used to identify the IDI format (the authority responsible for the IDI values) and the syntax of the domain-specific part (DSP).

initial domain identifier (IDI):   specifies the addressing domain and the network addressing authority for the DSP values. It is interpreted according to the AFI.

domain specific part (DSP):   contains the address determined by the network authority. It is an address below the second level of the addressing hierarchy and can contain addresses of user end systems on an individual subnetwork.

The NSAP RDATA record could then take the form of this type of address, with the number coded in accordance with the rules just explained. An example is: ACME.COM. NSAP (an OSI NSAP number). Figure 4.7 provides an illustration of a resource record and ties together several of the examples in the previous discussion. The top box shows the topology of two networks connected through a gateway (labeled G1). Host A is attached to network 128.11, as are workstations 1 and 2. Workstations 3 and 4 are attached to network 129.12. The Internet addresses are shown as 128.11 and 129.12 for the two networks. The local addresses are shown in the boxes next to the workstations, gateways, or hosts.

The bottom part of the figure shows the RRs for this domain. Note that this entry is written for pedagogical reasons and has been simplified, but it does contain the major parts of the records. The right part of the figure shows 11 notes. These notes describe the entries in the database and are explained next.

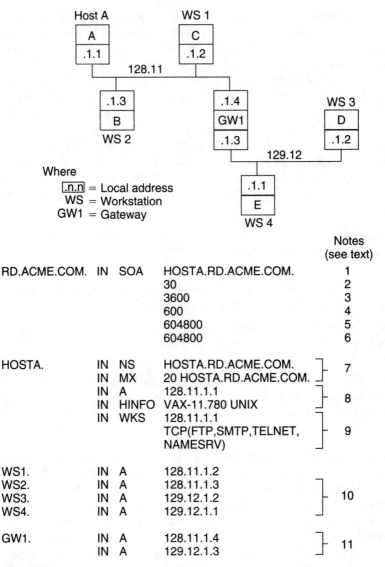

Figure 4.7 Example of Resource Record.

Note 1: This line describes the owner name as RD.ACME.COM. The IN identifies the class as the Internet. The SOA defines the type of RR record as the start of a zone authority. The right-most part of this line describes the first entry into the RDATA field for the SOA record. The HOSTA.RD.ACME.COM. describes the first field of the SOA RDATA segment called MNAME.

Note 2: The value of 30 is in the SERIAL field.

Note 3: The value of 3600 describes (in seconds) the time allotted to RE-FRESH the zone. This zone is to be refreshed every 60 minutes.

Note 4: The value of 600 describes (in seconds) the interval before a failed REFRESH must be reattempted. In this example, the value is 10 minutes.

Note 5: The value of 604800 specifies an upper limit (in seconds) on the time that can elapse before the zone is no longer considered authoritative. This value translates into one week.

Note 6: This field describes the minimum TTL value that should be exported from this zone. This value is 604800 seconds (one week).

Note 7: This note describes two entries in the RR file. The NS identifies the authoritative name server as HOSTA.RD.ACME.COM. The MX identifies the host for the mail exchange support operations. The precedence field of 20 is irrelevant because only one MX is identified.

Note 8: This note shows the entry to identify HOSTA and its address of 128.11.1.1. Entry A is an example of a *glue* record. It specifies the address of the server and is used when the server for a domain is inside that same domain. HINFO provides information about the host.

Note 9: This line depicts a WKS RDATA entry. It establishes that host A, with an Internet address of 128.11.1.1, uses TCP to support the well-known services of FTP, SMTP, TELNET, and NAMESRV.

Note 10: Four entries exist to define the Internet addresses for workstations 1, 2, 3, and 4.

Note 11: This note shows the addresses for the gateway. The gateway is identified with two Internet addresses: 128.11.1.4 and 129.12.1.3.

The structure of the DNS permits relatively simple and easy addition of entries into the RR database. For example, assume that the networks depicted in Figure 4.7 are connected to another network. This network has its own name server for its zone. All that is required to reflect this additional interconnection is to add the entry of the name server to the local domain's name server database and reference the other network by its specific name server. The entries would use NS and A type records to indicate that the server on the other network is the authority for the newly connected network. Consequently, queries for that network would be directed to the identified name server. The new configuration is shown in Figure 4.8, along with the resulting code in the local name server database. Workstations, etc., are not shown on the new network for reasons of simplicity.

DNS Messages

Figure 4.9 shows the format of a DNS message. These messages are transferred between name servers to update the RRs. Consequently, some of the

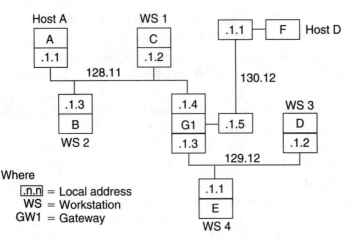

Where
[.n.n] = Local address
WS = Workstation
GW1 = Gateway

—Code added to name server database:

TRN.ACME.COM.   IN   NS   HOSTD.TRN.ACME.COM.

HOSTD.TRN.ACME.COM.   IN   A   130.12.1.1.

GW1.   IN   A   130.12.1.5

Figure 4.8 Adding Another Network and Server to Database.

fields in the message are similar to the format of the RR discussed in the previous section.

As indicated in the figure, the message consists of five major sections. The *header* (which is always present) contains fields about the nature of the query and response. (More about all these fields is discussed shortly.) The *question* section contains the data used to pose a query to the name

Header
Question
Answer
Authority
Additional

Figure 4.9 Format for DNS Message.

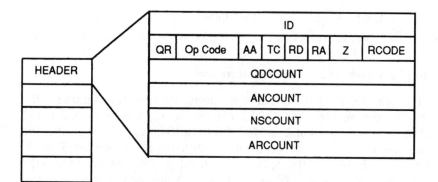

Figure 4.10 DNS Message Header.

server. The *answer* section contains the values of the RRs retrieved in response to the questions. The *authority* section contains RRs that point to the authoritative name server. The *additional record* section contains RRs to assist in the query; these RRs are not specifically related to the answers to the question.

Figure 4.10 shows the format of the header section. The first field is the *ID* field, which consists of 16 bits. This identifier is used both with the query and reply to match the two together. The *QR* field is a 1-bit field, specifying whether this message is a query (value of 0) or response (value of 1).

The *opcode* consists of 4 bits that contain the following information and values: 0 = standard query, 1 = inverse query, 2 = server status request, and 3 to 15 = reserved.

The *AA* (authoritative answer) bit is turned on (a value of 1) for a response and identifies that the responding name server is the recognized authority for the domain name being queried. The *TC* (truncation) bit is turned on to notify that this message was truncated because it was too long. The truncation depends on the length of the data unit permitted on the transmission link. The *RD* (recursion desired) bit is set to 1 to direct the name server to do a recursive query. The *RA* (recursion available) bit is used in a response message to indicate if a recursive query capability is available in the name server. The three *Z* bits are reserved for future use.

The *RCODE* consists of 4 bits set to the following values:

0   = No error occurred.

1   = A format error has occurred and the name server is unable to interpret the query.

2   = A problem has occurred at the name server.

3   = A problem has occurred with the domain reference in the query; the server cannot find it.

4   = The name server does not support this type of query.

5   = The name server cannot perform the operation for administrative or policy reasons.

6 to 15 = Values are reserved for future use.

The *QDCOUNT* is a 16-bit value that specifies the number of entries in the question section. The *ANCOUNT* is a 16-bit value specifying the number of RRs in the answer section. The *NSCOUNT* is a 16-bit value that specifies the number of server resource records in the authority record section. The *AR-COUNT* is a 16-bit field that specifies the number of resource records in the additional record section. These last four fields are used by the receiver of the message to determine how to interpret the boundaries of the four fields.

Figure 4.11 shows the formats for these four sections. The *QUESTION* section contains three entries. We learned earlier that this section is used to carry the question of the query messages. The *QNAME* contains the domain name. The format of the field consists of a length octet followed by the appropriate number of octets. The *QTYPE* field specifies the type of the query. The values in this field can contain the values of the type field discussed in the previous section (see Table 4.1). The *QCLASS* is the last field in the question section. It specifies the class of the query. Typically, this value would be IN for the Internet.

As shown in Figure 4.11, the *ANSWER, AUTHORITY,* and *ADDITIONAL* sections of the DNS message consist of the same format. The fields for this format are as follows:

NAME: This field identifies the domain name associated with the resource record.

TYPE: This field contains one of the RR type codes.

CLASS: This field specifies the data class contained in the RDATA field.

TTL: This is the time-to-live parameter discussed in the previous section.

RDLENGTH: This field specifies field length.

RDATA: This field contains the information associated with the resource. Its contents depend on the type and class of the resource record. For example, it could be an Internet address.

The *ANSWER, AUTHORITY,* and *ADDITIONAL* record sections contain a variable number of RRs. The contents and formats of these records were described earlier in conjunction with Figure 4.3.

RR Compression

It is likely that the exchange of RR messages entails duplicate domain names in succeeding occurrences of traffic on the communications link.

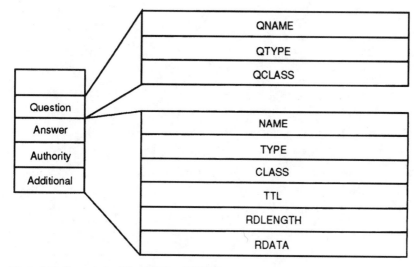

Figure 4.11   Formats for Other Fields of DNS Message.

With this in mind, the DNS provides for message compression. The process is quite simple. Any duplicate domain name (or a list of labels) is replaced with a pointer that identifies the previous occurrence of the traffic.

Summary

The DNS provides the first international standard for name server protocols. It allows Internet users to map names to addresses and addresses to names. It also supports mailbox operations and stores host profiles about operating systems, hardware, and applications architectures. Recent additions provide address and naming services for X.25 and ISDN systems. Many venders now run DNS as part of their directory and naming services.

The Internet Protocol

As discussed in Chapter 1, the Internet Protocol (IP) is an internetworking protocol developed by the Department of Defense. The system was implemented as part of the DARPA internetwork protocol project and is widely used throughout the world. This chapter examines IP in more detail, including its major features, its use of address and routing tables, and its relationships to other Internet, ISO, and IEEE protocols.

Major Features of IP

IP is quite similar to the ISO 8473 specification (the connectionless network protocol, or CLNP) explained in a later part of this chapter. Many of the ISO 8473 concepts were derived from IP.

IP is an example of a connectionless service. It permits the exchange of traffic between two host computers without any prior call setup. (These two computers can, however, share a common connection-oriented transport protocol.) Because IP is connectionless, it is possible that datagrams can be lost between the two end users' stations. For example, the IP router enforces a maximum queue length size, and if this queue length is violated, the buffers overflow. The additional datagrams are then discarded in the network. Thus, a higher-layer protocol (such as the TCP) is essential to recover from these problems.

IP hides the underlying subnetwork from the end user. In this context, it creates a virtual network to that end user, allowing different types of networks to attach to an IP gateway. As a result, IP is reasonably simple to install, and, because of its connectionless design, is quite robust. But, because IP is an unreliable, best-effort, datagram-type protocol, it has no reliability mechanisms. It provides no error recovery for underlying subnetworks. It has no flow-control mechanisms. The user data (datagrams) can be lost, duplicated, or even arrive out of order. It is not the job of IP to deal with most of these problems. As we discover later, most of the problems are passed to the next higher layer, TCP.

IP supports fragmentation operations. The term *fragmentation* refers to an operation wherein a PDU is divided or segmented into smaller units. This feature can be quite useful because all networks do not use the same size PDU. For example, X.25-based WANs typically employ a PDU (called a *packet* in X.25) with a data field of 128 octets. Some networks allow negotiations to a smaller or larger PDU size. The Ethernet standard limits the size of a PDU to 1500 octets. Conversely, proNET-10 stipulates a PDU of 2000 octets. Without the use of fragmentation, a router would be tasked with trying to resolve incompatible PDU sizes between networks. IP solves the problem by establishing rules for fragmentation at the routers and reassembly at the receiving host.

IP and Subnetworks

As seen in Figure 5.1, IP is designed to rest on top of the underlying subnetwork—transparently insofar as possible. This means that IP assumes little about the characteristics of the underlying network or networks. As stated earlier, from the design standpoint, this tendency is quite attractive to engineers because it keeps the subnetworks relatively independent of IP.

In Figure 5.1, as traffic (datagrams) is received at a router, the IP address is matched against a routing table. Based on the entries in the routing table, IP routes the datagram to the next network or directly to the receiving host. This example also illustrates that CLNP could be used to provide the same services as IP.

As you might expect, the transparency is achieved using encapsulation. The data sent by the host computer are encapsulated into an IP datagram, and the IP header identifies the address of the receiving host computer. The IP datagram and header are further encapsulated into the specific protocol of the transit network. For example, a transit network could be an X.25 network or an Ethernet LAN.

After the transit network has delivered the traffic to an IP gateway, its control information is stripped away. The router then uses the destination address in the datagram header to determine where to route the traffic. Typically, it then passes the datagram to a subnetwork by invoking the subnetwork access protocol (for example, Ethernet on a LAN or X.25 on a WAN). This protocol is used to encapsulate the datagram header and user data into the headers and trailers used by the subnetwork. This process is repeated at each router, and eventually the datagram arrives at the final destination, where it is delivered to the receiving station.

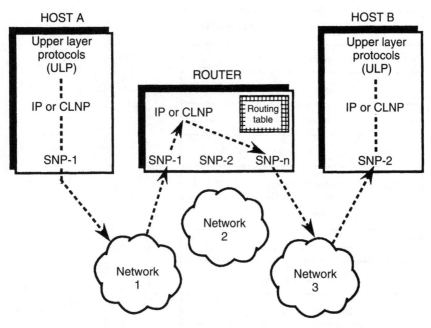

Figure 5.1 IP/CLNP Model.

An IP router is not completely unconcerned with the access protocol of an attached subnetwork. There is nothing magic about IP; the router interface must know how to access its connected networks. Consequently, some form of communications (however limited) must occur between the router and the attached subnetworks. (The section later in this chapter titled "IP Service Definitions and Primitives" discusses this topic.) The important point is that an IP module does not care about the operations inside the networks.

The IP Datagram

A productive approach to analyzing IP is first to examine the fields in the IP datagram (PDU) depicted in Figure 5.2. An abbreviated description of the fields in the datagram is provided in Table 5.1.

The *version* field identifies the version of IP in use. Most protocols contain this field because some network nodes might not have the latest release available of the protocol.

The *header length* field contains 4 bits set to a value that indicates the length of the datagram header. The length is measured in 32-bit words. Typically, a header without quality-of-service (QOS) options contains 20 octets. Therefore, the value in the length field is usually 5.

The *type-of-service (TOS)* field can be used to identify several QOS functions provided for in an internet. It is quite similar to the service field

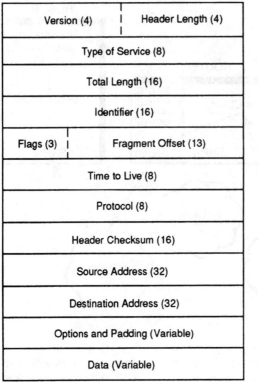

Figure 5.2 IP Datagram.

(*n*) = Number of Bits in Field

TABLE 5.1 IP Protocol Data Unit

Version field	Identifies the version of IP
Internet header length	Specifies the length of the IP header
Type of service	Stipulates quality-of-service functions
Total length field	Specifies the total length of the IP datagram, including the header
Identifier	Used with the address fields to identify the data unit uniquely (for fragmentation)
Flags	Used in the fragmentation operations
Fragmentation offset	Describes where this datagram belongs within the original PDU
Time to live	Used to determine how long the datagram is to remain in an internet
Protocol	Used to identify a next-level protocol that is to receive the user data at the final destination
Header checksum	Used to perform an error check on the header
Source and destination addresses	Identifies the source and destination hosts and their directly attached networks
Options	Used to request additional services for the IP user
Padding	Used to give the datagram a 32-bit alignment
User data	Contains user data

that resides in the CLNP PDU. Transit delay, throughput, precedence, and reliability can be requested with this field.

The TOS field is illustrated in Figure 5.3. It contains five entries consisting of 8 bits. Bits 0, 1, and 2 contain a precedence value used to indicate the relative importance of the datagram. Values range from 0 to 7, with 0 set to indicate a *routine precedence*. The precedence field is not used in all systems, although the value of 7 is used by some implementations to indicate a network control datagram. The precedence field could, however, be used to implement flow control and congestion mechanisms in a network, allowing gateways and host nodes to make decisions about the order of discarding datagrams in case of congestion.

The next three bits are used for other services. Bit 3 is the *delay bit (D bit)*. When set to 1, this TOS requests a short delay through an internet. The aspect of delay is not defined in the standard, and the vendor must implement the service. The next bit is the *throughput bit (T bit)*. It is set to 1 to request high throughput through an internet. Again, its specific implementation is not defined in the standard. The last bit used is the *reliability bit (R bit)*, which allows a user to request high reliability for the datagram. The next two bits, 6 and 7, are not currently used.

The *TOS field* is also not used in some vendors' implementations of IP. Nonetheless, it will be used increasingly in the future as the Internet capabilities are increased. For example, it is used in the open shortest path first (OSPF) protocol discussed in Chapter 8. Consequently, a user should examine this field for future work and ascertain a vendor's use or intended support of this field.

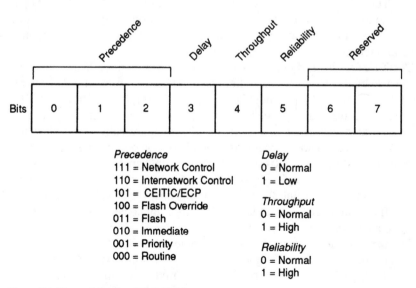

Precedence
111 = Network Control
110 = Internetwork Control
101 = CEITIC/ECP
100 = Flash Override
011 = Flash
010 = Immediate
001 = Priority
000 = Routine

Delay
0 = Normal
1 = Low

Throughput
0 = Normal
1 = High

Reliability
0 = Normal
1 = High

Figure 5.3 Type-of-Service (TOS) Field.

The *total length* field specifies the total length of the IP datagram. It is measured in octets and includes the length of the header and the data. IP subtracts the header length field from the total length field to compute the size of the data field. The maximum possible length of a datagram is 65,535 octets (2^{16}). Routers that service IP datagrams are required to accept any datagram that supports the maximum size of a PDU of the attached networks. Additionally, all routers must accommodate datagrams of 576 octets in length.

The IP protocol uses three fields in the header to control datagram fragmentation and reassembly. These fields are the *identifier, flags,* and *fragmentation offset.* The identifier field is used to identify uniquely all fragments from an original datagram. It is used with the source address at the receiving host to identify each fragment. The flags field contains bits that determine if the datagram can be fragmented. If it can be, one of the bits can be set to determine if this fragment is the last fragment of the datagram. The fragmentation offset field contains a value that specifies the relative position of the fragment to the original datagram. The value is initialized as 0 and is subsequently set to the proper number if the router fragments the data. The value is measured in units of eight octets. We devote a special section later in this chapter to fragmentation and reassembly and the use of these three fields.

The *time-to-live (TTL)* parameter is used to measure the time a datagram has been in an internet. It is quite similar to CLNP's lifetime field. Each router in an internet checks this field and discards it if the TTL value equals 0. A router is also required to decrement this field for each datagram it processes. In actual implementations, the TTL field is a number-of-hops value. Therefore, when a datagram proceeds through an IP node (a hop), the value in the field is decremented by a value of one. Implementations of IP might use a time counter in this field and decrement the value in one-second decrements.

The TTL field is used not only by the router to prevent endless loops, but it can also be used by the host to limit the lifetime that segments have in an internet. Be aware that if a host is acting as a router, it must treat the TTL field by the router rules. Check with the vendor to determine when a host throws away a datagram based on the TTL value. Ideally, the TTL value could be configured and its value assigned based on observing internet performance. Additionally, network management information protocols, such as those residing in simple network management protocol (SNMP) might wish to set the TTL value for diagnostic purposes. Finally, if your vendor uses a fixed value that cannot be reconfigured, make certain it is fixed initially to allow for your internet's growth.

The *protocol* field is used to identify the next-layer protocol above the IP that is to receive the datagram at the final host destination. It is quite similar to the type field found in the Ethernet frame. The Internet standards groups have established a numbering system to identify the most widely used upper-layer protocols. Table 5.2 lists and describes these protocols.

TABLE 5.2 Internet Protocol Numbers (Examples)

Decimal	Key word	Protocol
0	—	Reserved
1	ICMP	Internet Control Message Protocol
2	IGMP	Internet Group Management Protocol
3	GGP	Gateway-to-Gateway Protocol
4	—	Unassigned
5	ST	Stream
6	TCP	Transmission Control Protocol
7	UCL	UCL
8	EGP	Exterior Gateway Protocol
9	IGP	Interior Gateway Protocol
10	BBN-MON	BBN-RCC Monitoring
11	NVP-II	Network Voice Protocol
12	PUP	PUP
13	ARGUS	ARGUS
14	EMCON	EMCON
15	XNET	Cross Net Debugger
16	CHAOS	Chaos
17	UDP	User Datagram Protocol
18	MUX	Multiplexing
19	DCN-MEAS	DCN Measurment Subsystems
20	HMP	Host Monitoring Protocol
21	PRM	Packet Radio Monitoring
22	XNS-IDP	XEROX NS IDP
23	TRUNK-1	Trunk-1
24	TRUNK- 2	Trunk-2
25	LEAF-1	Leaf-1
26	LEAF-2	Leaf-2
27	RDP	Reliable Data Protocol
28	IRTP	Internet Reliable TP
29	ISO-TP4	ISO Transport Class 4
30	NETBLT	Bulk Data Transfer
31	MFE-NSP	MFE Network Services
32	MERIT-INP	MERIT Internodal Protocol
33	SEP	Sequential Exchange
34–60	—	Unassigned
61	—	Any host internal protocol
62	CFTP	CFTP
63	—	Any local network
64	SAT-EXPAK	SATNET and Backroom EXPAK
65	MIT-SUBN	MIT Subnet Support
66	RVD	MIT Remote Virtual Disk
67	IPPC	Internet Plur. Packet Core
68	—	Any distributed file system
69	SAT-MON	SATNET Monitoring
70	—	Unassigned
71	IPCV	Packet Core Utility
72–75	—	Unassigned
76	BRSAT-MON	Backroom SATNET Monitoring
77	—	Unassigned
78	WB-MON	Wideband Monitoring
79	WB-EXPAK	Wideband EXPAK
80–254	—	Unassigned
255	—	Reserved

The *header checksum* is used to detect any distortions that might have occurred in the header. Checks are not performed on the user data stream. Some critics of IP have stated that the provision for error detection in the user data would allow the router at least to notify the sending host that problems have occurred. (This service is indeed provided by a companion standard to IP, called the Internet control message protocol (ICMP), which is discussed in Chapter 6.) Whatever one's view on the issue, the current approach keeps the checksum algorithm in IP quite simple. It does not need to operate on many octets, but it does require that a higher-level protocol at the receiving host perform an error check on the user data if the receiving host cares about its data integrity.

IP carries two addresses in the datagram. These are labeled *source* and *destination addresses* and remain the same value throughout the life of the datagram. These fields contain the internet addresses examined in Chapter 3.

The *options* field is used to identify several additional services. As we see later, it is similar to the option part field of CLNP. The options field is not used in every datagram. The majority of implementations use this field for network management and diagnostics.

Figure 5.4 illustrates the format of the option field. Table 5.3 contains the values currently defined in the standard. The options field length is variable because some options are of variable length. Each option contains three fields. The first field is coded as a single octet containing the option code. The option code also contains three fields, whose functions are as follows:

Flag copy (1 bit)   0 = copy option into only the first fragment of a
                       fragmented datagram
                       1 = copy option into all fragments of a fragmented
                       datagram

Class (2 bits)   identifies the option class (Table 5.3):
                       0 = user datagram or network control datagram

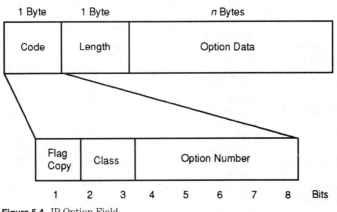

Figure 5.4 IP Option Field.

TABLE 5.3 Option Codes

Class	Number	Length	Description
0	0	0	End of option list
0	1	0	No operation
0	2	11	Security
0	3	var	Loose source routing
0	7	var	Record route
0	8	4	Stream ID (obsolete)
0	9	var	Strict source routing
2	4	var	Internet time-stamp

1 = reserved

2 = diagnostic purposes of debugging and measuring

3 = reserved

Option Number   identifies the option number (Table 5.3).

The next octet contains the length of the option. The third field contains the data values for the option. More detail about the option field is provided in the next section of this chapter.

The *padding* field can be used to ensure that the datagram header aligns on an exact 32-bit boundary. Finally, the *data* field contains the user data. IP stipulates that the combination of the data field and the header cannot exceed 65,535 octets.

Major IP Services

This section provides an overview of the major services of IP. Be aware that vendors have different products for IP and some of them might not support all the features described in this section.

Internet header check routine

When a router receives the datagram, it checks the header to determine the type of traffic it is processing. If the traffic is an internet datagram, it passes the datagram to the internet header check routine. This module then performs a number of editing and validity tests on the IP datagram header. The following checks are performed on the header:

- valid IP header length
- proper IP version number
- valid IP message length
- valid IP header checksum
- nonzero time to live field validity

If checks are performed and not passed, the datagram is discarded. If the checks are performed and passed, the internet destination address is examined to determine if the datagram is addressed to this router, or if the datagram is destined for another router. If it is not destined for this gateway, the datagram is passed to the IP forwarding routine for further routing.

IP source routing

IP can use a mechanism called *source routing* as part of its routing algorithm. Source routing allows an upper layer protocol (ULP) to determine how the IP routers route the datagrams. The ULP has the option of passing a list of internet addresses to the IP module. The list contains the intermediate IP nodes that are to be traversed during the routing of the datagrams to the final destination. The last address on the list is the final destination of an intermediate node.

When IP receives a datagram, it uses the addresses in the source routing field to determine the next intermediate hop. As illustrated in Figure 5.5, IP uses a pointer field to learn about the next IP address. If a check of the pointer and length fields indicates that the list has been completed, the destination IP address field is used for routing. If the list is not exhausted, the IP module uses the IP address indicated by the pointer.

The IP module then replaces the value in the source routing list with its own address. It then increments the pointer by one address (4 bytes) for

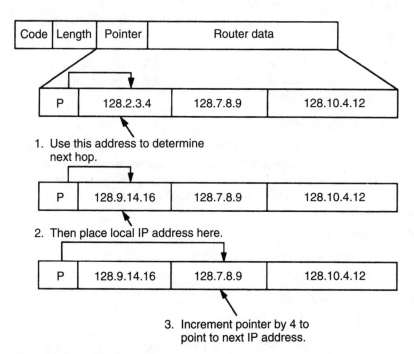

Figure 5.5 Source Routing.

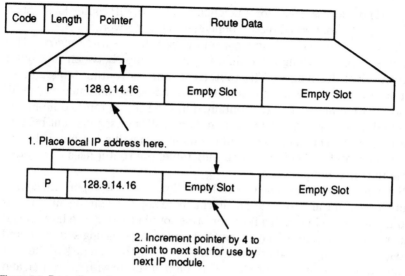

1. Place local IP address here.

2. Increment pointer by 4 to
point to next slot for use by
next IP module.

Figure 5.6 Route Recording.

the next hop to retrieve the next IP address in the route. With this approach, the datagram follows the source route dictated by the ULP and records the route along the way.

Figure 5.6 provides an example of route recording. In the first step, IP uses the pointer to locate the next address in the route data field. In this example, it locates address 128.2.3.4 and makes a routing decision based on this address. In the second step, it places its own address in the route data field in the same location as the current destination address. In the third step, it increments the pointer value to enable the next IP module to determine the next (or final) hop in the route.

Routing operations. The IP router makes routing decisions based on the routing list. If the destination host resides in another network, the IP router must decide how to route to the other network. Indeed, if multiple hops are involved in the communications process, then each router must be traversed and the router must decide the route.

Each gateway maintains a routing table that contains the next gateway (next node, or nn) on the way to the final destination network. In effect, the table contains an entry for each reachable network. These tables could be either static or dynamic, although dynamic tables are more common. The IP module makes a routing decision on all datagrams it receives.

The routing table contains an IP address for each reachable network and the address of a neighbor router (that is, a router directly attached to this network). The neighbor router is the shortest route to the destination network. If no address exists for a neighbor router, the IP router logic establishes that the router is directly connected to this network.

The IP routing is based on a concept called the *distance metric*. This value is usually nothing more than the fewest hops between the router and the final destination. The router consults its routing table and attempts to match the destination network address contained in the IP header with a network entry contained in the routing table. If no match is found, it discards the datagram, and an ICMP message is sent back to the IP source. This message would contain a "destination unreachable" code. If a match is found in the routing table, the router uses it to determine the outgoing port.

Some implementations of TCP/IP have allowed a host to perform source route forwarding and to act as an intermediate hop through the full route. If you use a system in which a host performs source routing, the host should adhere to all the rules of a conventional router in managing source routed datagrams. Again, this point is made to emphasize that the task of the host in any type of router function should be commensurate with the router, and the software should not be scaled down for purposes of efficiency. For example, the TTL field must be decremented by the host. The host should also be able to generate the ICMP destination-unreachable messages if the source route fails or in case fragmentation cannot be performed. The host must also be able to perform the time-stamp option (discussed shortly) in accordance with the proper rules of an IP router.

Loose and strict routing. IP provides two options in routing the datagram to the final destination. The first, called *loose source routing,* gives the IP modules the option of using intermediate hops to reach the addresses obtained in the source list, as long as the datagram traverses the nodes listed. Conversely, *strict source routing* requires that the datagram travel only through the networks whose addresses are indicated in the source list. If the strict source route cannot be followed, the originating host IP is notified with an error message. Both loose and strict routing require that the route recording feature be implemented.

Route recording option

The route recording option operates similarly to source routing, but also using the recording feature just discussed. Thus, any IP module that receives a datagram must add its address to a route recording list, illustrated in Figure 5.7. For the route recording operation to occur, the receiving IP module uses the pointer and length fields to determine if any space is available to record the route. If the route recording list is full, the IP module simply forwards the datagram without inserting its address. If it is not full, the

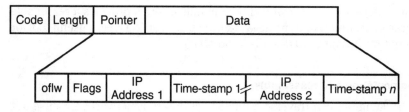

Figure 5.7 Time-Stamp Option.

pointer is used to locate the first empty full-octet slot, the address is inserted, and the IP module then increments the pointer to the next IP slot.

The time-stamp option

Another useful option in IP is the provision for time-stamping the datagram as it traverses each IP module through an internet. This idea allows a network manager to not only determine the route of the datagram through the internet but also the time at which each IP module processed the datagram. This capability can be useful in determining the efficiency of routers, networks, and routing algorithms.

The format for the options fields for time-stamp operations is shown in Figure 5.7. As with previous options, the length and pointer fields are used to identify the proper slot in which to place an IP address *and* the time-stamp related to the address. The pointer therefore increments itself across an IP address and time-stamp for the address. The *oflw* field is used only when an IP module cannot register a time-stamp because of a lack of resources (for example) or a too-small option field. This value is incremented by each module that encounters this problem.

A 4-bit flags field is used to provide guidance to each IP module about the time-stamp operations. The values of this field are described as follows:

0 = only time-stamps are to be recorded and stored in consecutive 32-bit words.

1 = each time-stamp is to be preceded by the IP address of the relevant module.

3 = IP addresses are already specified by the originator, and the router is tasked with recording the time-stamp in its relevant IP address area.

The time used with the time-stamp is based on milliseconds (ms) using universal time (previously called Greenwich Mean Time). Obviously, the use of universal time does not guarantee completely accurate time-stamps between machines, because machines' clocks can vary slightly. Nonetheless, in most networks, the universal time in milliseconds provides a reasonable degree of accuracy, and the network time protocol (NTP) is a useful tool for this option (Chapter 10 describes the NTP).

Fragmentation and reassembly

An IP datagram can traverse a number of different networks that use different PDU sizes. All networks have a maximum PDU size, called the *maximum transmission unit (MTU)*. IP thus contains procedures for dividing (fragmenting) a large datagram into smaller datagrams. It also allows the ULP to stipulate that fragmentation can or cannot occur. Of course, IP must also use a reassembly mechanism at the final destination that places the fragments back into the order originally transmitted.

When an IP router module receives a datagram that is too big to be transmitted by the transit subnetwork, it uses its fragmentation operations. It divides the datagram into two or more pieces, aligning the pieces on 8-octet boundaries. Each of the fragmented pieces has a header attached that contains identification, addressing, and (as another option) all options pertaining to the original datagram. The fragmented packets also have information attached to them defining the position of the fragment within the original datagram, as well as an indication if this fragment is the last fragment.

Referring to Figure 5.3, the flags (the 3 bits) are used as follows:

Bit 0: reserved

Bit 1: 0 = fragmentation

      1 = do not fragment

Bit 2 (M bit): 0 = last fragment

      1 = more fragments

Interestingly, IP handles each fragment operation independently. That is, the fragments can traverse different routers to the intended destination, and they can be subject to further fragmentation if they pass through networks that use smaller data units. Each router uses the offset value in the incoming fragment to determine the offset values of fragmented datagrams. If further fragmentation occurs at another router, the fragment offset value is set to the location that this fragment fits relative to the original datagram and not the preceding fragmented packet. Figure 5.8 shows an example of multiple fragmentation operations across two routers.

Subnet 128.3 uses a 1500-octet PDU size. It passes this data unit to router A. Router A decides to route the PDU to subnet 21.4, which supports a 512-octet PDU size. The router fragments the 1500 data unit into three smaller data units of 512, 512, and 476 octets. Thus, 1500 = 512 + 512 + 476. The last segment containing 476 octets is filled (padded) with zeros to

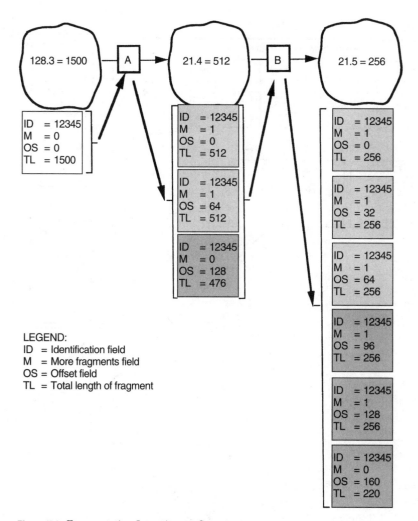

Figure 5.8 Fragmentation Operations at Gateways.

equal a total size that is a multiple of 8. Therefore, this data field is 480 (480 = 476 + 4, which is an even multiple of 8).

Router A passes the data to subnetwork 21.4, which delivers it to router B. This router determines that datagram fragments are to be delivered to subnetwork 21.5. Because the router knows that this network uses a PDU size of 256 octets, it performs further fragmentation. It divides the 512 octet fragments into yet smaller data units and, using the offset values in the three incoming fragments, accordingly adjusts the offset values in the outgoing data units. Notice that the offset values are reset at router B, and their values are derived from the offset values contained in the preceding fragments.

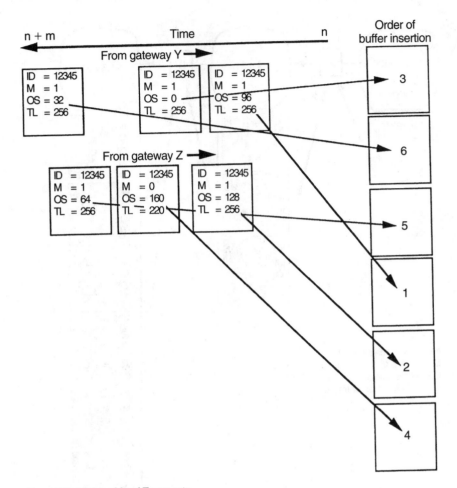

Figure 5.9 Reassembly of Fragments.

Figure 5.9 illustrates the reassembly of the packets, which occurs at the receiving host. The IP module sets up buffer space when the first fragment is received. A buffer is reserved for each fragment, and the fragment is placed in an area within the buffer relative to its position in the original datagram. As the fragments arrive, they are placed into the proper location in the buffer (pigeonholing). When all the fragments have been received, the IP module passes the data to the ULP in the same order that it was originally sent from the sending ULP.

For discussion purposes, assume that the datagram fragments depicted in Figure 5.8 are routed to other routers, say routers Y and Z. To continue the analysis, Figure 5.9 shows that the fragmented datagrams arrive from routers Y and Z in the order depicted by the "time arrow," with earliest arrival at time n and latest time of arrival at time $n + m$. The fragments therefore arrive in the following order (using the offset values in the figure to identify the fragment):

First: fragment with offset value of 96

Second: fragment with offset value of 128

Third: fragment with offset value of 0

Fourth: fragment with offset value of 160

Fifth: fragment with offset value of 64

Sixth: fragment with offset value of 32

The receiving machine has a rather easy job of figuring out where the fragments are to be placed. The IP module simply multiplies the offset value by 8 to determine which slot in the buffer is to receive the fragment. For example, the first arriving fragment's relative position in the buffer is computed as 96 × 8 = 768, or memory address 768. (If you wish to test the calculations, use position 0, not 1, as the first position.)

In Figure 5.9, the reassembling host does not know the length of the complete IP datagram until it receives the fourth fragment, which contains the M = 0 bit (no more fragments), the offset value, and the fragment length. Because the offset value is 160 and the length is 220 octets, the host now knows that the total datagram is 1500 octets, or (160 offset values) × (8 octets per value) + (220 octets in final fragment).

You now see why the M bit is so important. Because the length field in the fragment does not refer to the size of the original datagram but to the size of the fragment, the only method to determine the original length (and the final fragment) is the M = 0 indicator.

If some fragments do not arrive or have been discarded because they exceeded the TTL parameter, IP discards the fragments of the partially reassembled datagram. In addition, upon detection of the arrival of the first fragment, the receiving computer turns on a reassembly timer. This timer, which is set by the network manager, can be used to ensure that all fragments arrive in a timely manner. If the timer times out before all fragments have arrived, the received fragments are discarded.

If a user does not want fragmentation to occur, the fragment flag can be turned to 1, which indicates that fragmentation must not occur. This might be desirable if fragmentation creates excessive overhead because the reassembly timer continues to discard fragments that require retransmission from higher-layer protocols. This situation, however, must be weighed against the fact that turning on the "don't fragment" flag means that datagrams will be discarded by routers if the MTU exceeds the size of the subnetwork capability.

Packet reassembly at the router.   Connectionless routers that use dynamic routing (such as IP) do not reassemble datagrams. The task is impossible because all fragments belonging to the original datagram might not be processed by the same routers. As a consequence, the router does not know how to compute the offset values for fragments it does not receive.

In contrast, connection-oriented routers can perform intermediate reassembly because, by the very nature of the system, all PDUs pass through the same routers. For example, imagine in Figure 5.8 that router A is a connection-oriented router. It could reassemble the fragments for transmission over a higher-capacity subnetwork by detecting the M = 0 in the fragment, as well as the offset value of 128 and length of 476, or 1500 octets (128 offset values × 8 octets per offset + 476 octets in final fragment).

Fragments retained upon retransmission of other fragments. Several of my clients have expressed concern about IP discarding fragments based on the expiration of the fragmentation timer. In some instances, this discarding can create significant replicated traffic on a network. This brief discussion, however, should shed some light on the problem.

First, we assume that discarded fragments are retransmitted by a higher-layer protocol (e.g., TCP). The traffic is fragmented (once again) by the originator and sent to the receiver. The retransmitted fragments contain the same values in the IP identification field as the original submission. Assuming that the receiver's software does not discard the fragments acceptable in the original transmission, one could argue that the identification field could be used to reconstruct a complete data unit by using the fragments of the retransmissions. Of course, if a pigeonhole is full, the received duplicate fragment would be discarded.

A brief analysis shows that this method is not worth the effort. Filling vacant pigeon holes with retransmitted fragments is almost pure chance because some of the retransmitted fragments might undergo different fragmentation operations because the fragments were routed differently the second time. It is especially onerous if the transmitting end must determine which fragments should be transmitted and which should not. Making IP this smart also makes IP more complicated, which should be avoided.

Also, be aware that the reassembly timeout is based on the remaining value of the TTL field in the IP header. This value does not work very well because the vast majority of TTL values are implemented with a hop-count metric rather than a time metric. Implementation of the reassembly timeout should therefore be based on an actual clock.

Before leaving the subject of the options within IP, let us reexamine the flag copy feature (shown in Figure 5.4). A network administrator should determine if the flag copy can be used for certain options. For example, is it useful for all fragments to have the route-recording option? After all, if these fragments move through different routes in an internet, the receiver might have difficulty determining a single list of routes. On the other hand, such a feature still does not preclude examining the routes to determine the efficiency of the internet routers and IP modules. For purposes of simplicity, however, it might make sense (and the IP standard so requires) to stipulate that a route recording option is only used in one of the fragments of a fragmented datagram.

Next, consider when the option should be copied into all fragments. One situation that comes to mind is source routing. If the user wants source routing to be applied to a datagram, it is logical to assume the user wants it to be applied to all fragments of a fragmented datagram.

IP Address and Routing Tables

IP uses routing and address tables to send the data through the internet. Routing tables store routes within them, and address tables store the individual addresses of entities within a network. Both types of tables are discussed in the following subsections.

Address tables

The Internet Activities Board (IAB) has published the definition for the IP address table in RFC 1213. This table is depicted in Figure 5.10; it consists of five columns and anywhere from one to n rows. Each row pertains to an IP address at an entity (a host, router, etc.). More than one row entry can exist if the machine has more than one IP address. The contents of this table are as follows:

The *Entry Address* contains the IP address for this entry's interface.

The *entry ifIndex* contains the interface number (port number) pertaining to this entity's connection to a subnetwork.

	Entry Address	Entry IfIndex	Entry Net Mask	Broadcast Address	Maximum Size of Datagram
Address Entry 1					
Address Entry 2					
Address Entry *n*					

Figure 5.10 IP Address Table.

The *entry net mask* column contains the subnet mask associated with the IP address in the entry address column.

The *broadcast address* contains a value for the least-significant bit in the IP broadcast address. It is used for sending datagrams on the local interface and is associated with the IP address of this row.

The *maximum size of datagram* column represents the maximum size of a datagram that can be processed by this IP module.

Routing tables

Until 1990, an IP routing table was designed based on an individual vendor's perception of the need for the entries in the table. With the publication of the Internet Management Information Base (MIB), a more formal definition of the IP routing table is now available. Figure 5.11 shows the IP routing table as defined in the MIB standard, which was published as RFC 1213.

Each row of the IP routing table contains an entry for each route that is known to the IP module storing this table. The columns represent the information available on each route. A brief description of each column follows.

The *destination* entry contains the IP address of the destination for this route. If this column is coded as 0.0.0.0, the route is considered a default route.

The *ifIndex* entry stands for the interface index. It identifies the local interface (more commonly known as a physical port), through which the next hop in the route can be reached.

	Destination	IfIndex	Metric 1 /	Metric 5	Next Hop	Route Type	Routing Protocol	Route Age	Routing Mask	Route Information
Route 1										
Route 2										
Route 3										
Route *n*										

Figure 5.11 One Possibility for IP Routing Table.

The next five columns are labeled *metric*. The metric entries contain information about the cost metric used for determining the route. With most systems, the cost metric is the number of hops to reach the destination. With the evolution of more sophisticated route discovery protocols (such as OSPF), however, it is possible that more than one cost metric can be used in calculating the route. As the table indicates, up to five cost metrics can be stored.

The *next hop* entry contains the IP address identifying the next hop for this route.

The next column in the table is the *route type*. It is set to one of four values to provide the following information:

1 = none of the following

2 = an invalid route

3 = a directly connected route (a directly connected subnet)

4 = indirect (an indirect connection to reach this destination)

The next column is labeled *routing protocol*. This entry identifies the route discovery protocol by which this route was learned. If the route is discovered with the routing information protocol (RIP), the value in this column must be 8; if it is discovered with the Cisco internal group routing protocol, it must be set to 11; and so on.

The *route age* column is the time, in seconds, since the route was updated or verified.

The next field in the table contains the *route mask* for this route. This mask is logical ANDed with the destination address in the IP datagram before being compared to column 1 in this table (labeled *destination*).

The last column, labeled *route information*, allows a reference to an MIB definition that pertains to a particular routing protocol. Its value depends on the type of routing protocol used in this row entry. As an example of a row entry in the IP routing table, refer back to Chapter 3, Figure 3.10. This figure shows one of the destination networks as 14.0.0.0. Consequently, from the perspective of the routing table at router 8, the column entries for this network are as follows:

destination = 14.0.0.0

interface (port) index = 3

metric 1 = number of hops (the remaining metric columns are empty)

next hop = 13.0.0.2

route type = indirect (4)

routing protocol = egp (5) (for example)

route age = 5 seconds (for example)

route mask = several options

route information = value that depends on routing protocol entry.

IP Service Definitions and Primitives

IP uses two primitives to define the services it provides to the adjacent ULP. The transmitting ULP utilizes the SEND primitive to request the services of IP. In turn, IP uses the DELIVER primitive to notify the destination ULP of the arrival of data. The interface of IP with the upper layer is quite simple because IP is designed to operate with diverse ULPs.

IP/ULP primitives

IP's service definitions (implemented with primitives) are somewhat abstract to allow them to be tailored to the specific host operating system. For example, the SEND and RECV services on a UNIX-based system can be implemented with UNIX system library calls (see Chapter 13).

The relationship of IP and the ULP is shown in Figure 5.12, which depicts host A sending data to host B. The arrows are reversed if host B sends data to host A. The parameters associated with the primitives inform the ULP and IP about the operation requested from the ULP (SEND) and performed by IP (RECV).

The SEND parameters are also used to create the IP header. Consequently, they correlate closely to the IP header fields of a transmitted datagram, shown in Figure 5.2. Likewise, the parameters in the RECV primitive correlate closely to the parameters of the received datagram. The SEND primitive contains the following information:

Source address: IP address of the host sending the data

Destination address: IP address of host to receive the data

Protocol: name of the recipient ULP (e.g., TCP, UDP, etc.)

TOS indicators: relative transmission quality associated with unit of data: precedence, reliability, delay, and throughput

Identifier: optional, for fragmentation control

Don't fragment indicator: yes or no

Time to live: in number of hops

Data length: length of data being transmitted (0 if no data)

Buffer pointer: pointer to the datagram

Option data: options requested by a ULP (security, loose or strict source routing, record routing, stream identification, or time-stamp)

Data: present when data length is greater than 0

Result: result of this SEND request; either (1) datagram sent or (2) error in arguments or network error

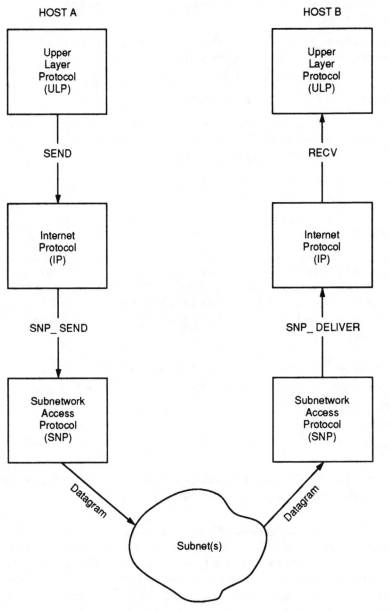

Figure 5.12 IP Primitives.

The RECV primitive contains the following information:

Source address: IP address of sending host

Destination address: IP address of recipient host

Protocol: name of recipient ULP as supplied by the sending ULP (e.g., TCP, UDP, etc.)

TOS indicators: relative transmission quality associated with unit of data: precedence, reliability, delay, and throughput

Data length: length of received data

Buffer pointer: pointer to the datagram

Option data: options requested by source ULP (security, loose or strict source routing, record routing, stream identification, or time-stamp)

Data: present when data length is greater than 0

Result: result of this RECV request

IP/SNP primitives

The primitives between IP and the subnetwork access protocol (SNAP) are similar to the IP/ULP primitives. As shown in Figure 5.12, two primitives are invoked for the IP/SNP operations. The SNP_SEND primitive is used by IP to invoke a service of the SNP; the SND_DELIVER is used by the SNP to deliver a datagram to the IP module. The SNPSEND primitive contains the following information:

Local destination address: Subnetwork address of the destination

TOS indicators: relative transmission quality associated with unit of data: precedence, reliability, delay, and throughput

Length of datagram

Datagram

The SNP_DELIVER primitive contains the datagram and error indicators (the latter is optional and not defined in the standard).

Other IP/SNP service definitions. Many IP modules rest on top of IEEE LANs and interface with IEEE 802.2 (logical link control, or LLC). Chapter 3 (Figure 3.5) explains the method by which LLC and IP use the LSAP header extension to coordinate their operations. As of this writing, no RFC exists to explain the relationship of the IEEE 802.2 LLC primitives and IP. The next section, however, provides this explanation.

Network layer/LLC primitives

The IP/SNP primitives explained in the previous section are not designed for the LLC interface. If an implementation only uses the LLC connection-less data transfer service, the interface is simple. A brief explanation of this service follows, and is shown in Figure 5.13.

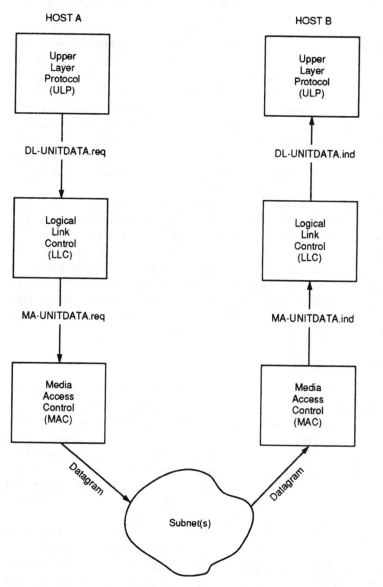

Figure 5.13 IP over LLC in IEEE LAN.

Two primitives are used for connectionless data transfer. They are passed between LLC and its upper-layer protocol (which could be IP or some other module).

- *DL-UNITDATA.request* (source-address, destination-address, data, priority)

- *DL-UNITDATA.indication* (source-address, destination-address, data, priority)

The request primitive is passed from the network layer to LLC to request that a link service data unit (LSDU) be sent to a remote link service access point. The address parameters are equivalent to a combination of the LLC SAP and MAC addresses. The priority field is passed to the media access control (MAC) and implemented (except for in 802.3, which has no priority mechanism). The indication primitive is passed from LLC to the network layer to indicate the arrival of an LSDU from a remote entity.

A comparison of Figures 5.12 and 5.13 reveals close similarities between IP/SNP and ULP/LLC operations, but differences do exist in the parameters associated with the IP/SNP and ULP/LLC primitives.

If IP is placed on top of LLC, a convergence protocol must be implemented to map the SNP_SEND primitive and its parameters to the DL-UNITDATA.request and its parameters. The protocol must also map the SNP_DELIVER primitive and its parameters to the LLC DL-UNITDATA.indication and its parameters. The address fields present no major problem if RFC 1042 is followed (see Chapter 2, "Extension of LSAP Header"). A potential problem is deciding how to handle the TOS parameters. Perhaps the best approach is to ignore them at the LLC and MAC levels, as they are mostly irrelevant for use in a high-capacity LAN.

Multicasting

Similar to the physical layer, the Internet network layer supports multicasting. The concept is quite similar to LAN multicasting, in which a single PDU (in this case an IP datagram) is sent to more than one host. The set of hosts forms a *multicast group.*

IP multicasting allows hosts to operate on one or multiple physical networks. A host can belong to more than one multicast group or a permanent multicast group (a *well-known* group), or it can dynamically enter and leave groups as the need dictates. Also, a host does not have to be a member of the multicast group to send data to the group.

Multicasting is accomplished through the use of the IP class D address discussed in Chapter 3. The first 4 bits of the 32-bit address field are set to 1110; the next 28 bits identify the specific multicast group. Because of the structure of the address space, the classes of A, B, and C addresses are meaningless when using multicasting.

The permissible ranges for multicast addresses are from 224.0.0.0 through 239.255.255.255. The Internet does not allow the address space of 224.0.0.0 to be used, and the address space of 224.0.0.1 is reserved for an *all-hosts* group. An all-hosts group identifies all hosts and routers participating in an Internet IP multicast operation.

Figure 5.14 shows an example of how IP multicasting operates. Router 1 (R1) receives an IP datagram from another part of an internet. The destination IP address is a multicast address (a source address is not allowed to contain multicast values for obvious reasons). The router is responsible for interpreting the multicast address and forwarding it to the proper hosts (for which it has authority) and to other participating multicast routers (R2). In this example, hosts A, C, and E are members of the same multicast group. R2 and host F are also members.

One approach to sending this traffic to the proper host on a LAN is to map the IP multicast address to an Ethernet multicast address. The mapping is quite simple and proceeds as follows: The low-order 23 bits of the IP address are mapped into the low-order 23 bits of the Ethernet multicast address. This approach is not perfect because a one-to-one relationship does not exist between the 28 bits of the IP address and the 23 bits of the Ethernet address. It is a reasonable solution, however, because the chances are quite small that any two groups would choose the same 23 bits for the multicast address value. In any event, it is prudent to ensure that the receiving software can discard datagrams that are not appropriate.

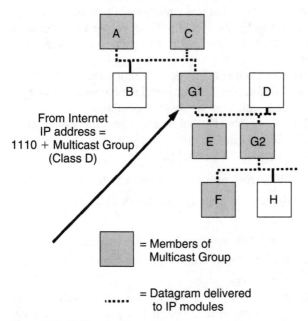

Figure 5.14 Multicasting Operations.

Hosts can be configured to either send or receive multicast datagrams. Alternately, hosts can be configured to send but not receive multicast datagrams or even not participate in any multicast operations.

To implement multicasting, the software must be capable of allowing a host to join or leave a multicast group. A means must be devised to allow hosts to inform other hosts about the relationships and status of memberships. The IP software must keep bookkeeping operations about which host belongs to separate multicast groups and delete and add hosts accordingly. These administrative tasks are accomplished through the Internet group management protocol (IGMP), which is discussed in the next section.

Internet Group Management Protocol

The IGMP allows routers and hosts to inform each other about multicasting operations, such as joining and leaving multicast groups. Additionally, it allows the machines to communicate status messages about multicasting information. IGMP works in a manner quite similar to the Internet control message protocol (ICMP). An IP datagram is used to transport the IGMP message between the machines. Be aware that IGMP is required for all machines that implement IP multicasting.

IGMP also has some similarities to a LAN token bus protocol in how a machine is added as a member to a group. When a host wishes to join a multicast group, it must send out a message (just as a LAN station sends out a set solicitor message in a token bus). This message is an all-host multicast address in which the host establishes that it is a member of a multicast group. The IGMP message is received by the local multicast router that performs the necessary operations to route the traffic to other multicast routers throughout an internet.

Once these operations have been performed, the multicast router must periodically query the host to determine if a host is still a member of a group. If the query does not get a response from the host, the multicast router is required to stop advertising membership for that host to other multicast routers.

The format for the IGMP message is quite simple and is illustrated in Figure 5.15. The message consists of five fields.

The *version* field gives the current protocol version, which is currently 1.

The *type* field identifies the field as a query (a value of 1) or a response (a value of 2).

Logically enough, the *unused* field is not used.

The *checksum* field checks for errors. The calculation uses the same algorithm as the IP and TCP protocols.

The *group address* field contains the group address for hosts to report their membership in the multicast group. This field has no meaning for a query message.

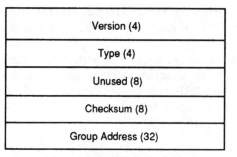

| Version (4) |
| Type (4) |
| Unused (8) |
| Checksum (8) |
| Group Address (32) |

Figure 5.15 IGMP Message Format.

(*n*) = number of bits in the field

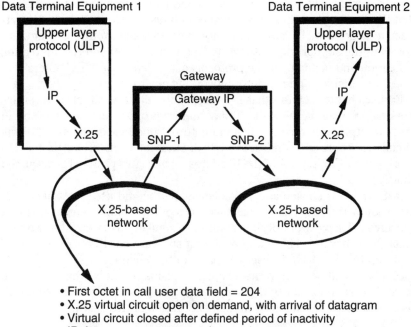

Data Terminal Equipment 1   Data Terminal Equipment 2

- First octet in call user data field = 204
- X.25 virtual circuit open on demand, with arrival of datagram
- Virtual circuit closed after defined period of inactivity
- IP datagrams sent as complete packet sequences using the M bit, if necessary
- Interrupts and D bit not used

Figure 5.16 X.25 and IP.

A number of organizations transmit IP datagrams through X.25 public and private networks. RFC 877 was published to provide guidance on how to transfer IP datagrams through an X.25 interface (see Figure 5.16).

The X.25 packet switch must react to datagrams on demand and create a virtual circuit when a datagram arrives. RFC 877 does not define the details of how IP addresses are mapped to corresponding X.25 data terminal equipment (DTE) addresses, nor does it define how long the virtual circuit remains open if no activity occurs from IP. The standard requires that the first octet in the X.25 call user data field be coded to decimal 204 (binary 11001100). This value identifies the IP.

IP datagrams are sent as complete packet sequences and, if necessary, the M bit is used to ensure that if the IP datagram is fragmented, it can be reassembled properly at the other end. Either user can close the virtual circuit at any time. Upper-layer protocols such as TCP, SNA path control, UDP, etc., are not affected by this implementation scheme.

Other Thoughts on IP

You might be surprised at the brevity of the discussion of IP. I am not shirking my responsibility in the analysis; rather, I am merely reflecting the fact that IP does not contain a great number of functions. Indeed, one of the attractive aspects of IP is its simplicity and efficiency. You might surmise, however, the supporting protocols to IP (such as TCP) and the addressing resolution and naming service protocols discussed in earlier chapters provide for a complex and rich internetworking environment.

Earlier chapters stated that IP is one of the most widely used internetworking protocols in the world. Today, hundreds of products are available in the marketplace that use the IP architecture. Nonetheless, the use of IP will diminish as users and vendors move to another internetworking protocol to overcome the limitations of the IP address space (this protocol is discussed shortly).

If ISO 8473 is chosen as a replacement IP, the end user most likely will never know that the change has taken place if the implementation is well conceived. The network designer will see a similarity between the two protocols, but they are different enough that software must be written almost from scratch. ISO 8473 is discussed later in this chapter.

A subsequent section in this chapter explains the CLNP, but before we leave IP, it is important to discuss some of the problems relating to the IP address, which are examined in the next section of this chapter.

Possible Replacements to IP

Because the IP address space of 32 bits will be exhausted within a few years, the Internet has been examining ways to either enhance IP to accommodate larger addresses or replace IP. Several ideas are under consideration; one of these is called the simple internet protocol (SIP).

SIP is designed to overcome the shortcomings of IP, eliminate the features of IP that were not used much (if at all) and utilize a larger and more flexible address space. The latter problem is considered the most serious. As Figure 5.17 shows, the number of networks connected to the Internet is doubling every year. Even if the growth slows, the limited and relatively flat address space of IP must be corrected.

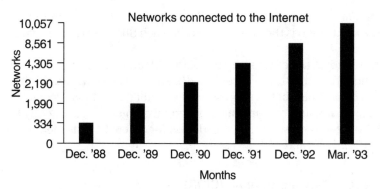

Figure 5.17 Growth of the Internet.

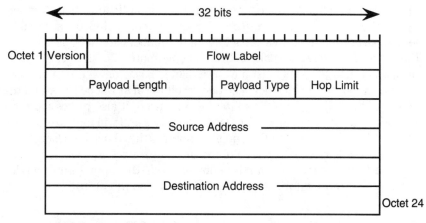

Figure 5.18 SIP Header.

Figure 5.18 shows the format of the SIP datagram. The SIP header is 24 octets in length, with an optional header not shown in this figure. The version field identifies the version of the protocol and is used to distinguish a SIP datagram from an IP datagram.

The flow label field is an enhancement to the IP TOS field. Labels of 0_31 correspond to the IP TOS field of 5 bits ($2^5 = 32$). Labels greater than 31 have not been defined (and will likely be optional), but will be used to identify special features for handling the SIP datagram.

The payload type field specifies the length of the datagram (excluding header), and the type of header that follows the SIP header. For the latter operation, headers, such as TCP or UDP, can be identified—in which case, values of the ongoing IP field are employed. SIP permits multiple headers to follow the SIP header; the headers are chained together. For example, a source routing header could precede a TCP header. This feature thus takes care of the options field of the IP datagram.

The hop limit field is similar to the IP time-to-live field. It is set to non-zero by the sender and is then decremented at each SIP node until the value reaches zero.

As of this writing, the exact structure of the SIP address has not yet been defined—nor will it be to the extent of IP's strict definitions. Rather, the boundaries of the fields in the address will be defined by bit masks or some other means. A number of companies, government agencies, and individuals have proposed the use of the OSI address for a new IP. This idea is examined further in Chapter 14.

Classless Inter-Domain Routing (CIDR)

Chapter 3 stated that the Internet IP address organization was changed in 1993. With this change, the concept of a class for an IP address is dropped, hence the term *classless routing*. Routing is conducted on a variable-length part of the IP address. In addition, IP numbers are to be assigned on the basis of topology to make CIDR concepts more effective. The change means that IP addresses must now be assigned based on where the IP user is connected into the Internet. The end result of CIDR will be to extend the length of time the current IP address can be used. It also places more restrictions on the assignment of Class B addresses and will increase the use of Class C addresses. One final point is noteworthy. Blocks of Class C addresses are released (delegated) to the Internet service providers, and it is the user's task to obtain an IP number from the appropriate service provider. For more information, read RFC 1466 and RFC 1481.

Connectionless-Mode Network Service (ISO 8473)

ISO 8473 is a specification that describes the architecture for connectionless-mode network service. It is also called the connectionless network protocol (CLNP). It is quite similar to IP in the functions it performs, but it is not compatible with IP.

ISO 8473 is designed to operate with the hosts attached to public and private networks and the routers that service the hosts and networks. The protocol does not involve itself with the particular characteristics of the underlying subnetworks. Like IP, the basic idea is to demand little in the way of services from the subnetworks, except to transport the PDU.

The protocol communicates by exchanging internetwork PDUs (IPDUs) in a connectionless (datagram) fashion. Each IPDU is treated independently and does not depend on the state of the network for any particular establishment connection time (because no connection exists in a connectionless network). Routing decisions are made independently by each forwarding internetworking node. It is also possible for the source user to determine the routing by placing the routing information in the IPDU source routing field.

The ISO 8473 connectionless-mode network service is provided by two primitives: N-UNITDATA.request and N-UNITDATA.indication. These two primitives are quite similar to the primitives used by the IP. Note that the protocol uses no connection and clear primitives, which is a rather obvious indication of its connectionless attributes. The two primitives each contain four parameters:

- NS-source-address
- NS-destination-address
- NS-quality-of-service
- NS-userdata

The ISO 8473 PDU

A brief description of the fields of the 8473 PDU is provided in Table 5.4. As you review this material, you will see the similarity to the IP datagram. Figure 5.19 shows the format of the data unit. The next sections discuss how the fields are used in 8473 operations.

TABLE 5.4 Functions of Fields in ISO 8473 PDU

Protocol identifier	Identifies the protocol as ISO 8473
Length indicator	Describes the length of the header.
Version/protocol	Identifies the version of ISO 8473.
Lifetime	Represents the lifetime of the PDU. It is coded in units of 500 ms.
Segmentation permitted	Indicates if segmentation is permitted. The originator of the PDU determines this value, and it cannot be changed by any other entity.
More segments	Indicates if more user data is forthcoming. It is used when segmentation takes place. When the bit equals 0, it indicates that the last octet of the data in this PDU is the last octet of the user data stream (the network service data unit, NSDU).
Error report	Indicates that an error report is to be generated back to the originator if a data PDU is discarded.
Type code	Describes the PDU as a data PDU or an error PDU.
PDU segment length	Specifies the length of the PDU (header and data). If no segmentation occurs, the value of this field is identical to the value of the total length field.
Checksum	Calculated on the entire PDU header. A value of 0 in this field indicates that the header is to be ignored. A PDU is discarded if the checksum fails.
Destination and source addresses and address lengths	Because the source and destination addresses are variable in length, the length fields are used to describe their length The actual addresses are network service access points (NSAPs).
Data unit identifier	Identifies an initial PDU to reassemble a segmented data unit correctly.

TABLE 5.4 Functions of fields in ISO 8473 PDU (Continued)

Protocol identifier	Identifies the protocol as ISO 8473
Segmentation offset	If the original PDU is segmented, this field specifies the relative position of this segment in relation to the initial PDU.
Total PDU length	Contains the entire length of the original PDU which includes both the header and data. It is not changed for the lifetime of the PDU.
Options	Optional parameters are placed in this part of the PDU such as route recording, quality-of-service parameters, priorities, buffer congestion indication, padding characters, and designation of security levels.
Data	Contains the user data

Protocol identifier
Length indicator
Version/protocol ID extenion
Lifetime
Segment/more/error/report/type code
Segment length
Checksum
Destination address length
Destination address
Source address length
Source address
Data unit identifier
Segmentation offset
Total PDU length
Options
Data

Figure 5.19 ISO 8473 PDU format.

Quality-of-service functions

An underlying subnetwork can provide several quality-of-service (QOS) functions. The services are negotiated when the primitives are exchanged between layers. Of course, the primitive parameters must be based on *a priori* knowledge of the availability of the services within the subnetwork. It does little good to ask for a QOS feature if the subnetwork does not provide it. Be aware that the values of QOS apply to both ends of the network connections (NC), even if the NC spans several subnetworks that offer different services.

Use of ISO 8348. For QOS choices, ISO 8473 uses the following QOS functions described in ISO 8348:

Transit delay: Establishes the elapsed time between a data request and the corresponding data indication. This QOS feature applies only to successful PDU transfers. The delay is specified by a desired value up to the maximum acceptable value. All values assume a PDU of 128 octets. User-initiated flow control is not measured in these values.

Residual error rate (RER): ratio of total incorrect, lost, or duplicated PDUs to total PDUs transferred:

$$RER = \frac{N(e) + N(1) - N(x)}{N}$$

where RER = residual error rate; N(e) = PDUs in error; N(1) = lost PDUs; N(x) = duplicate PDUs; N = number of PDUs.

Cost determinants: defines the maximum acceptable cost for a network service. It can be stated in relative or absolute terms. Final actions on this parameter are left to the specific network provider.

Priority: determines preferential service in the subnetwork. Outgoing transmission queues and buffers are managed based on the priority values contained in the PDU header options field.

Protection against unauthorized access: directs the subnetwork to prevent unauthorized access to user data. [xul1]

Protocol functions

ISO 8473 includes several optional or required protocol functions. Each function provides a specialized service to the network user. In a sense, the ISO 8473 protocol functions are similar to the QOS features, except that they are performed as an integral part of the protocol.

Traffic management between subnetworks

This section provides an illustration of how a connectionless-mode internetwork protocol transfers data between subnetworks. While different vendors use various techniques for the provision of connectionless service, many use the concepts described herein.

When the protocol receives the NS-source-address and NS-destination-address parameters in the N-UNITDATA.request primitive from an upper layer, it uses them to build a source address and destination address in the header of the PDU. The source address and NS-quality-of-service parameters are used to determine which optional functions are to be selected for the network user. At this time, a data unit identifier is assigned to identify this request from other requests. This identifier remains unique for the lifetime of the initial PDU and any segmented PDUs in the networks. Subsequent or derived PDUs are considered to correspond to the initial PDU if they have the same source address, destination address, and data unit identifier. At first glance, this rule might appear to be connection-oriented, but it applies only to PDUs created as a result of segmentation.

The PDU is then forwarded through any subnetworks. Each hop examines the destination address to determine if the PDU has reached its destination. If the destination address equals a network service access point (NSAP) served by the network entity, it has reached its destination. Otherwise, it must be forwarded to the next node.

When the PDU reaches its destination, the receiver removes the protocol control information (PCI) from the PDU. It also uses the addresses in the header to generate the NS-source-address and NS-destination-address parameters of the UNITDATA indication primitive. It preserves the data field of the PDU until all segments (if any) have been received. The options field of the PDU header is used to invoke any QOS parameters at the receiving end.

Unlike connection-oriented networks, an ISO 8473 connectionless-mode network has more flexibility in terminating service to a user. For example, if a new network connection request is received with a higher priority than an ongoing data transfer, the network can release the lower-priority transfer. Moreover, users can also have priorities established for the data transfers. The network connections with a higher priority have their requests serviced first, and the remaining resources of the network attempt to satisfy the lower-priority network connections.

User data is given a specific *lifetime* in networks. This mechanism is useful for several reasons. First, it prevents lost or misdirected data from accumulating and consuming network resources. Second, it gives the transmitting entity control over the disposition of aged data units. Third, it greatly simplifies congestion control, flow control, and accountability logic in the networks. Discarded data units, however, can be recovered by the transport layer.

The lifetime field in the PDU header is set by the originating network entity. The value also applies to any segmented PDUs and is copied into the header of these data units. The value contains, at any given time, the remaining lifetime of the PDU. It is decremented by each network entity that processes it. The value is represented in units of 500 ms and is decremented by one unit by each entity. If delays exceed 500 ms, the value is decremented by more than one unit.

If the lifetime value reaches zero before it reaches its destination, it is discarded. If the error report bit is on, an error report data unit is generated to inform the originator of the lost data. Some consider this feature to be a connection-oriented service. Whatever its name, it is obviously very useful if end-to-end accountability is required.

In addition to discarding aged data units, the network can also discard data for other reasons:

- Checksum reveals an error (if checksum is used).
- A PDU that contains an unsupported function is received, such as a QOS function.
- Local congestion occurs at the receiver.
- Header cannot be interpreted accurately.
- A PDU cannot be segmented and is too large for the underlying network to handle.
- The destination address is not reachable, or a path route is not acceptable to the network serving the PDU.

The PDU is transferred on a hop-to-hop (next-node) basis. The selection of the next system in the route can be influenced by the QOS and other optional parameters. For example, the next hop might be chosen because it supports the QOS requests.

Internetwork routing. The routing technique in ISO 8473 is called *source routing* and is quite similar to IP source routing. The originator of the PDU determines the route by placing a list of the intermediate routes in the options field of the PDU header. The route indicators are called *titles*. The relaying is accomplished by each network entity, which routes the PDU to the next title in the list. The indicator is updated by each relay point to identify the next stage of the route.

The protocol provides two types of routing: complete source routing and partial source routing. *Complete source routing* requires that the specified route be used in the exact order as in the route list. If this route cannot be taken, the PDU must be discarded with the option of returning an error report to the originator. *Partial source routing* allows a system to route to intermediate systems not specified in the list.

Another routing option, called the *record route function,* requires intermediate systems to add their title to a record route list in the options field of the header. The list is built as the PDU is forwarded to its destination. This list can be used for troubleshooting internet or subnet problems. It can also be used as a tool for efficiency analysis, audit trails, or simply as a "directory" for a returning PDU.

If this option is invoked, either complete route recording or partial route recording is used. With the former, all intermediate systems are recorded, and PDU reassembly is performed only if all derived PDUs took the same route. Otherwise, the PDU is discarded. The partial route recording also requires the full list but does not require that the derived PDUs visit the same intermediate systems.

CLNP and IP

The ISO 8473 standard was derived from the IP. From a design standpoint, the routing of the network should remain the same when an organization migrates to ISO 8473 from IP. The network topology should not be affected either by the transition to ISO 8473. So, the good news is that the two protocols are similar, but the bad news is that the conversion still requires rewriting a lot of software.

Summary

The IP is a widely used internetworking protocol. It is implemented on both LANs and WANs and is designed to operate in a connectionless mode. It does, however, support a number of quality service options called type-of-service (TOS). IP remains transparent to the underlying network. Consequently, it can be placed on a variety of networks. IP does not perform route discovery. Instead, it uses routing tables created by route discovery protocols.

Internet Control
Message Protocol

The Internet Protocol (IP) has no error-reporting or error-correcting mechanisms; it relies on a module called the internet control message protocol (ICMP) to report errors in the processing of a datagram, and provide for administrative and status messages. This chapter examines the major features of ICMP and provides guidance on its effective use.

ICMP resides in either a host computer or gateway as a companion to the IP (see Chapter 1, Figure 1.7). As illustrated in Figure 6.1, the ICMP is used between hosts or gateways when datagrams cannot be delivered, when a gateway directs traffic on shorter routes, or when a gateway does not have sufficient buffering capacity to hold and forward protocol data units.

ICMP notifies the host if a destination is unreachable. ICMP also manages or creates a time-exceeded message if the lifetime of the datagram expires. Finally, ICMP performs certain editing functions to determine if the IP header is in error or otherwise unintelligible.

Certain implementations of TCP/IP have been rather relaxed in returning ICMP datagrams when an error is detected. We discuss when ICMP error messages should be used prudently and there are some instances when they should not be used at all. Check the product being used in your installation to ensure that ICMP datagrams are generated for errors and are generated logically. For example, a phenomenon in this protocol suite exists nicknamed the "black hole disease": datagrams are sent out, but nothing is returned, not even ICMP errors. This happenstance implementation of ICMP makes troubleshooting very difficult.

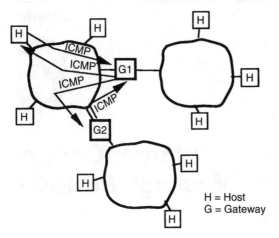

Figure 6.1 ICMP Activities.

The following aspects of ICMP need to be emphasized:

- ICMP is a user of IP. IP encapsulates the ICMP data unit into IP datagrams for transport across an internet.

- IP must use ICMP.

- ICMP does not make IP reliable; its function is to report errors. Even with the use of ICMP, datagrams can still be lost or delivered out of sequence. Reliability is the responsibility of a higher-layer protocol, such as the transmission control protocol (TCP) or even an application-layer protocol.

- ICMP reports errors on IP datagrams, but it does not report errors on ICMP data units. To do so would create a catch-22 situation, wherein infinite repetitions could occur in error reporting.

- If IP uses fragmented datagrams, ICMP reports an error only on the first fragment of the datagram received.

- ICMP is not required to report errors on datagram problems. In actual situations, however, gateways generally create ICMP error messages. Reporting is less certain with regard to a host computer generating ICMP messages; check for individual variations in your vendor's product line.

ICMP Message Format

The ICMP message format is shown in Figure 6.2. ICMP messages are carried in the user portion of the IP datagram. The protocol field in the IP header is set to 1 to signify the use of ICMP. All ICMP messages contain three fields:

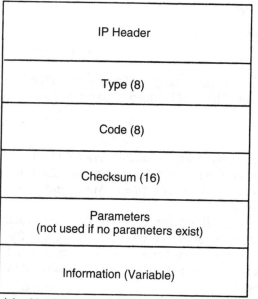

| IP Header |
| Type (8) |
| Code (8) |
| Checksum (16) |
| Parameters
(not used if no parameters exist) |
| Information (Variable) |

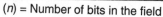

(*n*) = Number of bits in the field

Figure 6.2 ICMP Message Format.

- the type field, which defines the type of message
- the code field, which describes the type of error or status information
- a checksum field, which computes a 16-bit one's complement on the ICMP message.

The ICMP error-reporting message also carries the internet header and the first 64 bits of the user data field. These bits are useful for trouble-shooting and problem analysis.

ICMP Error- and Status-Reporting Procedures

The error- and status-reporting services reported by ICMP are listed below. They are explained further in the following material.

- time exceeded on datagram lifetime
- parameter unintelligible
- destination unreachable
- source quench for flow control
- echo and echo reply
- redirect

- time-stamp and time-stamp reply
- information request or information reply
- address mask request and reply

As stated earlier, the type code identifies the type of message and the format of the ICMP protocol data unit. This field is coded as shown in Table 6.1.

Time exceeded

This service is executed by a gateway when the time-to-live field in the IP datagram expires (its value becomes zero), and the gateway has discarded the datagram. This service is also invoked if a timer expires during reassembly of a fragmented datagram.

The ICMP message consists of the IP header and 64 bits of the original data in the first fragments (if fragmentation is used) of the datagram. The ICMP code field is set to 0 if time-to-live has been exceeded in transit or 1 if fragment assembly time has been exceeded. Code 0 can be generated by the gateway; code 1 by the host.

Parameter unintelligible

The destination host or gateway can invoke this service if it encounters problems processing any part of an IP header. Typically, this occurs if a field is unintelligible, and the host or gateway cannot process the datagram.

The ICMP message contains a pointer field whose value points to the byte that created the problem in the original datagram header. The ICMP data unit also carries the IP header and the first 64 bits of the problem datagram. The code field is set to 0 if a pointer is used. A code field set to 1 indicates a problem with the IP service options.

TABLE 6.1 ICMP Type Codes

Type code value	Type of ICMP message
0	Echo reply
3	Destination unreachable
4	Source quench
5	Redirect
8	Echo request
11	Time exceeded
12	Parameter unintelligible
13	Time-stamp request
14	Time-stamp reply
15	Information request
16	Information reply
17	Address mask request
18	Address mask reply

Destination unreachable

This service is used by a gateway or the destination host and is invoked if a gateway encounters problems reaching the destination network specified in the IP destination address. This service can also be used by a destination host if an identified higher-level protocol is not available on the host or if a specified port is not available (inactive).

The ICMP message contains the IP header and the first 64 bits of the problem datagram. The code field of the ICMP header is coded as follows:

0 = network unreachable

1 = host unreachable

2 = protocol unavailable

3 = port unavailable

4 = fragmentation needed

5 = failed source route

The gateway can send codes of 0, 1, 4, and 5; codes 2 and 3 are sent from the host.

Source quench

This service is a primitive form of the flow and congestion control invoked by a gateway and is used if the machine has insufficient buffer space for queuing incoming datagrams. If the datagram is discarded, the gateway can send this message to the host that originated the datagram. It performs the same function as the receive not ready (RNR) format in many other protocols. The destination host can use the source quench message service if datagrams are arriving too fast to process.

In actual operations, this service notifies the transmitting host to reduce the number of datagrams being transmitted to the destination host. This service thus acts as a flow control entity for an internet.

A gateway has the option of sending a source-quench message for every datagram it discards. Upon receiving this message, the source host should reduce the datagram traffic. ICMP has no message to reinstate transmission; flow control is reinitiated when the transmitting host no longer receives any source quench messages. Typically, the host can increase traffic (perhaps gradually) until running at full-transmit rate or until it receives another source quench message.

It is prudent to issue a flow-control signal before a machine's capacity is exceeded. Consequently, the source-quench message can also be issued when the machine's capacity is being approached. If this method is used, the datagram that initiates the flow-control message can be delivered.

The ICMP data unit contains the relevant type value of 4. The code is set to 0 and, as with other ICMP error messages, the internet header and the first 64 bits of the problem datagram reside within the unit.

Echo request and reply

Echo request and reply is a valuable tool to determine the state of an internet. It can be sent to any IP address, such as a gateway, which must return a reply to the originator. In this manner, a network administrator can find out about the state of the network resources because a reply is only sent in response to a request. If a problem exists, a reply is not returned.

The echo service can also determine if another host is active and available in the network. To initiate the service, a sender host sends the ICMP data unit with the address of the destination host and the IP address field. If the queried host is indeed active, it returns an echo reply to the querying host.

This service is called PING in some systems. It uses the ICMP echo and echo reply but embellishes the basic operation with additional features, including the ability to specify the interval between requests and the number of times to send the request. For example, the IBM version of PING can perform the following services:

PING LOOPBACK: verifies the operation of TCP/IP software

PING my-IP-address: verifies whether the network resource can be addressed

PING a-remote-IP-address: verifies whether the network can be accessed

PING a-remote-host-name: verifies the operation of the name server or name resolver

The ICMP message type field identifies an echo message with a 1 and an echo reply message with a 0.

Redirect

This service is invoked by a gateway to send the ICMP message to the source host. It is used to provide routing management information to the host by indicating that a better route is available. Typically, this message means the host should send its traffic to another gateway. Under most circumstances, the gateway generates a redirect message if its routing table indicates that the next hop, either host or gateway, is on the same network as the network contained in the source address of the IP header.

You might wonder why a host would not know the optimum route to a destination. In many installations, the host IP tables are created initially with very little routing information to simplify system generation at the host for the TCP/IP software and supporting tables. In the simplest form, a host routing table might begin with only an entry to one gateway. The table is then updated by gateways as the gateways discover paths through the internet. Consequently, a host might not know a route, but a redirect message can be sent from the gateway to the host to inform the host of a better choice. The redirect message is not sent if the IP datagram is using the source route option, even if a better route to the final destination exists.

The code field is coded to convey the following information:

0 = redirect datagrams for the network

1 = redirect datagrams for the host

2 = redirect datagrams for the type of service and network

3 = redirect datagrams for the type of service and host

A host computer should not be allowed to send an ICMP redirect because it is the gateway that should be tasked with this job; a host should only be tasked with updating its routing table according to receiving the redirect. Additionally, the rationale is to keep host machines out of the routing business as much as possible.

Time-stamp and time-stamp reply

This service is used by gateways and hosts to determine the delay incurred when delivering traffic through a network or networks. The ICMP data unit contains three time-stamp values:

Originate time-stamp: time the sender last processed the message before sending it (filled in immediately before sending).

Receive time-stamp: time the echoer first processed the message upon receiving it (filled in immediately upon receiving message).

Transmit time-stamp: time the echo last processed the message before sending it (filled in immediately before the reply is sent).

Request for Comments (RFC) 792 requires that the time-stamp values be in milliseconds elapsed since midnight universal time (UT). If the time is not available in milliseconds or it cannot be provided with respect to midnight UT, any time can be inserted in the time-stamp values as long as the high-order bit of the time-stamp is set to indicate that the time-stamp values are nonstandard.

At first glance it might appear that the time-stamp service provides a simple yet accurate method of synchronizing clocks between machines. Generally, this is indeed the case, especially if the machines are on a point-to-point connection without any intervening network between them. Because point-to-point lines have nonvarying transit delays (with rare exceptions), the three time-stamps can be used to coordinate the clocks between the two machines with acceptable accuracy. Even in this simple situation, however, problems can arise. For example, the message must be time-stamped immediately upon transmission for the originate time-stamp, immediately upon reception for the receive time-stamp, and immediately upon transmission for the transmit time-stamp to achieve accurate clocking. If delays occur at the machines because of buffering or computation problems, variations in the clocking coordination occur. When intervening networks are involved, the time-stamp and time-stamp reply fields could be significantly inaccurate because of the variable delay experienced through the internet subnetworks. The best approach for synchronizing clocks between machines is to use some form of smoothing with statistical analysis.

Realistically, the time-stamp and time-stamp reply are better used to ascertain delay through an internet. In this regard, the three time-stamps can be a valuable tool to perform diagnostics of the performance of the internet resources.

Information request or information reply

This service enables a host to identify the network to which it is attached. A host sends the ICMP message with the IP header source and destination address fields coded as 0, which conveys "this network." A replying IP module (one designated as a server authorized to perform this task) returns the reply with the address fully specified in both the source and destination address fields of the IP header. This service is similar to the reverse address resolution protocol (RARP), which enables a host to obtain its own IP address. It is not used much and has been replaced by RARP and BOOTP.

Address mask request and reply

This service is used by a host to obtain a subnet mask used on the host's network. (Chapter 3 provides a discussion on subnets and masks.) The requesting host can send the request directly to an IP gateway or can broadcast it.

While the address masked request and reply operations are quite useful, they must be approached with some forethought. At a minimum, an address mask reply should not be sent by any computer unless the computer is the authoritative originator of the address mask. The host should be designated as "an address mask agent." This approach can solve many problems in using this feature of ICMP, especially if the vendor knows how to format and reply to the IP address mask field.

Other Thoughts on ICMP

Some implementations of ICMP have resulted in the proliferation of unnecessary status or error messages. The key in using protocols as flexible as the TCP/IP suite is to accept almost anything and send out almost nothing.

ICMP messages that should not be sent are broadcast and multicast address messages. Sending error messages for this type of traffic has a tendency to create broadcast storms. As stated before, ICMP should not report on itself.

Additionally, ICMP messages should be sent cautiously on user datagram protocol (UDPs) traffic. Although we have not yet discussed UDPs, keep in mind that sending error messages relating to unidentified UDP ports could create significant problems with the ICMP destination-unreachable report. This problem can occur in computers that have not established a client for the destination port identifier in the UDP segment.

Summary

ICMP is used by an internet to provide error, status, and administrative messages between gateways and hosts. The protocol relies on IP to deliver its messages, although ICMP reports on the IP operations. ICMP is often used as a diagnostic tool because of its echo, time-stamp, parameters-unintelligible, and destination-unreachable features. It must be implemented as part of the IP operations.

Transmission Control Protocol and User Datagram Protocol

This chapter examines the widely used transport layer protocol known as the transmission control protocol (TCP). As discussed earlier, TCP was originally developed for use in ARPANET and the Internet, but it is now used throughout the world and found in many commercial and research centers and university networks. TCP has several similarities to the OSI transport protocol, and some of its features were incorporated into OSI's transport protocol class 4 (TP4). This chapter also examines the user datagram protocol (UDP), which is used in place of TCP in a number of applications. The rather abbreviated discussion of UDP in this chapter is not meant to diminish its importance. Rather, it is a reflection on UDP's simplicity and brevity of functions.

Value of the Transport Layer

In previous chapters, I emphasized that the Internet Protocol (IP) is not designed to recover from certain problems, nor does it guarantee traffic delivery. Moreover, IP discards datagrams that have exceeded the number of permissible transit hops in an internet.

Certain user applications require assurance that all datagrams have been delivered safely to the destination. Furthermore, the transmitting user might need to know that the traffic has been delivered at the receiving host. The mechanisms to achieve these important services reside in TCP; UDP, however, does not provide delivery assurance services.

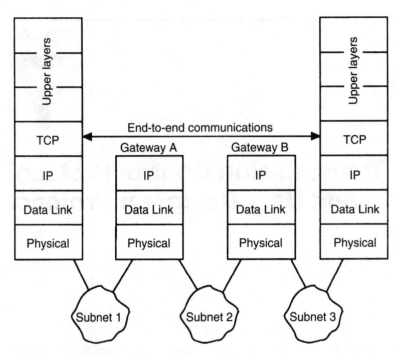

Figure 7.1 Relationship of Transport Layer to Other Layers.

The job of TCP can be quite complex. It must be able to satisfy a wide range of applications requirements and, equally important, accommodate a dynamic environment within an internet. TCP must establish and manage sessions (logical associations) between its local users and these users' remote communicating partners. Thus, TCP (and the computer's operating system) must constantly be aware of the user's ongoing activities to support the user's data transfer through the internet.

TCP Overview

As depicted in Figure 1.7 in Chapter 1 and Figure 7.1 here, TCP resides in the transport layer of the conventional seven-layer model. (Remember, however, the Internet layers do not include the session and presentation layers.) TCP is situated above IP and below the upper layers. Figure 7.1 also illustrates that TCP is not loaded into the router to support user data transfer. It resides in the host computer or a machine tasked with the end-to-end integrity of the transfer of user data. If TCP runs in the router, it does so to support activities such as network management, terminal sessions with the router, etc.[1]

---

[1] There are exceptions to this rule, especially in IBM token rings, where the router uses TCP to account for user traffic.

Figure 7.1 also shows that TCP is designed to run above IP. Because IP provides no sequencing or traffic acknowledgment, and is connectionless, the tasks of reliability, flow control, sequencing application session, opens, and closes are given to TCP. Although TCP and IP are tied together so closely that they are used in the same context (TCP/IP), TCP can also support other protocols. For example, another connectionless protocol, such as the International Standards Organization (ISO) 8473 connectionless network protocol (CLNP), could operate with TCP with certain adjustments to the interface between the modules.

The application protocols, such as the file transfer protocol (FTP) and the simple mail transfer protocol (SMTP), rely on the services of TCP. Many of the TCP functions (such as flow control, reliability, and sequencing) could be handled within an application program. It makes little sense, however, to code these functions into each application. Moreover, applications programmers are usually not versed in error-detection and flow-control operations. The preferred approach is to develop generalized software that provides community functions applicable to a wide range of applications and then invoke these programs from the application software. This approach allows the application programmer to concentrate on solving the application problem and thus isolates the programmer from the nuances and problems of network control.

Major Features of TCP

TCP provides the following services to the upper layers.

- connection-oriented data management
- reliable data transfer
- stream-oriented data transfer
- push functions
- resequencing
- flow control (sliding windows)
- multiplexing
- full-duplex transmission
- precedence and security
- graceful close

TCP is a *connection-oriented protocol*. This term refers to the fact that TCP maintains status and state information about each user data stream flowing into and out of the TCP module. TCP also is responsible for the end-to-end transfer of data across one network or multiple networks to a receiving user application (or the next upper layer protocol). Referring to

Figure 7.1, TCP ensures that the data are transmitted and received between the two hosts across three networks (subnet 1, subnet 2, and subnet 3) by using sequence numbers and positive acknowledgments.

A sequence number is assigned to each byte transmitted. The receiving TCP module uses a checksum routine to check the data for damage that might have occurred during transmission. If the data are acceptable, TCP returns a positive acknowledgment (ACK) to the sending TCP module. If the data are damaged, the receiving TCP discards the data and uses a sequence number to inform the sending TCP about the problem. TCP timers ensure that the lapse of time is not excessive before remedial measures are taken for transmitting acknowledgments from the receiving site or retransmitting data at the transmission site.

TCP receives the data from an upper layer protocol (ULP) in a *stream-oriented* fashion. This operation is in contrast to many protocols in the industry. Stream-oriented protocols are designed to send individual characters, *not* blocks, frames, or datagrams. The bytes are sent from a ULP on a stream basis, byte-by-byte. When they arrive at the TCP layer, the bytes are grouped into TCP *segments*. These segments are then passed to the IP (or another lower-layer protocol) for transmission to the next destination. Segment length is determined by TCP, although a system implementor can determine how TCP makes this decision.

Implementors of TCP who have worked with block-oriented systems, such as IBM's operating systems, might need to adjust their thinking regarding TCP performance. TCP allows the use of variable-length segments because of its stream-oriented nature. Thus, applications that normally work with fixed blocks of data (such as a personnel application that sends fixed employee blocks or a payroll application that transmits fixed payroll blocks) cannot rely on TCP to present this fixed block at the receiver. Action must be taken at the application level to delineate the blocks within the TCP streams.

TCP also checks for duplicate data. If the sending TCP retransmits the data, the receiving TCP discards any duplicate data. Duplicate data could be introduced into an internet when the receiving TCP entity does not acknowledge traffic in a timely manner, which results in the sending TCP entity retransmiting the data.

In consonance with the stream-transfer capability, TCP also supports the concept of a *push* function. This operation is used when an application wants to ensure that all the data passed to the lower-layer TCP has been transmitted. In so doing, this function governs TCP's buffer management. To use the push, the ULP issues a send command to TCP with the push parameter flag set to 1. The operation requires TCP to forward all buffered traffic in one or more segments to the destination. As we shall see later, the TCP user can use a close-connection operation to provide the push function as well.

In addition to using the sequence numbers for acknowledgment, TCP uses them to *resequence* the segments if they arrive at the final destination out of order. Because TCP rests upon a connectionless system that might employ dynamic, multiple routes in an internet, it is possible that duplicate datagrams could be created in the internet. As stated earlier, TCP also eliminates duplicate segments contained in the duplicate datagrams.

TCP uses an inclusive acknowledgment scheme that acknowledges all bytes up to and including the acknowledgment number minus one. This approach provides an easy and efficient method of acknowledging traffic. For example, suppose that 10 segments have been transmitted, yet, due to routing operations, these segments arrive out of order. TCP is only obligated to acknowledge the highest contiguous number received without error. It is not allowed to acknowledge the highest arrived byte number until all intermediate bytes have arrived. Therefore, the transmitting TCP entity eventually times-out and retransmits the traffic not yet acknowledged.

The receiver's TCP module can also *flow control* the sender's data, which is very useful in preventing buffer overrun and possible saturation of the receiving machine. The concept used with TCP is somewhat unusual among communications protocols. It is based on issuing a "window" value to the transmitter. The transmitter can transmit a specified number of bytes within this window, after which the window is closed and the transmitter must stop sending data.

TCP also has a facility for *multiplexing* multiple user sessions within a single host computer onto the ULPs. As we shall see, multiplexing is accomplished using simple naming conventions for ports and sockets in the TCP and IP modules. TCP provides *full-duplex transmission* between two TCP entities, permitting simultaneous two-way transmission without waiting for a turnaround signal (required in a half-duplex situation).

TCP also provides the user with the capability to specify levels of *security* and *precedence* (priority level) for the connection. These two features are not implemented on all TCP products, but they are defined in the TCP DOD standard. TCP also provides a *graceful close* to the connection between the two users. A graceful close ensures that all traffic has been acknowledged before the connection is removed.

Another Look at Ports and Sockets

You might recall that a TCP upper-layer user in a host machine is identified by a *port* number (see Chapter 3, Figure 3.5). The port value is concatenated with the IP internet address to form a *socket*. This value must be unique throughout the internet. A pair of sockets uniquely identifies each end-point connection. For example,

Sending socket = source IP address + source port number
Receiving socket = destination IP address + destination port number

TABLE 7.1 Common Internet Port Numbers (Not Exhaustive)

Number	Name	Description
5	RJE	Remote job entry
7	ECHO	Echo
11	USERS	Active users
13	DAYTIME	Daytime
20	FTP-DATA	File transfer (data)
21	FTP	File transfer (control)
23	TELNET	TELNET
25	SMTP	Simple mail transfer
37	TIME	Time
42	NAMESERV	Host name server
43	NICKNAME	Who is
53	DOMAIN	Domain name server
67	BOOTPS	Bootstrap protocol server
68	BOOTPC	Bootstrap protocol client
69	TFTP	Trivial file transfer
79	FINGER	Finger
101	HOSTNAME	NIC host name server
102	ISO-TSAP	ISO TSAP
103	X400	X.400
104	X400SND	X.400 SND
105	CSNET-NS	CSNET mailbox name server
109	POP2	Post office protocol 2
111	RPC	SUN RPC portmap
137	NETBIOS-NS	NETBIOS name service
138	NETBIOS-DG	NETBIOS datagram service
139	NETBIOS-SS	NETBIOS session service

Although mapping ports to higher-layer processes can be handled as an internal matter in a host, the Internet publishes numbers for frequently used higher-level processes. Table 7.1 lists the commonly used port numbers, along with their names and descriptions.

Although TCP establishes specific numbers for frequently used ports, the numbers and values above 255 are available for private use. These values above 255 have the low-order 8-bits set to zero and are available to any organization to use as it chooses. The numbers 0 through 255 are always reserved, however, and should be avoided.

Examples of port assignments and port bindings

Figure 7.2 shows how port numbers are assigned and managed between two host computers. In event **1**, host A sends a TCP segment to host C. This segment is a request for a TCP connection to communicate with a higher-level process. In this instance, it is the well-known port 25, which is the assigned number for the SMTP. The destination port value is fixed at 25. The source port identifier, however, is a local matter. A host computer can choose any number convenient to its internal operations. In this ex-

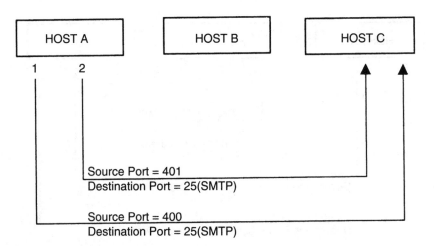

Figure 7.2 Establishing Sessions with a Destination Port.

ample, a source of 400 is chosen for the first connection. The second connection, noted by the numeral **2,** is also destined for host C to use SMTP. Consequently, the destination port of 25 remains the same. The source port identifier is different; in this instance, it is set to 401. The use of two different numbers for FTP access prevents any confusion between the two sessions in hosts A and C.

Figure 7.3 shows how the two segments establish the connections in Figure 7.2. Hosts A and C typically store the information about the TCP connections in *port tables*. Notice the inverse relationship of these tables in relation to the source destination. In the host A port table, the sources are 400 and 401, and the destination is 25 for both connections. Conversely, in

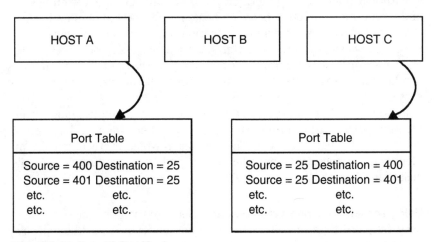

Figure 7.3 Binding with Port Numbers.

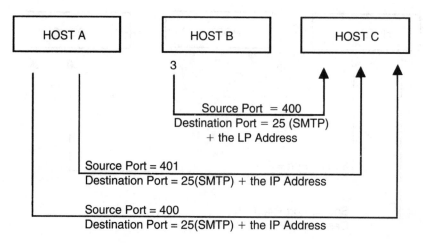

Figure 7.4 Distinguishing between Port Identifiers.

the host C port table both sources are 25 and the destinations are 400 and 401. Thus, the TCP modules reverse the source and destination port numbers to communicate back and forth.

Murphy's Law is alive and well, even with TCP. It is possible for another host to send a connection request to host C with the source port and destination port equal to the same values. It certainly would not be unusual for the destination port to be the same value because well-known ports are frequently accessed. In this case, a destination port of 25 would identify the SMTP. Because source port identifiers are a local matter, you can see in Figure 7.4 that host B has chosen its source port to be 400.

Without an additional identifier, the first connection between hosts A and C and the connection between hosts B and C are in conflict because they use the same source and destination port numbers. In these cases, host C can easily discern the difference by using the IP addresses in the IP header of these datagrams. In this manner, the source port numbers can be duplicates while the internet address distinguishes between the sessions.

In addition to IP addresses and port numbers, many systems further identify a socket using a *protocol family* value. For example, IP is a protocol family; DECnet is another. The manner in which protocol families are identified is dependent upon the vendor and the operating system, discussed in Chapter 13.

Using sockets to support multiplexing. Because the port numbers can be used by more than one end-point connection, users can simultaneously share a port resource. That is, multiple users can simultaneously be multiplexed across one port. In Figure 7.4, three users are sharing port 25 (UDP also supports port multiplexing, as explained later).

Passive and Active Opens

Two forms of establishing a connection are permitted with TCP ports: passive-open and active-open. The *passive-open* mode allows the ULP (for example, a server) to tell the TCP and the host operating system to wait for the arrival of connection requests from the remote system (for example, a client process) rather than issue an *active-open*. Upon receiving this request, the host operating system assigns an identifier to this end. This feature could be used to accommodate communications from remote users without encountering the delay of an active-open.

The applications process requesting the passive-open can accept a connection request from any user (given a profile that matches requirements). If any call can be accepted (without profile matching), the foreign socket number is set to all zeros. Unspecified foreign sockets are allowed only on passive-opens.

The second form of connection establishment, the active-open, is used when the ULP designates a specific socket through which a connection is to be established. Typically, the active-open is issued to a passive-open port to establish a connection.

TCP supports a scenario in which two active-opens are issued at the same time to each other. TCP then makes the connection. This feature allows applications to issue an open at any time without concern that another application has also issued an open.

TCP provides conventions on how the active- and passive-opens can be used together. First, an active open identifies a specific socket and, as options, its precedence and security levels. TCP grants an open if the remote socket has a matching passive open or if it has issued a matching active-open. Certain implementations of TCP define two types of passive-opens:

Fully specified passive open: The destination address in the active- and passive-open are the same. Therefore, the local passive-open operation has fully specified the foreign socket. The security parameter in the active-open is within the range of the security parameter in the passive-open.

Unspecified passive-open: Addresses need not match, but the security parameters should be within an acceptable range. Alternatively, no security parameters are checked at all.

An example of a TCP process that requires little or no authentication during an open is anonymous FTP. This service is offered by a number of organizations through the Internet. It requires the user to identify itself to the FTP server with a password such as "guest," which, of course, is no password at all.

The Transmission Control Block

Because TCP must remember several things about each connection, it stores information in a *transmission control block (TCB)*. Among the entries stored in the TCB are the following:

- local and remote socket numbers
- pointers to the send and receive buffers
- pointers to the retransmit queue
- security and precedence values for the connection
- current segment

The TCB also contains several variables associated with the send and receive sequence numbers. These variables are described in Table 7.2, and the next section examines how they are used.

TCP Window and Flow-Control Mechanisms

Using the entries in Table 7.2, we examine in this section how TCP/IP provides flow-control mechanisms between two connection end points. To begin this analysis, examine Figure 7.5. The boxes labeled A and B depict two TCP modules. Module A is transmitting two units of data, or two bytes, to module B (although it is unusual to send just two octets, this example keeps matters simple). These segments are labeled SEQ = 1 and SEQ = 2. The effect of this transfer can be seen by examining the send variables in the box at the bottom part of the picture. The SND UNA vari-

TABLE 7.2 Send and Receive Variables

Variable name	Purpose
	Send sequence variables
SND.UNA	Send unacknowledged
SND.NXT	Send next
SND.WND	Send window
SND.UP	Sequence number of last octet of urgent data
SND.WL1	Sequence number used for last window update
SND.WL2	ACK number used for last window update
SND.PUSH	Sequence number of last octet of pushed data
ISS	Initial send sequence number
	Receive sequence variables
RCV.NXT	Sequence number of next octet to be received
RCV.WND	Number of octets that can be received
RCV.UP	Sequence number of last octet of received urgent data
RCV.IRS	Initial receive sequence number

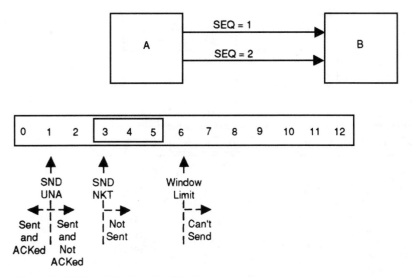

Figure 7.5 TCP Send Window Variables.

able identifies the bytes not yet acknowledged (byte 2). Also, as indicated by the arrows below this variable name, the values less than this range have been sent and acknowledged (byte 0). Numbers greater (bytes 1 and 2) have been sent but not acknowledged. The SND NXT identifies the sequence number of the next octet of data to be sent (byte 3). The window limit indicator is the largest number that can be sent before the window is closed. The send window value is derived from the value in the TCP window segment field. At the box at the bottom of Figure 7.5, the window limit is computed as SND UNA + SND WND. This value is 5 because SND UNA = 2 and SND WND = 3.

Because A has transmitted units 1 and 2, its remaining send window is 3 units. That is, A can transmit units 3, 4, and 5, but not unit 6. This window is indicated in the figure by the boxed area.

TCP is somewhat unusual compared to other protocols in that it does not use just the acknowledgment number for window control. As just stated, it has a separate number carried in the TCP segment that increases or decreases the sending computer's send window. This concept is illustrated in Figure 7.6, where B returns a segment to A. The segment contains, among other fields, an acknowledgment field of 3 and a send window field of 6. The acknowledgment field simply acknowledges previous traffic. Used alone, it does not increase, decrease, open, or close A's window. Window management is the job of the send-window field. Its value of 6 states that A is allowed to send octets based on this value of 6 plus the acknowledgment value. Hereafter, the window limit = ACK + SND WND. As depicted in the

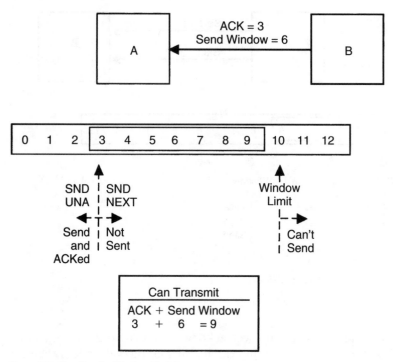

Figure 7.6   Results of a Window Update.

bottom part of this figure, the window is 9 (3 + 6). The window is thus expanded as indicated by the boxed area in the figure.

The size of the window could have been reduced by computer B. The send window field permits the window to be expanded or contracted as necessary to manage buffer space and processing. This approach is more flexible than using the acknowledgment field for both traffic-acknowledgment and window-control operations. (Be aware that window shrinkage can seriously affect traffic flow. At best, it complicates matters.)

TCP is allowed to send an urgent data segment even if its transmit window is closed. This segment contains a bit (the urgent bit) set to 1 if urgent data need to be transmitted. This bit is explained in more detail shortly.

Retransmission Operations

TCP has a unique way of accounting for traffic on each connection. Unlike many other protocols, it does not have an explicit *negative acknowledgment (NAK)*. Rather, it relies on the transmitting entity to issue a timeout and retransmit data for which it has not received a *positive acknowledgment (ACK)*. This concept is illustrated in Figure 7.7, which shows eight operations labeled with bold numbers (1 through 8). Each of these operations is described in order. For the purposes of simplicity, the window values and pointers described in Figures 7.5 and 7.6 are not included in Figure 7.7.

Event 1: TCP machine A sends a segment of 300 bytes to TCP machine B. This example assumes a window of 900 octets (bytes) and a segment size of 300 octets. The sequence (SEQ) number contains the value of 3.

Event 2: TCP B checks the traffic for errors and sends back an acknowledgment with a value of 303. Remember, this value is an inclusive acknowledgment that acknowledges all traffic up to and including 302, or SEQ

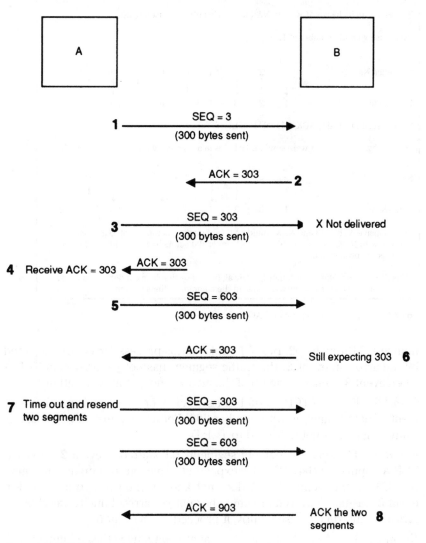

Figure 7.7 TCP Retransmission Schemes.

I once sat in a meeting with two of my clients (who were writing code for a proprietary transport layer). We were discussing sliding windows, rejects, selective rejects, and inclusive ACKs for a 512-byte PDU. These two individuals got into a rather heated debate on whether the inclusive ACK number should be 512 or 513. I told them the answer depended on whether the number 0 was used as part of the *initial sequence (ISS)* number. Consider the following (for a 10-byte PDU, for simplicity). First, using an ISS of 0,

	ISS									
Sequence No.	0	1	2	3	4	5	6	7	8	9
	↓	↓	↓	↓	↓	↓	↓	↓	↓	↓
Bytes Sent	1	2	3	4	5	6	7	8	9	10

Therefore, an inclusive ACK = 10, NAK = 0. (This protocol used NAKs.)

Next, using an ISS number of 1,

	ISS									
Sequence No.	1	2	3	4	5	6	7	8	9	10
	↓	↓	↓	↓	↓	↓	↓	↓	↓	↓
Bytes Sent	1	2	3	4	5	6	7	8	9	10

Therefore, an inclusive ACK = 11, NAK = 1.

So, for Fig. 7.7, if TCP A were sending 10 bytes in a segment with an ISS number of 3,

	ISS									
Sequence No.	3	4	5	6	7	8	9	10	11	12
	↓	↓	↓	↓	↓	↓	↓	↓	↓	↓
Bytes Sent	1	2	3	4	5	6	7	8	9	10

The inclusive ACK = 13 and NAK would be 3 (although remember that TCP does not know how to NAK.) Because this example sends 300 octets in a segment, the ACK value of 303 is the proper value.

This discussion might seem somewhat trivial, but these simple misunderstandings can cause problems and result software bugs in the communications system.

Box 7.1 Sequence Numbering and ACKs.

numbers 3 through 302. Box 7.1 explains this process further. As depicted by the arrow in event **2**, the traffic segment has not yet arrived at TCP A when event **3** occurs. (The tip of the arrow is not yet at A's location.)

Event 3: Because TCP A still has its window open, it sends another segment of data beginning with number 303. For any number of reasons, this traffic segment is not delivered to TCP B.

Event 4: The acknowledgment segment transmitted in event **2** arrives at TCP A stipulating that TCP B is expecting a segment beginning with number 303. At this point, TCP A does not know if the traffic transmitted in event **3** was not delivered or simply has not yet arrived due to variable delays in an internet. Consequently, it proceeds with event **5**.

Event 5: TCP A sends the next segment beginning with the number 603. It arrives error-free at TCP B.

Event 6:   TCP B successfully receives the segment number 603, which was transmitted in event **5**. TCP B then sends back a segment with ACK 303 because it is still expecting segment number 303.

Event 7:   Eventually, TCP A times out and resends the segments for which it has not yet received an acknowledgment. In this example, it must resend the segments beginning with numbers 303 and 603.

The idea depicted in event **7** has its advantages and disadvantages. It makes the protocol quite simple, because TCP simply goes back to the last unacknowledged segment number and retransmits all succeeding segments. On the other hand, it likely retransmits segments not in error, such as the segment beginning with number 603, which had arrived error-free at TCP B. Nonetheless, TCP operates in this fashion for the sake of simplicity even at the risk of degraded throughput.

Event 8:   All traffic is accounted for after TCP B receives and error checks segments 303 and 603 and returns an ACK value equal to 903.

Estimating Timers for Timeouts and Retransmissions

This section describes the approach taken by TCP to estimate a value for the timeout and retransmission. The discussion begins with earlier approaches and concludes with recent changes to the TCP retransmission algorithm.

Choosing a value for the retransmission timer is deceptively complex. The reason for this complexity stems from the following facts:

- the delay of receiving acknowledgments from the receiving host varies in an internet

- segments sent from the transmitter can be lost in the internet, which obviously invalidates any round-trip delay estimate for a spurious acknowledgment

- acknowledgments from the receiver can also be lost, which further invalidates the round-trip delay estimate.

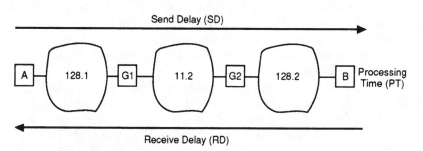

Figure 7.8 Round Trip Time (RTT).

Because of these problems, TCP does not use a fixed retransmission timer. Rather, it utilizes an adaptive retransmission timer derived from an analysis of the delay encountered in receiving acknowledgments from remote hosts.

Returning to Figure 7.8, the round-trip time (RTT) is derived from adding the send delay (SD), the processing time (PT) at the remote host, and the receive delay (RD). If delay were not variable, this simple calculation would suffice for determining a retransmission timer. Because delay in the Internet is often highly variable, however, other factors must be considered.

The approach taken with earlier versions of TCP was to analyze each round-trip sample and develop an average RTT for the delay. This simple formula for RTT is a weighted value based on the following:

$$SRTT = (\alpha \times OSRTT) + ([1 - \alpha] \times NRTT)$$

where
  SRTT = smoothed round-trip time
  α = smoothing factor (ranging near 1 for accommodating the changes that last for a short period)
  OSRTT = old smoothed RTT (near 0 to respond to delays quickly)
  NRTT = the new RTT sample

The next step in computing the timer is to apply a weighting factor to RTT as follows:

$$VT = \beta \times SRTT$$

where
  VT = value for timeout
  β = a constant weighting factor that must be greater than RTT

Some implementations varied this formula, as follows:

$$VT = min\ (Ubound,\ max\ [Lbound,\ \{\beta \times SRTT\}])$$

where
  Ubound = an upper bound on the timeout
  Lbound = the lower bound on the timeout

This method of calculating the variable for the timeout did not work well because of the variable delay and loss of acknowledgments in an internet. Ideally, the timeout timer should be quite close to RTT. Due to the variable nature of RTT, however, the timeout timer expired too quickly in many instances and resulted in unnecessary segments being reintroduced into the internet. On the other hand, using a small value for the timeout allows segment loss to be handled more quickly.

One solution to the problem was provided by Phil Karn and is known as Karn's algorithm. The approach is twofold: TCP does not modify its estimate for any retransmitted segments and the timeout is increased each time the timer expires and initiates a retransmission. You might recognize that this approach is quite similar to the Ethernet back-off algorithm, except that Ethernet uses an exponential back-off because of increased traffic collisions on the network.

The Karn formula is

$$NVT = MF \times VT$$

where

NVT = new value for timeout

MF = a multiplication factor (usually a value of 2 or a table of values)

The approach is to recalculate the RTT on a segment that was not retransmitted. It works well enough except in an internet with large RTT variations.

RFC 1122 concedes that the original TCP approach to timeout and retransmission is inadequate. With new systems, the *Van Jacobsen's* slow-start approach is used: Upon a timeout, TCP shuts its window to one. Upon receiving an ACK, it opens its window to half the size the window was before the timeout occurred.

The newest TCP implementations take advantage of Poisson distribution and network utilization factors regarding RTT. This approach uses additional computations that take into account varying delay as a function of network utilization.

These learning timers, while very valuable, can have a negative effect on an application's performance and throughput. In essence, the operation makes TCP "courteous," because it backs off when network congestion is high. So, "non-courteous" protocols (such as UDP) have no back-off operation and can continue to transmit. Under high-traffic conditions, the courteous protocols are not sending much traffic but the non-courteous protocols are.

TCP and User Interfaces

TCP works with the service definition/primitive concept to interface with an upper-layer user. The interface is achieved with the commands and messages summarized in Table 7.3. Be aware that primitives are abstract and their actual implementation is dependent on a host's operating system. Furthermore, RFC 793 defines those interfaces generally; vendor implementations vary. (Chapter 13 provides more information on this topic.) Figure 7.9 shows the relationship of the ULP, TCP, and IP.

TABLE 7.3 Typical TCP User Interfaces

Command	Parameters
Service request primitives (ULP to TCP)	
UNSPECIFIED-PASSIVE	Local port, ULP timeout (1),* timeout action (1), precedence (1)
OPEN	Security (1), options (1) → local connection name
FULL-PASSIVE-OPEN	Local port, destination socket, ULP timeout (1), timeout action (1), precedence (1), security (1), options (1)

TABLE 7.3 Typical TCP User Interfaces (Continued)

Command	Parameters
ACTIVE-OPEN	Local port, foreign socket, ULP timeout (1), ULP timeout action (1), precedence (1), security (1), options (1)
ACTIVE-OPEN WITH DATA	Source ports, destination address, ULP timeout (1), ULP timeout action (1), precedence (1), security (1), data, data length, push flag, urgent flag (1)
SEND	Local connection name, buffer address, byte count, push flag, urgent flat, ULP timeout (1), ULP timeout action (1)
RECEIVE	Local connection name, buffer address, byte count, urgent flag, push flag
ALLOCATE	Local connection name, data length
CLOSE	Local connection name
ABORT	Local connection name
STATUS	Local connection name
	Service response primitives (TCP to ULP)
OPEN-ID	Local connection name, foreign socket, destination address
OPEN-FAILURE	Local connection name
OPEN-SUCCESS	Local connection name
DELIVER	Local connection name, buffer address, byte count, urgent flag
CLOSING	Local connection name
TERMINATE	Local connection name, description
STATUS RESPONSE	Local connection name, source port and address, foreign port, connection state, receive and send window, amount-waiting-ACK and -receipt, urgent mode, timeout, timeout action
ERROR	Local connection name, error description

* A notation of (1) means parameters are optional.

The service definitions between TCP and its lower layer are not specified in the TCP standard. It is assumed in the TCP operations that TCP and the lower layer can pass information to each other asynchronously. TCP expects the lower layer to specify this interface. (The OSI Model follows the same practice.) This lower-layer interface is defined in the IP specification (see Chapter 6) if IP rests below TCP.

Segments

The PDUs exchanged between two TCP modules are called *segments*. Figure 7.10 illustrates the format for a segment. We examine each of the fields in this section.

The segment is divided into two parts, the header and the data. As depicted in Figure 7.10, the data follows the header. The first two fields of the segment are the *source port* and *destination port*. These 16-bit fields are used to identify the upper-layer application programs using the TCP connection.

The next field is labeled *sequence number*. This field contains the sequence number of the first octet in the user data field. Its value specifies the position of the transmitting module's byte stream. Within the segment, the first user data octet in the segment is specified.

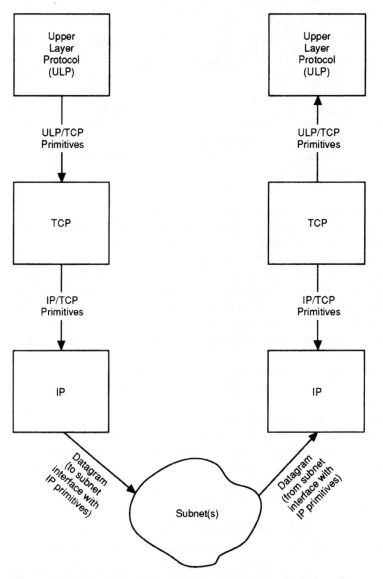

Figure 7.9 Relationships of Upper Layer, Transmission Control, and Internet Protocols.

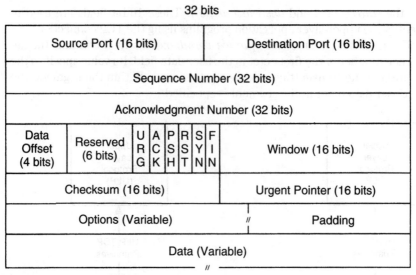

Figure 7.10 TCP Segment (PDU).

The sequence number is also used during a connection management operation. If a connection-request segment is used between two TCP entities, the sequence number specifies the *initial send sequence (ISS)* number to be used for subsequent numbering of user data.

The *acknowledgment number* is set to a value that acknowledges data previously received. The value in this field contains the value of the sequence number of the next expected byte from the transmitter. Because this number is set to the next expected octet, it provides an inclusive acknowledgment capability in that it acknowledges all octets up to and including this number minus 1.

The *data offset* field specifies the number of 32-bit aligned words that constitute the TCP header. This field is used to determine where the data field begins.

As you might expect, the *reserved* field is reserved. It consists of 6 bits that must be set to zero. These bits are reserved for future use.

The next six fields are called *flags*. They are used as control bits by TCP, and they specify certain services and operations to be used during the session. Some of the bits determine how to interpret other fields in the header. The six bits convey the following information:

URG: This flag signifies if the urgent pointer field is significant.

ACK: This flag signifies if the acknowledgment field is significant.

PSH: This flag signifies that the module is to exercise the push function.

RST: This flag indicates that the connection is to be reset.

SYN: This flag indicates that the sequence numbers are to be synchronized; it is used as a flag with the connection-establishment segments to indicate that handshaking operations are to take place.

FIN: This flag indicates that the sender has no more data to send; it is comparable to the end-of-transmission (EOT) signal in other protocols.

The next field is labeled *window*. Its value indicates how many octets the receiver is willing to accept. The value is established based on the value in the acknowledgment field (acknowledgment number). The value in the window field is added to the value of the acknowledgment number field.

The *checksum* field performs a 16-bit one's complement of the one's complement sum of all the 16-bit words in the segment, including the header and text. The purpose of the checksum calculation is to determine if the segment has arrived error-free from the transmitter. It uses a similar pseudo-header as UDP, which is explained in the UDP section.

The next field in the segment is labeled the *urgent pointer*. This field is only used if the URG flag is set. The purpose of the urgent pointer is to signify the data byte in which urgent data is located. Urgent data is also called *out-of-band* data. TCP does not dictate what happens for urgent data; it is implementation-specific. TCP only signifies where the urgent data are located. The urgent data, at least, are the first byte in the stream; the pointer also indicates where the urgent data end. The receiver must immediately inform the application using TCP that urgent data have arrived. Urgent data could be control signals such as interrupts, checkpoints, terminal control characters, etc.

The *options* field was conceived to provide for future enhancements to TCP. It is constructed in a manner similar to that of the IP datagrams option field, in that each option specification consists of a single byte containing an option number, a field containing the length of the option, and the option values themselves. The option field is quite limited in its use. Currently, only three options are defined for the TCP standard:

0: end-of-option list

1: no operation

2: maximum segment size

Finally, the *padding* field is used to ensure that the TCP header is filled to an even multiple of 32 bits. After that, as the figure illustrates, user *data* follows.

Effect of segment size (length) on performance. Because TCP is designed to support variable-length segments, the options field can be used by the receiver to inform the transmitter of the maximum buffer size that can be accommodated. In this manner, a limit is placed on the size (length) of the segment to be transmitted to the receiver. Otherwise, segments can vary in length up to the maximum length. If this is the case, the length of the segments could affect the length of the frames on the network because the segments are encapsulated into the frames.

Frame length is an important aspect of network performance, and it can affect bridges and gateways. To illustrate these points, imagine that two variable-length frames are sent across an Ethernet network. One set of frames each contains 1500 bytes; another set of frames each contains 64 bytes. Large frames provide better throughput on a local area network (LAN) because the number of user bytes per overhead segment and Ethernet frame header is a greater ratio than the smaller 64-byte frame. Moreover, a point that is often overlooked is the *interframe gap*, which is the time between frames when no transmission occurs. TCP cannot directly affect the interframe gap; it is determined by lower-layer protocols. However, the effect of using a larger frame gives a bridge or gateway more time to examine and make decisions on the frame than if a smaller frame is arriving with the same interframe gap as the large frame. Indeed, how TCP segments data and the speed at which these segments are sent to a lower layer should be examined carefully because the ability of a bridge to forward traffic and filter irrelevant traffic is a function of both frame length and interframe gap.

This is not to say that TCP is solely responsible for these operations. As mentioned before, some of these activities are determined by the lower LAN layers. Nonetheless, the situation warrants examination to tune the upper layers to the LAN protocol layers. Some internet access services notify the user of the maximum segment size permitted as part of the logon process to an internet.

The TCP Connection Management Operations

TCP is a state-driven protocol. As such, its operations must conform to many rules on how and when specific segments are exchanged between the TCP entities. These rules are described in a state transition diagram. A general depiction of the TCP connection management operations is illustrated in Figure 7.11. We use this figure to explain several features of TCP.

Examples of TCP operations

The TCP operations of open, data transfer, and close are explained in the following sections. Before explaining these TCP operations, we first need to pause briefly and define the terms *type* and *instance* in a communications protocol.

A type describes an object. In this example, TCP is an object. An instance describes the manifestation of an object. Therefore, each time TCP is invoked, it manifests itself. Because many user processes can use TCP simultaneously, each user session invokes the TCP logic, and each invocation is an instance of type TCP. In more pragmatic terms, each user invocation of

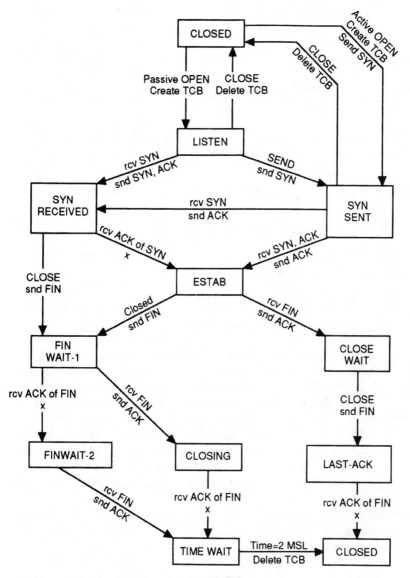

Figure 7.11 TCP Connection Management State Diagram.

TCP represents executing some of TCP's services to support a session. Each instance of TCP requires that TCP maintain information about the event. These pieces of information are kept in the TCB about *each* user session.

TCP open. Figure 7.12 illustrates the major operations between two TCP entities establishing a connection. TCP A's user has sent an active-open primitive to TCP. The remote user has sent a passive-open to its TCP

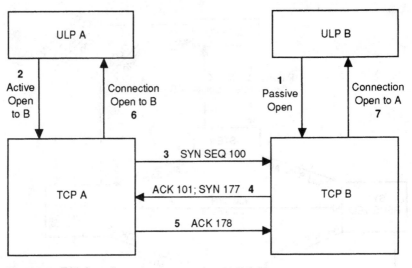

Figure 7.12   TCP Open Operations

provider. These operations are listed as events **2** and **1**, respectively, although either event could have occurred first.

Invoking an active-open requires TCP A to prepare a segment with the SYN bit set to 1. The segment is sent to TCP B and is depicted in the figure as **3** and coded as SYN SEQ 100. In this example, sequence (SEQ) 100 is used as the ISS number, although any number could be chosen within the rules discussed earlier (the most common approach is to set the value to 0). The SYN coding simply means the SYN bit is set to 1.

Upon receiving the SYN segment, TCP B returns an acknowledgment with sequence number of 101. It also sends its ISS number 177. This event is labeled as **4**. Upon receipt of this segment, TCP A acknowledges with a segment containing the acknowledgment number 178, depicted as event **5** in the figure.

Once these handshaking operations have occurred with events 3, 4, and 5 (which is called a *three-way handshake*), the two TCP modules send opens to their respective users, as in events **6** and **7**.

We can now use Figure 7.13 to illustrate the relationship of the operations of Figure 7.12 to the state diagram rules of Figure 7.11. The information in Figure 7.11 is condensed and redrawn as Figure 7.13, which shows the relationship of the open operations with the segment exchanges and state transactions. The top of the figure is derived from Figure 7.12 but contains only the segment flow between the two TCP entities and not the operations between the upper and TCP layers in each machine.

The bottom part of Figure 7.13 shows the relevant portion of the state diagram for the open. The labels are shown in bold print as **A**, **B**, **A-3**, **A-4**, **B-3**. These indicators can be matched to the bold event numbers at the top of the figure to show how both TCP modules use the segments and the state diagrams.

For help in following the operations of Figure 7.13, look at the event labeled **3** at the top part of the figure. It shows TCP A issuing SYN SEQ 100. Prior to the transmission of this segment, TCP A is in state = CLOSED for this specific user session. Its state is changed to SYN-SENT after it sends the segment to TCP B.

Next, refer to the bottom diagram. The notation **A** indicates that TCP A is in the CLOSED state in regard to this user session. The state transition labeled **A-3** is matched to the segment issued by TCP A in the top part of the figure, labeled as **3**. When the segment is issued, TCP A enters the SYN-SENT state and creates a TCB entry for the connection, as shown in the state diagram.

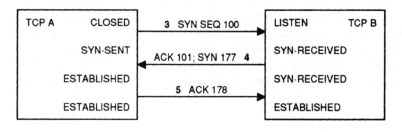

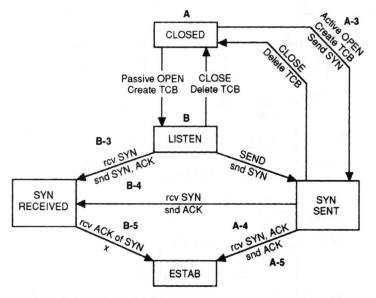

Figure 7.13 Relationship of Open Operations, Segment Exchanges, and State Transitions.

Next, we examine TCP B. As the top part of the figure shows, it is in the LISTEN state. The state diagram LISTEN state is labeled as **B**. The top part of the figure shows that upon receiving the SYN SEQ 100 segment, TCP B moves to the SYN-RECEIVED state. These events are shown in the state diagram with the label **B-3**, which also shows that TCP B sent back the SYN and ACK in event 4 at the top of the figure and **B-4** at the bottom of the figure. Figure 7.13 can be further analyzed by continuing to match the numbers and events between the top and bottom part of the figure.

A newcomer to TCP often asks if TCP modules can initiate an open to a closed TCP socket. That is, must there be a passive-open before a connection can occur? TCP does indeed permit opens to closed sockets. Figure 7.14 shows this activity, as well as how TCP handles opens that might be issued simultaneously from the two TCP modules. To answer the question about issuing an open to a closed TCP socket, the major requirement is that the open call must contain a local socket identifier as well as the foreign socket identifier. The open call can also contain precedence, security, and user timeout information. If this information is available, the TCP module issues the SYN segment. In Figure 7.14, opens are sent from A and B at approximately the same time. The events in this figure occur as follows:

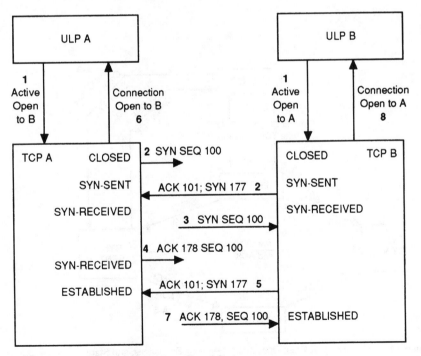

Figure 7.14 Simultaneous Opens from Closed States.

Event 1:   After receiving these opens, the TCP modules create new transmission control blocks to hold the connection information.

Event 2:   The SYN segments are sent from TCP A and B at approximately the same time. The position of the arrows are used in this figure to indicate the relative time sequence of the traffic. Consequently, the SYN segment from TCP A has not yet arrived at TCP B when TCP B's segment arrives at TCP A.

Event 3:   The SYN segment from TCP A finally arrives at TCP B. The results of the SYN segments in event **2** move the two TCP modules from CLOSED to SYN-SENT to SYN-RECEIVED.

Events 4 & 5:   Both TCP modules issue an ACK segment, which, as we learned earlier, is to acknowledge the SYN segments. TCP B's segment in event **5** arrives before TCP A's segment in event **4**. This somewhat asynchronous aspect of TCP simply results from the variable delay in an internet. The delay varies in both directions.

Event 6:   Upon receipt of the ACK at TCP A (in event **5**), TCP A sends a connection open signal to its ULP.

Event 7:   The ACK segment from TCP A finally arrives at TCP B.

Event 8:   To complete the connection, TCP B sends a connection open to its ULP.

Notice the effect of the arrival of the ACKs in events **5** and **7** when the ULPs are issued the open primitives in events **6** and **8**.

Receiving a call at a receiving module in which a TCP does not exist results in an error condition if the operating system has not generated some control information indicating that the user does have access to the connection identified in the open call.

TCP data transfer operations.   Figure 7.15 shows the TCP entities after they have successfully achieved a connection. In event **1**, ULP A sends data to TCP A for transmission with a SEND primitive. Assume that 50 bytes are to be sent. TCP A encapsulates this data into a segment and sends the segment to TCP B with sequence number of 101, as depicted in event **2**. Remember that this sequence number identifies the first byte of the user data stream.

At the remote TCP, data is delivered to the user (ULP B) in event **3**, and TCP B acknowledges the data with a segment acknowledgment number of 151, depicted in event **4**. The acknowledgment number of 151 acknowledges inclusively the 50 bytes transmitted in the event **2** segment.

Next, the user connected to TCP B sends data in event **5**. This data is encapsulated into a segment and transmitted as event **6** in the diagram. The initial sequence number from TCP B was 177; therefore, TCP begins its sequencing with 178. In this example, it transmits 10 octets.

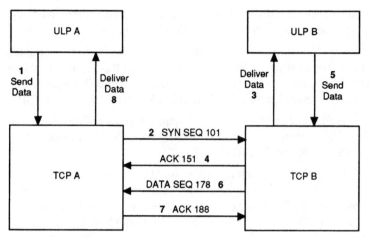

Figure 7.15 TCP Data Transfer Operations.

TCP A acknowledges TCP B's 10 segments in event **7** by returning a segment with acknowledgment number of 188. In event **8**, this data is delivered to TCP A's user.

Data transfer operations pertaining to retransmission and timeouts were discussed in an earlier section (see Figure 7.6).

TCP close operations. Figure 7.16 shows a close operation. Event **1** illustrates that TCP A's user wishes to close its operations with its upper peer layer protocol at TCP B. The effect of this primitive is shown in event **2**, where TCP A sends a segment with the FIN bit set to 1. The sequence number of 151 is a continuation of the operation of Figure 7.15 and is the next sequence number the TCP module is required to send.

The effect of this segment is shown as event **3** from TCP B. TCP B acknowledges TCP A's FIN SEQ 151. Its segment has SEQ = 188 and ACK = 152. Next, it issues a closing primitive to its user, which is depicted as event **4**.

In this example, the user application acknowledges and grants the close as event **5**. The application might or might not choose to close, depending on the state of its operations. For simplicity, assume the event depicted in **5** does occur. This primitive is mapped to event **6**, which is the final segment issued by TCP B. Notice that in event **6**, the FIN flag is set to 1, SEQ = 188, and ACK = 152. TCP A acknowledges this final segment with event **7** as ACK = 189. The result of all these operations is shown in events **8** and **9**, where connection-closed signals are sent to the user applications.

To complete this analysis of TCP connection management, Figure 7.17 shows the close operations in relation to the relevant part of the state diagram. Again, the top part of the figure is a scaled-down version of Figure 7.16, in which only the segment transmissions are shown. The effect of

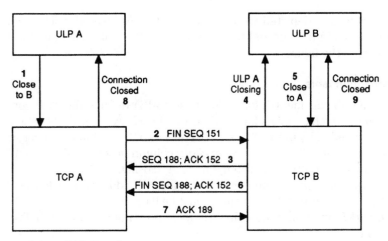

Figure 7.16   TCP Close Operations.

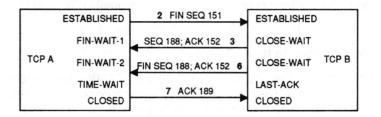

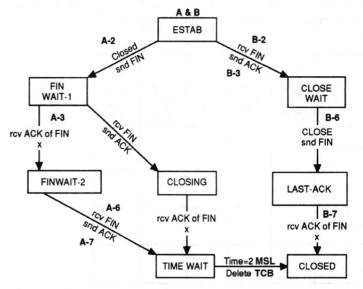

Figure 7.17   Relationship of Close Operations, Segment Exchanges, and State Transitions.

these operations is depicted with the state notations located inside each box and the bold numbers and figures shown on the state diagram in the bottom part of the figure.

TCP connection table

The Internet Management Information Base (MIB) defines the TCP connection table, which contains information about each existing TCP connection. As depicted in Figure 7.18, the table consists of five columns and a row for each connection. The *Connection State* column describes the state of each TCP connection (closed, listen, finWait 1, closing, etc.).

The *Local Address* column contains the local IP address for each TCP connection. In a listen state, this value must be 0.0.0.0.

The *Local Port* column contains the local port number for each TCP connection.

The *Remote Address* column contains the remote IP address for each TCP connection.

The *Remote Port* column contains the remote port number for each TCP connection.

Other Considerations in Using TCP

As explained earlier in this chapter, the TCP stream data are acknowledged by the receiver on a byte basis, not on a PDU. The acknowledgment number, returned by the receiver, refers to the highest byte received in the data stream. The sending TCP software keeps a copy of the data until it has been acknowledged. Once acknowledged, it turns off a retransmission timer and deletes the segment copy from a retransmission queue.

	Connection State	Local Address	Local Port	Remote Address	Remote Port
Connection 1					
Connection 2					
Connection 3					
Connection n					

Figure 7.18 TCP Connection Table.

If necessary, TCP retransmits lost or errored data. The term associated with this technique is *inclusive acknowledgment*. It works well on systems that deliver data in sequential order, but, as you know, the underlying IP might deliver data out of order or discard data. In such an event, TCP has no way to notify the sender that it has received certain segments of a transmission. It can only relay the value of the contiguous, accumulated bytes. Consequently, the sending TCP software can timeout and resend data segments that have already been successfully received.

A *push* function is available to force the TCP to send data immediately. This function is used to ensure that traffic is delivered and avoid deadlock at the other end. The stream concept does not deal with structured data streams, and it cannot delineate between records in a file transfer. Therefore, applications must have some means of identifying the logical records before they begin their communications.

We also learned that TCP has a function similar to the OSI TP4 credit scheme. It is called the *window advertisement* field. A value in this field is returned to the sending TCP to inform it of the number of bytes of additional data the receiver is prepared to receive. If the sender receives a larger value in the window advertisement field than in the transmit window, it can change the transmit window accordingly. It is not advisable to shrink the window advertisement past the previously acceptable positions in the data stream unless accompanied by a complementary acknowledgment. That is, the window size can change as it slides forward.

Finally, TCP can provide considerable information to the network manager (for example, if TCP is sending excessive retransmissions, it might provide a clue to problems in the network, such as dead routers or timers that are not functioning properly). The positive acknowledgments also could be used to determine how well the components in an internet are functioning.

User Datagram Protocol

Previous chapters have discussed the concepts of a connectionless protocol. Recall that the connectionless protocol provides no reliability or flow-control mechanisms. It also has no error recovery procedures. The UDP is classified as a connectionless protocol, although the operating system must maintain information about each active UDP socket. Perhaps a better description of UDP is that it is connection-oriented, but does not employ the extensive state management operations normally used in connection-oriented protocols. It is sometimes used in place of TCP in situations where the full services of TCP are not needed. For example, the trivial file transfer protocol (TFTP), the simple network management protocol (SNMP), and the remote procedure call (RPC) use UDP.

UDP serves as a simple application interface to the IP. Because it has no reliability, flow-control, or error-recovery measures, it serves principally as a port multiplexer/demultiplexer for the receiving and sending of IP and applications traffic. Figure 7.19 illustrates how UDP accepts datagrams from IP.

UDP uses the port concept to direct the datagrams to the proper upper layer applications. The UDP datagram contains a destination port number and a source port number. The destination number is used by the UDP module to deliver the traffic to the proper recipient.

Format of the UDP message

Perhaps the best way to explain this protocol is to examine the message and fields that reside in the message. As Figure 7.20 illustrates, the format is quite simple and contains the following fields:

Source port: This value identifies the port of the sending application process. The field is optional, and, if not used, a value of 0 is inserted.

Destination port: This value identifies the receiving process on the destination host machine.

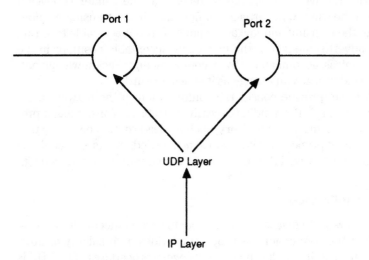

Figure 7.19   UDP Multiplexing.

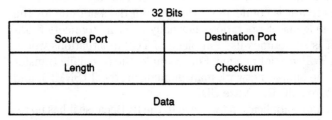

Figure 7.20   Format for UDP Datagram.

Length: This value indicates the length of the user datagram, including the header and data. This value implies that the minimum length is 8 octets.

Checksum: This optional value is the 16-bit one's complement of the one's complement sum of the pseudo-IP header, the UDP header, and the data. It also performs a checksum on any padding (if the message needed to contain a multiple of two octets).

The pseudo-header (also used in TCP) ensures that the UDP data unit has arrived at the proper destination address. Therefore, the pseudo header includes the IP addresses and is included as part of the checksum calculation. The final destination performs a complementary checksum on the pseudo-header (and, of course, the remainder of the UDP data unit) to verify that the traffic is not altered and it reached the correct destination address. There is not a lot more to be said about UDP. It is a minimal level of service used in many transaction-based application systems that is quite useful if the full services of TCP are not needed.

Summary

TCP provides a simple set of services for the ULPs of an internet. TCP has relatively few features, but the features are designed to provide end-to-end reliability, graceful closes, unambiguous connections, handshakes, and several quality-of-service operations. The internet transport layer also provides a connectionless operation called the UDP. UDP is a minimal level of service, principally offering source and destination ports for multiplexing. With UDP, the user application is typically tasked with performing some of the end-to-end reliability operations that would normally be done by TCP.

8

Route Discovery Protocols

Because the TCP/IP protocol suite is based on the concept of internetworking, routers play a very important role in TCP/IP-based networks. Indeed, the IP protocol is designed around the concept of internetworking host computers with gateways and routers. This chapter is devoted to the various types of route discovery protocols used in internet networks. It also examines the types of routers and networks that are administered by public and private authorities. The last part of the chapter discusses several newer techniques used in internetworking and router operations. You should be familiar with routers, bridges, and gateways, described in Chapter 2, prior to reading this chapter. In this discussion, the terms *gateway* and *router* are used interchangeably. More concise definitions are available in Chapters 2 and 3. Remember as you read this chapter that IP is not a route discovery protocol. It uses routing tables filled in by the protocols explained in this chapter.

Terms and Concepts

A computer acting as a switch can join together individual networks. As discussed in Chapter 2, the switch operations are programmed to route the traffic to the proper network by examining a destination address in the PDU and matching the address with entries in a routing table. Those entries indicate the best route to the next network or next gateway (one hopes).

Although these individual networks can be administered by local authorities, it is common practice for a group of networks to be administered as a whole system. From the perspective of an internet, this group of networks is called an *autonomous system,* and is administered by a single *authority.* Examples of autonomous systems are networks located on sites such as college campuses, hospital complexes, and military installations. The networks located at these sites are connected together by a gateway. Because these gateways operate within an autonomous system, they often choose their own mechanisms for routing data.

The routing of data between autonomous systems is, however, usually controlled by a single (global) administrative authority. Thus, the local administrative authorities must agree on how they provide information (advertise) to each other on the reachability of the host computers inside the autonomous systems. The advertising responsibility can be given to one or a number of gateways.

The autonomous systems are identified by autonomous system numbers. How this is accomplished is up to the administrators, but the idea is to use different numbers to distinguish different autonomous systems. Such a numbering scheme is helpful if a network manager does not wish to route traffic through an autonomous system. Even if the network is connected to the manager's network, the network might be administered by a competitor or might not have adequate or proper security services. By using routing protocols and numbers that identify autonomous systems, the gateways can determine how they reach each other and how they exchange routing information.

Route discovery operations are classified as either distance-vector or link state metric protocols. The distance-vector protocol determines a best route to a destination based on the distance (the fewest number of hops) to a vector (a destination end point usually identified by an address). The link state metric protocol uses a value that is assigned to each communications link attached to each router in an internet, or within a subnet or area in an internet. This value can represent delay, line speed, or anything the network administrator wishes. The route is determined by examining these values and deciding which output line from a node represents the best route. In both operations, the best path is the smallest value computed by summing the hop count or total link state values from the source to the destination for all possible routes. For large networks, do not attempt to calculate this best path by hand. Although the formula is simple, it requires too many iterations.

Routing based on fewest hops (distance-vector)

The vast majority of gateway products route traffic based on the idea that it is best to transmit the datagram through the fewest number of networks and gateways (hops). In the past, network designers believed that this approach led to the most efficient route through an internet and, perhaps more to the point, it was easy to implement. The value of the fewest-hops approach could be debated, but we confine ourselves to how the approach works rather than its relative merits. Later in this chapter, the newer routing techniques are explored in considerable detail.

Figure 8.1 shows an example of how a fewest-hops routing directory (table) can be employed. This figure actually shows a topological database, but it serves our purposes for this discussion. The next section explains a condensed version of the topological database, which can be used as the routing directory, or table.

The routing directory contains values that represent the number of intermediate gateways (hops) between the originator of the traffic (for ex-

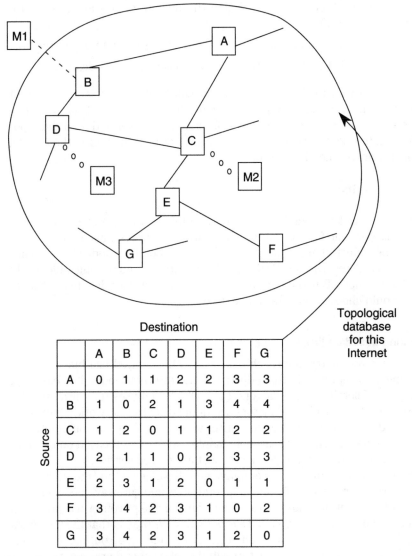

Destination

	A	B	C	D	E	F	G
A	0	1	1	2	2	3	3
B	1	0	2	1	3	4	4
C	1	2	0	1	1	2	2
D	2	1	1	0	2	3	3
E	2	3	1	2	0	1	1
F	3	4	2	3	1	0	2
G	3	4	2	3	1	2	0

Source

Topological database for this Internet

Figure 8.1 Routing Based on Fewest Number of Hops.

ample, the source at node A) and the receiver (for example, the destination at node G). For simplicity, the intervening networks are not shown in this figure. The datagrams are routed to the adjacent gateway closest to the final destination. A datagram at gateway A destined for a network connected to gateway G would be routed to gateway C, because C is closer to the destination than gateway B.

Each gateway typically maintains its own routing directory. In this example, each gateway routes the traffic as follows:

1. Access the directory to determine the neighbor gateways (source-to-destination = 1).

2. Route the datagram to the gateway on the shortest path to the destination.

3. Repeat steps 1 and 2 until the datagram has reached its destination.

This approach works well enough but can be more efficient. Instead of maintaining all the entries in the table as shown in Figure 8.1, a node can create a different table—one that still reflects the information in the topological database, but is shorter and more concise. To illustrate, the routing table for node A need only reflect:

```
Destination? Then next node
```

Other entries are needed in the routing table and are explained later in this chapter, but for this simple illustration, node A's next node choices would be reflected in a routing table as either node B or node C. For example, if node A receives a PDU destined for address N, its routing table would reveal that node B is the next node. If it received a PDU destined for node G, it would choose node C as its next node.

Routing based on link state metrics

The link state metric approach has seen rather limited use but is rapidly gaining in acceptance in the industry. In the Internet model, it is based on the type-of-service (TOS) factors. (The OSI Model uses the term *quality-of-service factors*.) These factors are defined by the network administrators and users and can include criteria such as delay, throughput, and reliability needs. The path through an internet is chosen based on the ability of the gateways and networks to meet a required service.

Some implementations use adaptive and dynamic methods to update the directories to reflect traffic and link conditions and gateway queue lengths. More often, routing changes occur only when a line or router has problems or fails. Such a situation is called a *topological change* in that the network's physical characteristics have changed. With adaptive routing, the datagrams can take different paths through the internet and arrive out of order at the final destination. As we learned in Chapter 5, the receiving host machine then resequences the datagrams before passing them to the end user.

Figure 8.2*a* shows an example of adaptive routing, with estimated delay as the service criterion as viewed by A. Datagrams are to be transported from A to J. The numbers on the links between the gateways reflect traffic conditions between the two gateways connected to the link. The larger numbers are weighted to indicate more delay. Each gateway communicates with its neighbor gateways (those directly connected to it) by exchanging status messages. If the information in the message indicates that the status of the neighbor has changed, the routing table is changed. This new information is broadcast to all other gateways and used to update their routing tables.

In Figure 8.2*b*, the dashed lines show that the datagrams follow the path A → C → D → E → G → I → J. The total time-weighted value for the end-to-end path is 15, which represents the path that has the shortest overall delay between A and J.

The datagrams from A can take different paths and traverse different gateways en route to J. If link, gateway, or network conditions change, as in Figure 8.2*c*, the end-to-end path could be changed (on the E-F, F-H, G-H, H-J, and I-J links). In this example, the datagrams now follow the path A → C → D → E → F → H → J. Care must be taken in the design and implementation of adaptive routing schemes to prevent the datagrams from oscillating in an internet. If the routing tables are updated too frequently because of unstable network performance, datagrams might take circuitous routes and perhaps never reach their final destination. It is easy to understand the value of the time-to-live parameter in the IP datagram in this situation. Oscillating datagrams are eventually discarded and then retransmitted later by the TCP module at the originating host computer.

Core and noncore gateways

Internet gateways have been classified as *core* or *noncore*. The terms are not used as much today, however, as they were in the past. Core gateways are administered by a single authority. In the case of the Internet, it is the Internet Network Operation Center (INOC). Noncore gateways are outside the control of the single administrative authority and are controlled by individual groups. From the perspective of the Internet, they are not controlled by the INOC.

When ARPANET was first implemented, it consisted of a single backbone network. As it evolved and grew, ARPANET provided attached gateways to local Internet networks. The *gateway-to-gateway protocol (GGP)*, was used for these core gateways to inform each other about their attached local networks. Traffic passing between two local networks passed through two gateways, and each core gateway had complete routing information on the other.

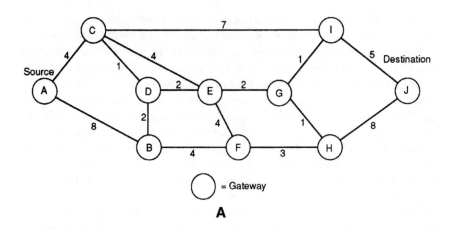

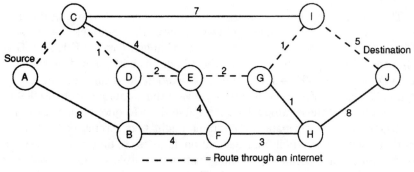

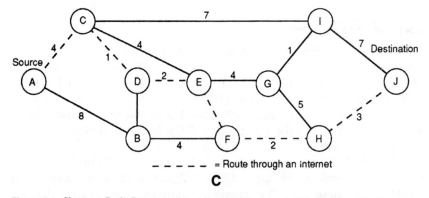

Figure 8.2 Shortest Path Routing with Adaptive Directories (*a*) Adaptive Routing with Shortest Path or Leqast-Cost Algorithm (*b*) Shortest Path from A to J (*c*) Revised Route for Datagrams of A.

Because these gateways had complete routing information, they did not need the default route described in Chapter 3. Things changed, however, and the Internet grew. Backbone networks were added to the original backbone, and local networks were attached to other local area networks (LANs). The same growth also occurred on many private internets. The concept of a gateway holding the complete routing information of an internet thus became too unwieldy.

Exterior and interior gateways

To solve this problem, gateways were given responsibilities for only part of an internet. In this manner, a gateway did not need to know about all other gateways of an internet, but relied on neighbor gateways and gateways in other autonomous systems to reveal their routing information. Indeed, if the gateways had insufficient knowledge to make a routing decision, they simply chose a default route. This change resulted in two other terms: *exterior gateways* and *interior gateways*. An exterior gateway supports the exchange of routing information between different autonomous systems. Interior gateways belong to the same autonomous system.

From these definitions we derive two other definitions. An *exterior neighbor* is a gateway that exchanges routing information between two autonomous systems. An *interior neighbor* exchanges information within the same autonomous system. Figure 8.3 shows the relationship between external and internal gateway protocols. A set of packet-switched networks is labeled as autonomous system 1 and is connected to another set of packet-switched networks, labeled autonomous system 2. Gateway 1 (G1) and gateway 2 (G2) use an *external gateway protocol (EGP)* to exchange data and control information. The two internets use their own *internal*

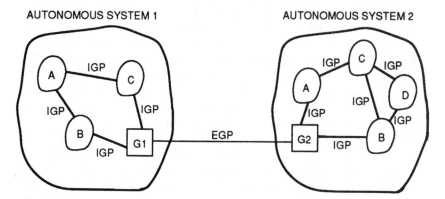

Figure 8.3 External Gateway Protocols and Internal Gateway Protocols.

gateway protocols (IGP) for route management inside each autonomous system. It is not unusual for a gateway to support two (or more) route discovery protocols, depending on where the traffic is destined. These gateways use an IGP within their autonomous systems and an EGP between each autonomous system.

Border routers and boundary routers

The terms described thus far would seem to cover all bases (or at least all nodes). Not quite. It is now accepted that an autonomous system might need to be further divided to achieve efficient and manageable routing tables and protocols. Therefore, an autonomous system can be divided into *areas*.

Areas can contain one to *n* subnets that exchange information through an IGP. In turn, areas have a designated *border* gateway that exchanges information with other border gateways. Finally, designated *boundary* gateways exchange information between autonomous systems.

If some of these terms seem redundant to other terms described in the previous sections, you are following this narrative quite well because some of them *are* redundant. For example, an EGP gateway is the same as a border router. So why did the Internet authorities expand the vocabulary? The terms *border* and *boundary routers* were added to the Internet vocabulary with the publication of the open shortest path first (OSPF) standard, which is described later in this chapter.

How autonomous systems or areas exchange information

Figure 8.4 is a slight alteration of Figure 8.1 but shows internetworking concepts in more detail. For simplicity, the networks between the gateways are not included in this figure. Be aware that this example is a generic example of route discovery. In later sections, we examine the specific rules for each internet gateway protocol. Gateways C and X are designated as gateways for autonomous systems 1 and 2, respectively. This section uses the term *autonomous systems*, but the same concepts apply to areas. In Figure 8.4*a*, gateway C's routing table (shown in the box) is sent to gateway X, which uses it to update its routing table containing reachability information pertaining to gateways A, B, C, D, E, F, and G. Gateway X is not concerned with how this information was obtained by gateway C. The internal operations of gateway C remain transparent to gateway X.

To expand this discussion, let us assume gateways F and K also exchange routing information. An autonomous system is not restricted to one core gateway, but an area usually designates only one router for each area. Now assume (as in Figure 8.4*b*) that the link or network connection is lost between E and F. Gateway C discovers this problem through its IGP and typically enters a value symbolizing infinity in its routing table entry for F (16, 256, or whatever the protocol stipulates to represent infinity). An "F = 16 through C" message is sent to gateway X, as shown by the arrow from C to X in Figure 8.4*b*.

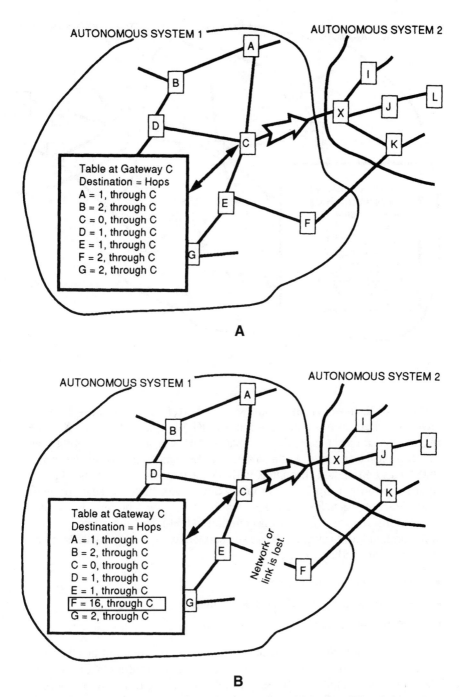

Figure 8.4 (*a*) Interactions of Autonomous Systems or Areas (*b*) Losing a Network Connection (*c*) Receiving Routing Information from Gateway X.

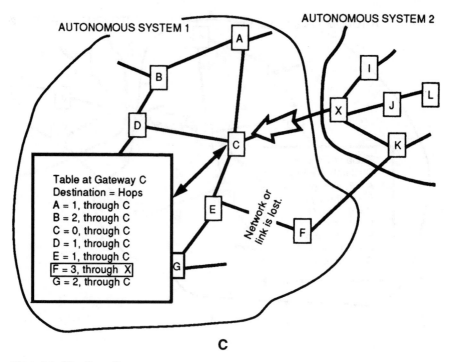

Figure 8.4 *(Continued)*

Gateway X, however, likely knows of a better route. Because F and K have exchanged routing information, the IGP exchange between X and K reveals that a better path than 16 exists to F. X stores in its routing table that this path is through K. It also sends an EGP message to core gateway C that F can be reached through X with a cost metric of 3. Because 3 is less than 16, gateway C updates its routing table accordingly, as seen in Figure 8.4*c*. This process is known as *repairing partitions*. The term is not used much in internet networks but is common in OSI-based networks.

In summary, the routing tables are changed at the gateways when an arriving message indicates that

- a new network has been found
- a better path to a network has been found
- a former "better" path must be degraded

In an actual internetworking situation, a network might not be allowed to repair its partition with another network. While the routers might be capable, a network administrator (say, of network A) might not want a foreign network's traffic to flow through network A. Moreover, the software might not be designed to support this operation.

Who participates in exchanging routing information and in executing routing logic?

As stated in previous chapters, both hosts and gateways can execute routing logic, and it is possible for a host to fulfill both functions. I have also said that the use of a host computer as a gateway must consider the issues of delay, throughput, and efficiency. Typically, the host in an internet does not have as much knowledge as the gateway has about the network. The host usually routes traffic through the IP routing algorithm and default values in the routing tables; in general, it routes traffic to gateways. These gateways thus have a more thorough knowledge of the network and perform more elaborate routing functions.

The internet protocols are based on the use of partial routing tables at some gateways and full routing tables at others. This approach represents a compromise between, at one extreme, loading full routing tables in all machines and, at the other extreme, using schemes without directories. The practice of using full routing tables could be unduly burdensome for a number of reasons. First, all machines do not need to know the locations of all other machines. Second, excessive memory could be consumed storing complete routing information in large tables. Third, searching the tables to extract the routing information could consume considerable CPU processing time. In any event, these factors should be considered very carefully before making a decision to load these tasks onto an applications processor or a specialized switching processor.

The practical approach is to use a relatively small number of gateways that maintain complete routing tables for the networks. The outlying gateways keep only partial information (the host might have even more limited routing tables). With this approach, the managers of outlying networks need not concern themselves with the onerous task of maintaining large tables of routing information. They need only be concerned with their specific networks.

In summary, the principal advantages to partial routing tables are storage saving, CPU cycle saving, and the ability of the outlying network managers to manage their routing operations in a relatively simple fashion without affecting other networks.

Clarifying terms

Before we move to an examination of specific gateway protocols, we should define several terms introduced earlier in this chapter·

GGP: gateway-to-gateway protocol; provides routing information between core gateways.

EGP: provides routing information between autonomous systems.

IGP: provides routing information within an autonomous system and perhaps within an area.

It is important to remember that some people use these three terms generically to describe a concept. This practice is acceptable, as long as it is understood how the terms are used.

The terms *GGP* and *EGP* also identify two specific Internet gateway standards examined in this chapter. The term *IGP* does not identify a specific standard but rather a concept, and a family of interior gateway protocols.

Now that we have analyzed the general concepts of gateways, we can turn our attention to the specific gateway protocols. First, we introduce GGP; next, we examine EGP. We then examine IGPs, notably the routing information protocol (RIP) and the OSPF standard.

The Gateway-to-Gateway Protocol

The GGP has seen limited use during the past few years, but it is discussed here because it is a good example of a distance-vector protocol and employs several concepts present in many other route discovery protocols: connecting to neighbor gateways, routing advertisements with neighbors, and maintaining an awareness of neighbors' presence.

We speak of it in the present tense because some networks still use variations of this protocol. The name is derived from the routing update message that contains pairs of values (D, V), in which V (the vector) identifies the destination, and D (the distance) identifies the number of intermediate hops (networks or gateways) to the destination. It is similar to the earlier example in this chapter of fewest-hops networks.

Vector-distance protocols require that all gateways exchange information because an option route must be computed based on a sum of the distance between each gateway. Moreover, information is only exchanged between adjacent gateways that share a common network.

To begin our analysis of GGP, imagine that a GGP gateway is brought up (initialized) in a network. Assume that it has no knowledge of the network or its neighbors. Indeed, when a network gateway begins operations, it assumes that its neighbors are down, and it is not connected to them. The distance to any other node in the routing table would therefore be an infinite number of hops (known as infinity).

The first order of business is to determine if a gateway can connect to its directly attached networks. It sends messages to these networks to determine the state of the physical attachments. These operations are not defined in GGP and are network dependent. A gateway might actually send messages to itself to determine if it can communicate with a network. Thus, a gateway periodically polls an attached network to determine if it can receive messages from the network.

Neighbor connectivity analysis

Assuming that the gateway is operational, it ascertains its connectivity to its neighbors by using the Internet K-out-of-N algorithm. Every 15 seconds, the gateway sends a status message (called an echo message) to each of its neighbors. In turn, the neighbors send back an echo reply. If there is no reply to K-out-of-N echo messages, the neighbor is considered inoperable. The Internet standard states the value of K as 3, and the value of N as 4.

On the other hand, if a neighbor is down and the gateway subsequently receives J-out-of-M echo replies, the neighbor is then declared to be up. The Internet standard states the value of J as 2 and the value of M as 4. The values of J, K, M, and N, however, can be set to any number deemed appropriate for autonomous systems.

Exchanging routing information

GGP gateways maintain several variables and numbers to manage the routing information exchanged within an internet. Figure 8.5 shows an example of a gateway and its neighbor exchanging routing information. I use this example to introduce the numbers and variables, as well as the basic operations for the information exchange messages.

A sending gateway maintains a send sequence number N at its node. This number is used to sequence its updates to its neighbors. Upon transmission of an update message, N is incremented by one. (It can be initialized to any value.) A neighbor also maintains a number; it is designated the receive sequence number R. Upon receiving an update from a gateway, the neighbor compares its value R with the send sequence number contained in the message. The sequence number in Figure 8.5 is labeled S.

The neighbor performs the comparison operation by subtracting R from S. If this value is greater than or equal to 0, it accepts the routing update message. This condition is true in the figure. It then sends back an ac-

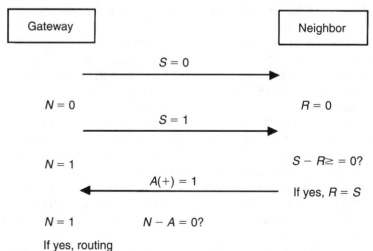

Figure 8.5 GGP: Exchanging Routing Information.

knowledgment (labeled A(+) = 1 in the figure) and replaces the value R with the value S. The acknowledgment is returned to the original sender (the gateway) in the acknowledgment message unit. In the example, the A value signifies an acknowledgment and the plus sign signifies a positive acknowledgment. The value 1 signifies the update value acknowledged.

Upon receiving this acknowledgment message, the transmitting gateway subtracts A from N. If the result of this calculation is equal to 0, it knows that the routing update has been acknowledged by its neighbor. If it does not equal 0, the gateway knows that an old routing update has been acknowledged, and it continues to transmit the S = 1 message until the neighbor sends the proper acknowledgment value back.

Figure 8.5 also indicates that the first message sent (S = 0) was not acknowledged by the neighbor. GGP states that if a second routing update is received before the first routing update is acknowledged, the neighbor need only acknowledge the second routing update.

If negative acknowledgments are received, the gateway uses the A and N values in several checking routines to determine at which point to begin retransmitting. The gateway must retransmit routing updates periodically until the messages are acknowledged and whenever its send sequence number changes. By use of the J, K, M, N algorithms, the gateway knows not to send updates to neighbors that are down.

Computing routes

The Internet procedure for exchanging routing information is described in Request for Comments (RFC) 823. The algorithms are summarized in this section.

An update to a routing table consists of a list of networks reachable through the gateway and the number of hops required to reach each of these networks. For example, Figure 8.6 shows gateways 1 through 6 (labeled G1, G2, etc.) in which G2 is sending a routing update to G1. This routing update occurs because G2 thinks it is closer than G1 to G3. G2 must therefore pass this information to G1 for G1 to make an efficient routing decision.

Figure 8.6 shows that G2 is labeled with variable J, and the network attached to G3 is labeled with variable I. The routing protocol works with the vector of dm(I,J), which contains the distance to I from J as reported by J. Because J is one hop away from I via G3, dm(I,J) = 1.

Upon receiving the routing update message, G1 copies several of its fields into a routing table. It copies the information from G2 into the Jth entry of this table, which is the connectivity between G1 and its Jth neighbor. This entry is represented as d(J).

Next, G1 calculates a minimum distance vector that contains the minimum distance to each gateway from G1. In Figure 8.6, G3 is represented as

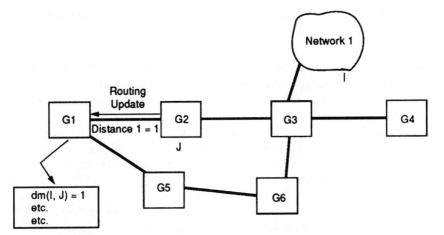

Figure 8.6 Computing Routes.

the Ith entry in this vector. The Ith entry is represented as MinD(I) and is calculated as

$$\text{MinD(I)} = \text{minimum over all neighbors of } d(J) + dm(I,J)$$

where d(J) is the distance between G1 and G2 (the Jth neighbor) and dm(I, J) is the distance from G2 (the Jth neighbor) to G3 (the Ith network attached to G3).

G1 would not store neighbor G5's distance to network I in MinD(I) because G5's dm(I, J) value to network I is greater than G3's.

After the routes have been recomputed, G1 determines if it should notify its neighbors with routing update messages. It only sends updates if all three of the following conditions occur:

- A routing update from a neighbor is different from a previously received update.

- A gateway's interface has changed its state.

- A gateway's neighbor gateway has changed its state.

Adding new networks. Adding a new network to the routing tables is fairly simple. Upon receiving a routing update message, the gateway compares the address list to its list of neighbor addresses. If the address is not in the table, it adds the address to the table of neighbor addresses. The gateway can use a polling message later to determine if the neighbor is up. It also adds the new network to its hop count matrix using the procedures discussed earlier.

Nonrouting gateways. The Internet standards allow the gateway to participate in forwarding datagrams without using the GGP routing operations. If such a topology is implemented, the gateways situated behind the nonrouting gateway must be known by the routing gateways.

GGP message formats.   The GGP message format is depicted in Figure 8.7. This message is encapsulated into an internet datagram, so the internet header precedes the message fields, although the header is not shown in the figure.

The first field is the *type* field. This 8-bit field specifies that the message is, for example, a routing update message. This field contains the value of 12 to distinguish it from other GGP messages. The next field is an *unused* field and is not defined at this time.

The *sequence number* field consists of 16 bits. It is used to sequence the routing updates between the sender and the receiver. The initialization of the sequence number must be agreed upon between both parties.

The next field is the *need update* field. This field is set to the value of 1 if the source gateway needs a routing update for the destination gateway. Otherwise, it is set to 0.

The next field, labeled *number of distance groups*, is an 8-bit field. (This field is also labeled *n-distance*.) It contains the number of groups reported in this update message. Each distance group must contain a distance value and the number of networks, followed by the actual network identification numbers reachable at that distance. GGP does not require that all the distances be reported.

Because the gateway protocols need not deal with the host address of the internet address structure, the GGP does not require that the host portion of the address be included in the address fields. Therefore, the network address fields can vary in length (1, 2, or 3 octets). GGP does not need a length field for the address fields; it need only examine the first bits of the network identifier to determine the number of octets in each address field.

The *distance D1* field contains the hop count or another distance indicator applicable to the distance group 1. The field labeled *number of networks at D1* (often labeled *n1 - dist*) contains the value representing the number of networks reported within distance group 1. The fields *first network at D1* and *last network at D1* contain the identification of the networks in the group. These are the actual IP addresses of the networks concerned. The GGP message format then repeats itself until the last distance group has been described, labeled *Dn* in Figure 8.7.

Figure 8.8 depicts the GGP acknowledgment message. The type acknowledgment, labeled *type* in this figure, simply identifies whether the acknowledgment is positive (type value of 2) or negative (type value of 10). The *sequence number* is used to acknowledge (either negatively or positively) previous traffic.

Figure 8.9 shows the format for the echo request and echo reply messages. These messages are used by the gateways to notify each other about

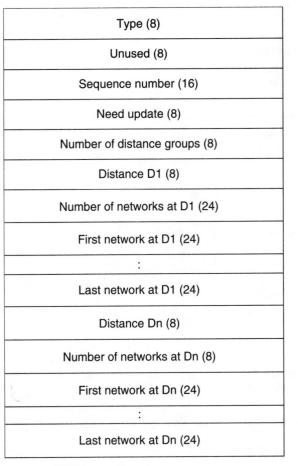

| Type (8) |
| Unused (8) |
| Sequence number (16) |
| Need update (8) |
| Number of distance groups (8) |
| Distance D1 (8) |
| Number of networks at D1 (24) |
| First network at D1 (24) |
| : |
| Last network at D1 (24) |
| Distance Dn (8) |
| Number of networks at Dn (8) |
| First network at Dn (24) |
| : |
| Last network at Dn (24) |

Figure 8.7   GGP Message Format.

| Type (8) |
| Unused (8) |
| Sequence number (16) |

Figure 8.8   GGP Acknowledgement Message.

their status and to test if the other gateway is responding properly. The message is a very simple structure consisting of the *type* of message (8 signifies echo, 0 signifies echo reply). The *source address* in the internet IP header is used in these messages to identify the two neighbors participating in the echo exchange.

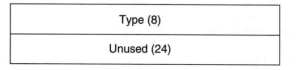

Type (8)
Unused (24)

Figure 8.9 GGPEcho Request/Reply Message.

Type (8)
Unused (24)

Figure 8.10 GGP Network Interface Status Message.

Figure 8.10 shows the format for the network interface status message. It is used by a gateway to determine if the gateway can send and receive traffic. Because the gateway might send these messages to itself, the *IP destination address* contains the address of the network interface of the gateway. The *type* field is set to 9.

Example of a GGP update message

Figure 8.11 shows an example of a GGP update message in relation to the internet topology examples discussed in previous sections. In this figure, the networks between the gateways have been labeled with the network portion of an internet address. The update message in this figure would be issued by gateway C to gateway X. Three distance groups are reported:

0 = networks directly attached to C

1 = networks one hop away from C

2 = networks two hops away from C

As stated earlier, GGP is not used much today, but its distance-vector concepts and neighbor operations have found their way into several other route discovery protocols, which are discussed in the following sections.

External Gateway Protocol

The EGP provides network reachability information between neighboring gateways. Although the name of the protocol includes the term *exterior*, these gateways can exist in the same or different autonomous systems. The more common approach is to use EGP between gateways that do not belong to the same autonomous system.

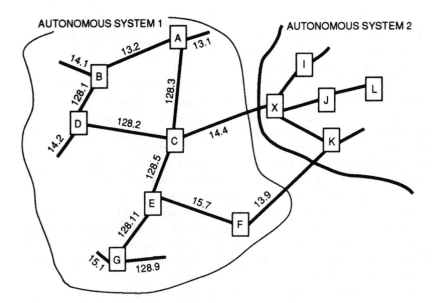

Type = 12
Unused
Sequence number = 24 (for example)
Need update = No (for example)
Number of distance groups = 3
Distance D1 = 0
Number of networks at D1 = 4
14.4, 128.5, 128.3, 128.2
Distance D2 = 1
Number of networks at D2 = 6
15.7, 128.11, 14.2, 128.1, 13.1, 13.2
Distance D3 = 2
Number of networks at D3 = 4
15.1, 128.9, 13.9, 14.1

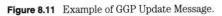

Figure 8.11 Example of GGP Update Message.

You might wonder why yet another gateway protocol is needed. After all, why not use GGP to handle the exchange of routing information between autonomous systems? To understand the need for EGP, consider the following situation, shown in Figure 8.12.

Gateways A, B, C, and D are core gateways and used to manage the routing of traffic between networks 1, 2, 3, 4, and 6. These gateways can use GGP operations to exchange routing information. The gateways use internet addresses to support routing between these networks. A problem is encountered, however, when an attempt is made to route datagrams to networks 5 and 7. From the perspective of the core gateways, networks 5 and 7 do not exist; they are hidden from view behind network 6.

How can we provide information about networks between core gateways and noncore gateways? The situation is somewhat complex in that we must decide who is responsible for exchanging information with whom. The answer to the problem is to develop concise rules concerning which gateway is responsible for providing information to the core network about the existence and reachability of the *hidden* networks.

The internet solution is a scheme that allows an autonomous system to send *reachability* information to any other autonomous system. These messages must also go to at least one core gateway. In practice, one gateway in an autonomous system usually assumes the responsibility for these tasks. From the perspective of Figure 8.12, gateway D assumes this responsibility. Thus, gateway D belongs to an autonomous system consisting of networks 5, 6, and 7, as well as gateways E and F. EGP therefore serves to partition the responsibility for maintaining and updating routing tables to specific gateways in an internet.

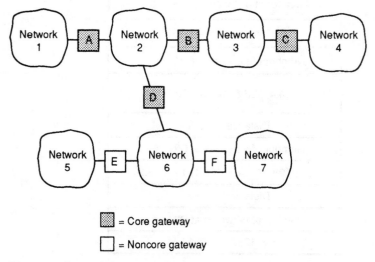

Figure 8.12   Core and Noncore Gateways.

Major operations of EGP

EGP contains procedures for the following:

- acquire neighbors
- exchange information messages between neighbors
- monitor the reachability of neighbors

EGP uses polling procedures that allow the gateways to monitor each other and exchange routing update messages.

The EGP states

EGP is a state-driven protocol, which means that its operations are described with state tables and state transition procedures. EGP contains five states, numbered 0 through 4. If a machine has a number of neighbors, it maintains a state table for each. The states are described next and further clarify how the protocol operates within a gateway.

Idle state (state 0): Defines a gateway that has no resources and is not involved in any protocol activity. It can respond to initiation messages, but it must ignore all other types of messages. Upon receipt of a message denoting a request, it can transition to a down state or, if it chooses to begin activities, to an acquisition state.

Acquisition state (state 1): Allows the gateway to transmit request messages periodically. It can, however, receive messages and move to the down state or return to the idle state.

Down state (state 2): The gateway is down. It is not allowed to process polling messages, and it is not allowed to send them. The gateway can receive certain types of traffic, discussed in more detail shortly.

Up state (state 3): Used to declare the neighbor gateway to be up. With this state, the gateway can process and respond to all EGP messages. This state is used for transmitting polling commands.

Cease state (state 4): As the name implies, this is the state in which the gateway ceases updating operations, although it does continue to send a cease command and receive a cease-ACK response.

Types of messages

The EGP messages are classified as commands, responses, or indications. Commands require some type of action to be performed. Responses give an indication of the status of an action, and indications can be sent at any time. Table 8.1 lists the commands, along with the permissible responses as defined in the state transition tables.

TABLE 8.1 EGP Commands,
Responses, and Indications

Command	Responses/Indications
Request	Confirm, refuse, error
Cease	Cease-ACK, error
Hello	I-H-U (I heard you), error
Poll	Update, error

As with many protocols, EGP uses state transition tables in conjunction with timers, sequence numbers, parameters, and state variables to control the sending and receiving of messages. Table 8.2 lists and briefly describes the sequence numbers, timers, and variables. Later discussions show examples of their use. The parameters P1 through P5 are fixed, although their values (in parentheses) are suggested by RFC 904. All other values are set during an initial handshake (request/confirm exchange) between neighbors. The one exception is send sequence number S.

EGP message types

EGP operates with 10 message types, listed and briefly explained in Table 8.3. Figure 8.13 shows the format for the header included on all EGP messages. It consists of seven fields and can be followed by other fields. The EGP *version* number identifies the current version of the protocol. Its current value is 2. The value is used by communicating EGP modules to ensure that they are using compatible software.

TABLE 8.2 EGP Timers and Other Parameters

Name	Description
R	Receive sequence number
S	Send sequence number
T1	Interval between Hello command retransmissions
T2	Interval between Poll command retransmissions
T3	Interval during which neighbor-reachability indications are counted
M	Hello polling mode
t1	timer 1—retransmission timer (for Request, Hello, and Cease)
t2	timer 2—poll retransmission timer (for Poll command)
t3	timer 3—abort timer
P1	Minimum interval acceptable between successive Hello commands received (30 seconds)
P2	Minimum interval acceptable between successive Poll commands received (2 minutes)
P3	Interval between Request or Cease command retransmissions (30 seconds)
P4	Interval during which state variables are maintained in the absence of command/responses (in Up/Down stages) (1 hour)
P5	Interval during which state variables are maintained in the absence of responses in the Acquisition and Cease states (2 minutes)

TABLE 8.3 EGP Messages

EGP message	Function of message
Request acquisition	Request the acquisition of neighbor and/or initialize polling variables
Confirm acquisition	Confirm acquisition of neighbor and/or initialize polling variables
Refuse acquisition	Negative response to acquisiton of neighbor
Cease request	Request deacquisition of neighbor
Cease-ACK response	Confirm deacquisition of neighbor
Hello	Request neighbor reachability
I-H-U (I heard you)	Confirm neighbor reachability
Poll	Request network reachability update
Update	Network reachability update information
Error	Error response to a message

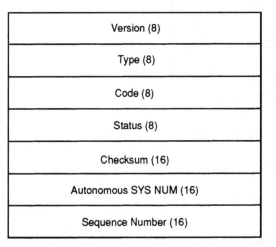

Figure 8.13 EGP Message Header.

The *type* field identifies the type of message, such as a neighbor acquisition request. The *code* field contains a value to identify the code or subtype of message, such as a cease command. The value of the *status* field depends on the message type.

The *checksum* field is used to perform error detection on the message. The algorithm used is the same one used by IP. The *autonomous system number* identifies the specific autonomous system of the sending gateway. The *sequence number* sequences the messages properly between the gateways.

Figure 8.14 shows the format for the neighbor acquisition message. The fields in the message are coded to convey the following information (note that when the field information is same as in Figure 8.13, it is not repeated here):

Type: This field is always set to 3 to identify a neighbor acquisition message.

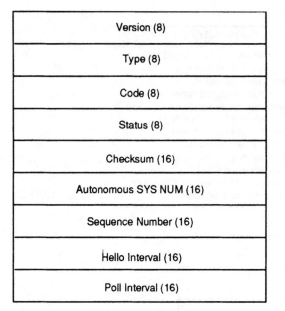

| Version (8) |
| Type (8) |
| Code (8) |
| Status (8) |
| Checksum (16) |
| Autonomous SYS NUM (16) |
| Sequence Number (16) |
| Hello Interval (16) |
| Poll Interval (16) |

Figure 8.14   EGP Neighbor Acquisition Message.

Code: This field is set to one of five values:
0 = request command
1 = confirm response
2 = refuse response
3 = cease command
4 = cease-ACK response

Status: This field is set to one of eight values:
0 = unspecified
1 = active mode
2 = passive mode
3 = insufficient resources
4 = administratively prohibited
5 = going down
6 = parameter problem
7 = protocol violation

Hello interval: Specifies the minimum hello command polling interval in seconds.
Poll interval: Specifies the minimum poll command polling interval in seconds.

The hello interval and poll interval are used only with request and confirm messages.

The status field is used by EGP to provide further information between communicating modules. Briefly, a code of 0 is used when the protocol can find nothing else appropriate to place in the status field. A value of 1 is used when the message indicates an active status mode. The value 2 indicates a passive status mode.

If the gateway does not have sufficient resources to process a request, it sets the status code to 3. RFC 904 suggests that this code be used if the machine is out of memory for the table management operations or otherwise out of system resources. A status code of 4 indicates that the proposed action is not allowed. For example, the value in the autonomous system field cannot be identified, or the gateway suggests the use of another gateway.

A status code of 5 indicates that the gateway is going down through an operator-initiated stop or through the expiration of the t3 abort timer. A status code of 6 indicates a parameter problem with the incoming message; possible scenarios include unintelligible parameters or the inability to assume a compatible mode. Finally, a status code of 7 signifies that a protocol violation has occurred because an incoming command or response message is incompatible with the state of the machine.

Figure 8.15 shows the format for the neighbor reachability messages. The *type* field is equal to 3. The *code* field is equal to 0 for a Hello command and 1 for an I-H-U response. The *status* field is equal to 0, which the standard identifies as indeterminate. A value of 1 signifies an up state, and a value of 2 a down state. Information for the other fields remains the same as described for Figure 8.13.

Figure 8.16 shows the format for the poll command. The *type* field is set to a value of 2. The *code* field is set to a value of 0. The *status* field is set to 0, which the standard states is indeterminate. A value of 1 signifies an up

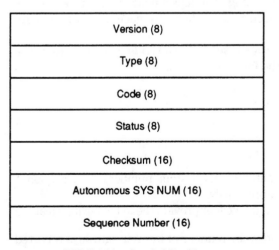

Figure 8.15   EGP Neighbor Reachability Message.

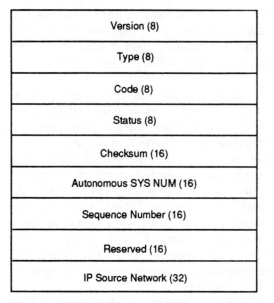

Version (8)
Type (8)
Code (8)
Status (8)
Checksum (16)
Autonomous SYS NUM (16)
Sequence Number (16)
Reserved (16)
IP Source Network (32)

Figure 8.16   EGP Poll Message.

state, and a value of 2 signifies a down state. The *IP source network* field contains the IP address of the network about which reachability information is required. It identifies a network common to the autonomous system of the neighbor receiving this message. As before, the information for the other fields remains the same as described previously.

Figure 8.17 shows the format for the update response/indication message. To understand the protocol, this message must be studied in more detail. As the figure shows, the message contains a header (on the left side of the figure) and a repeating occurrence of fields for each gateway being reported (called a *gateway block*).

The *type* field for this message is set to 1. The *code* field is set to 0. The *status* field is set to one of the following values:

0 = indeterminate

1 = up state

2 = down state

128 = an unsolicited message state

The version, checksum, autonomous system numbers, and sequence number have been described previously.

The three remaining fields in the header provide the following information:

Number of int. GWs: specifies the number of interior gateways reported in the message.

Number of ext. GWs: specifies the number of exterior gateways reported in the message.

IP source network: contains the IP address of the network about which reachability information is being reported.

The remainder of the message consists of the gateway blocks. The first field in a gateway block is the *gateway IP address*, which identifies the IP address of the gateway block. The # *distances* field contains the number of distances reported in the gateway block. The distance field's contents differ, depending on the architecture of the system. The # *nets* specifies the number of networks reported at each distance. Finally, the *net 1,1,1,1,1,2*, contains the IP address of the networks reachable through the gateway.

Example of an EGP update message

Figure 8.18 provides an example of an EGP update message using a network topology. Autonomous system 1 contains networks 128.1, 128.2,

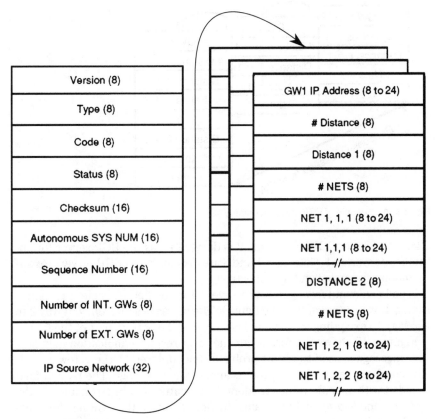

Figure 8.17   EGP Update Message.

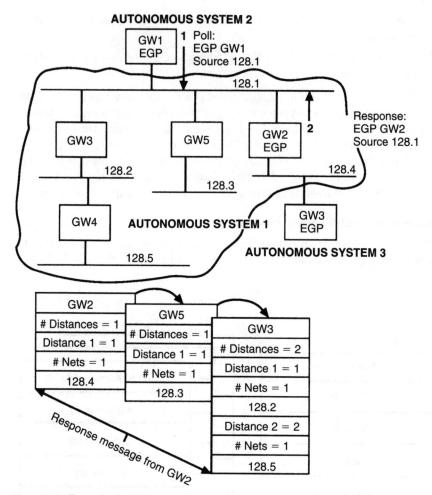

Figure 8.18 Example of EGP Message Update.

128.3, 128.4, and 128.5. Gateway 2 is designated as the EGP server for autonomous system 1. Gateways 1 and 3 are designated as EGP servers for autonomous systems 2 and 3, respectively.

A poll command from gateway 1 (event **1** in the figure) elicits a response from gateway 2 (event **2** in the figure). The message sent from gateway 2 to gateway 1 (excluding the header) is shown at the bottom part of the figure.

Figure 8.19 shows the format for the error response/indication message. This message is used to report problems encountered by the gateway, usually based on the inability to process an incoming message. The *reason* field is coded with specific values to identify the nature of the error, and the *error message header* field contains the first 96 bits of the EGP header causing the problem. The other fields were described previously.

EGP events

EGP is based on an event list as well as state transition diagrams. The protocol defines 15 events that can cause state transitions. Table 8.4 lists the events and their names. These events are based on the receipt of certain messages, the expiration of timers, or intervention via operating system or

Version (8)
Type (8)
Code (8)
Status (8)
Checksum (16)
Autonomous SYS NUM (16)
Sequence Number (16)
Reserved (16)
Error Message Header (first 3 words of EGP header)

Figure 8.19 EGP Error Response/Indication Message.

TABLE 8.4 EGP Events

Name	Event
Up	At least j neighbor-reachability indications have been received within the last T3 seconds
Down	At most k neighbor-reachability indications have been received within the last T3 seconds
Request	Request command has been received
Confirm	Confirm command has been received
Refuse	Refuse response has been received
Cease	Cease command has been received
Cease-ACK	Cease-ACK response has been received
Hello	Hello command has been received
I-H-U	I-H-U response has been received
Poll	Poll command has been received
Update	Update response has been received
Start	Start event has been recognized due to system or operator intervention
Stop/3	Stop event has been recognized due to (a) system or operator intervention, or (b) expiration of the abort time t3
t1	Timer t1 has counted down to zero
t2	Timer t2 has counted down to zero

human operator. In conjunction with the state diagram logic, these events define the specific actions of the protocol.

To explain these events and state transition tables would entail explaining the entire protocol, which is beyond the scope of this book and best left to RFC 904. The next section does provide several examples of EGP operations during the up state to clarify the protocol.

EGP operations during the up state

Table 8.5 lists the activities and state transitions associated with each EGP event. The row entries are used as beginning discussion points for explaining how the protocol operates in the up state. Note that this example is a general overview of the activities of the gateway during the up state. You should have a general understanding of the protocol after this discussion. Some events have two parts for one state. They are read as n/a, where n = next state and a = action taken. Let's use the column labeled *3 Up* and the rows pertaining to the *3 Up* column as an example.

The row entry in the table labeled *Up* means that the proper j neighbor reachability indications have been received within the proper t3 time; therefore, the machine remains in the up state. The next row entry means the *Down* event takes the machine to state 2 (the down state). Consult Table 8.4 for definitions of each event. The machine stops timer t2, as polling transmissions are unnecessary.

The row entry labeled *Request* describes the actions taken when a request command message arrives at the gateway. This message is formatted as a neighbor acquisition message (see Figure 8.14) and is used to request the acquisition of a neighbor and set up the hello and polling intervals

TABLE 8.5   Events, Actions, and States in EGP

Name	0 Idle	1 Acquisition	2 Down	3 Up	4 Cease
Up	0	1	3/Poll	3	4
Down	0	1	2	2	4
Request	2/Confirm	2/Confirm	2/Confirm	2/Confirm	4/Cease
Confirm	0/Cease	2	2	3	4
Refuse	0/Cease	0	2	3	4
Cease	0/Cease-ACK	0/Cease-ACK	0/Cease-ACK	0/Cease-ACK	0/Cease-ACK
Cease-ACK	0	1	2	3	0
Hello	0/Cease	1	2/I-H-U	3/I-H-U	4
I-H-U	0/Cease	1	2/Process	2/Process	4
Poll	0/Cease	1	2	3/Update	4
Update	0/Cease	1	2	3/Process	4
Start	1/Request	1/Request	1/Request	1/Request	4
Stop/3	0	0	4/Cease	4/Cease	0
t1	0	1/Request	2/Hello	3/Hello	4/Cease
t2	0	1	2	3/Poll	4

whose values are transmitted in the message. The gateway must respond with a *Confirm* message. It also reinitializes all state variables and resets timer t1 to T1 seconds and timer t3 to P5 seconds.

The row entry labeled *Refuse* means the gateway has received a refuse message. It generally stays in the same state after receiving this message. The row entry labeled *Cease* means the gateway has received a neighbor acquisition message with a code of cease command (state 3). The gateway must respond with a *cease-ACK* response. This message stops all timers and enters the idle state.

The row entry labeled *Hello* means that the gateway has received a hello command message. Because this message determines neighbor reachability, the gateway responds with an I-H-U response and remains in the up state (state 3).

The row entry labeled *I-H-U* means that the gateway has received an I-H-U response. It processes the information and remains in the up state. The row entry labeled *Poll* means that the gateway has received a poll command. Remember that this message (Figure 8.16) is used to request a network-reachability update and contains the internet address of the network about which the sending gateway wishes reachability information. The responding gateway thus sends an update message (Figure 8.17), which contains the information to satisfy the polling query. As noted in Table 8.5, the gateway remains in the up state.

The receipt of an *Update* message (as seen in the table's row entry labeled *Update*) requires the gateway to process reachability information and remain in the up state. This message is sent to the gateway because of a prior polling command and can therefore act as an ACK to the poll.

The *Start* event is a result of an operator or operating system action. It results in a transition to the acquisition state and a request message. The *Stop* event occurs because of a problem or the expiration of the abort timer (t3). The protocol requires that a *Cease* message be sent to request the deactivation of neighbors (placing them in an idle state). Timer t1 is set to P3 seconds, and timer t3 is set to P5 seconds. The expiration of timer t1 requires that a hello message be transmitted. The expiration of timer t2 requires that a poll message be retransmitted. In both instances, the protocol entity remains in the up state.

Figure 8.20 shows several of the more important activities and the relationships of the messages at the gateway during the up state. Because EGP contains many more rules than covered here, you are encouraged to study RFC 904 for more information.

Other features of EGP

You should be aware that EGP is restricted to advertise reachability to those networks completely within the gateway's autonomous system. An

GATEWAY ACTIONS   MESSAGES

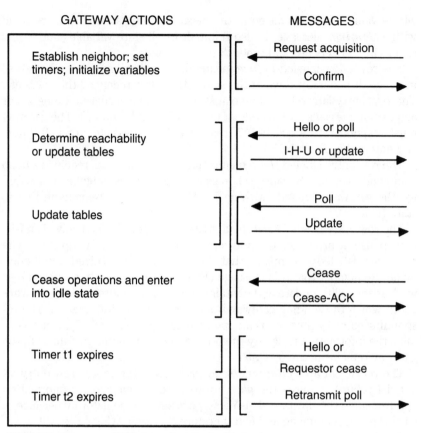

Figure 8.20   Summary of EGP Operations During Up State.

EGP gateway thus has a restricted authority. One of its values is to prevent a plethora of information from being transmitted around the network.

EGP is similar to GGP except that the EGP messages advertise multiple gateways. As we learned in this section, the EGP gateway is able to send a sequence of reachability information blocks relative to a specified network. EGP does not compute against the values contained in the routing update message. The software is designed only to establish that EGP can signify a path is available. The name *Distances field* in the update message is really a misnomer. EGP advertises reachability information and cannot function with elaborate topologies, including looping gateways.

The Border Gateway Protocol

The border gateway protocol (BGP) is an interautonomous system protocol and a relatively new addition to the family of route discovery protocols. It has been used since 1989 but not extensively until recently. It is intended for BGP to replace EGP. BGP is published in RFC 1267.

BGP has a number of significant advantages over EGP. First, it can operate with networks that have looped topologies, using algorithms that prune the loops out of the topology. Second, BGP does not have the "count-to-infinity" problem found in many route discovery protocols because it advertises all autonomous systems (transit machines) on the path to a destination address. Third, as a result of this full advertising, a node that receives more than one possible path (in advertisements) to a destination can, without ambiguity, choose the best path.

In addition, BGP does not care what type of intra-autonomous route discovery protocol is used. It does not care if multiple interautonomous protocols are employed.

BGP is designed to run with a reliable transport layer protocol, such as TCP. An implementor of BGP need not be concerned about reliable receipt of traffic, segmentation, etc., because these potential problems are handled by the transport layer.

BGP operations

BGP systems initially exchange routing information by sending an entire BGP routing table. Thereafter, only updates are exchanged. As with most routing exchange protocols, BGP uses keep-alive messages to ensure a connection is up.

The key aspect to BGP is the idea of *path attributes*, which are contained in the update messages, along with network addresses of the advertised networks. Several attributes are defined; the following is a summary of the major ones:

ORIGIN: defines the origin of the path information. It describes the origin as an IGP, EGP, or an origin of some other means.

AS_PATH: lists the autonomous systems (ASs) that must be traversed to reach the advertised networks.

NEXT_HOP: contains the IP address of the border router that is to be used as the next hop to reach the networks listed in an update message.

UNREACHABLE: notifies the speaker that a previously advertised route has become unreachable.

A BGP machine that sends BGP messages is called a *BGP speaker*. When a BGP speaker receives a new route advertisement from a BGP peer over an external BGP link (from another autonomous system), it advertises this route to all other BGP speakers in the autonomous system if the route is better than other known routes to the advertised network or if no acceptable routes are known. Unreachable routes are also advertised. This information is contained in the UPDATE message, and the path attributes are part of this message.

A BGP speaker must generate an update message to all peers when it selects a new route. Be aware that RFC 1267 does not define the rules for how alternate routes are selected and compared.

BGP messages

If you have studied this chapter, it is likely you are aware that the contents of the messages of routing exchange protocols are quite similar, but each has some aspect that makes it unique. BGP is no exception.

Figure 8.21a shows the header of the BGP message. The marker field is used for authentication, or to detect a loss of synchronization between BGP peer nodes. Its contents are application-dependent. The length field indicates the length of the entire message, including the header, in octets. The type field indicates the type of message: open, update, notification, or keep-alive.

The open message establishes a relationship with a peer BGP entity. Its contents are shown in Figure 8.21b. The version-number field contains the value of the current version of BGP (currently 3). The my-autonomous-number field contains the autonomous number of the sender of the message. Hold time indicates the maximum time expected between the receipt of successive keep-alive, update, or notification messages. The BGP identifier is an IP address of one of the sender interfaces; the value remains the same for all messages from all interfaces. The authentication code identifies the type of authentication procedure used to authenticate the sender; the meaning of the next field, authentication data; and the algorithm for computing the marker fields. Its contents are application-dependent.

The update message is used to exchange routing information between BGP peers. Its contents are shown in Figure 8.21c. The length field indicates the length of the path attributes field. The path attributes field contains a number of bits to indicate if the information is optional/required, partial/full, and other values. It also contains an attribute value that indicates the internet network numbers advertised in the message. The keep-alive and notification messages are not shown here. Their purpose is to ensure BGP peers are up and running and to exchange diagnostic messages.

Interior Gateway Protocols

I stated earlier in this chapter that the term *interior gateway protocol (IGP)* is a generic term that refers to a concept, as well as specific systems. Unfortunately, the Internet has no clear IGP "leader" because of the somewhat unsystematic way the IGPs were developed and promulgated. In fairness it should be stated that network administrators prefer different IGP approaches because of different internal network management require-

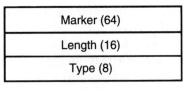

| Marker (64) |
| Length (16) |
| Type (8) |

A Header

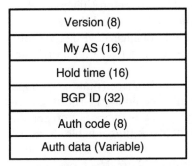

| Version (8) |
| My AS (16) |
| Hold time (16) |
| BGP ID (32) |
| Auth code (8) |
| Auth data (Variable) |

B Open message

| Total length (16) |
| Path attributes (Variable) |
| Network 1 (32) |
| Network n (32) |

C Update message

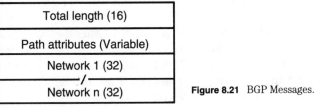

Figure 8.21 BGP Messages.

ments. Nonetheless, as this book's subject is TCP/IP and the internet protocols, our focus in this section is three internet-related IGPs: RIP, hello, and gated. The next section examines the OSPF, which is a better IGP.

Routing Information Protocol

The RIP system was developed based on research at the Xerox Palo Alto Research Center (PARC) and Xerox's PUP and XNS routing protocols. Interestingly, RIP's wide use was due to its implementation at the University of California at Berkeley (UCB) in a number of LANs. UCB also distributed RIP with its Unix system. It is rather ironic that RIP was designed for LANs yet is now used in wide area networks—if for no other reason than because it's there. Note that RIP is not standardized across vendor product lines, and most vendors offer value-added extensions to the protocol. This section describes the RIP version published in RFC 1058.

Because RIP was designed for LANs, it is based on a broadcast technology: a gateway periodically broadcasts its routing table to its neighbors. The broadcast aspect of RIP has brought forth complaints about its inefficiency.

RIP is classified as a distance-vector algorithm routing protocol. RIP routing decisions are based on the number of intermediate hops to the final destination. Early descriptions of this type of protocol were provided by L. R. Ford and D. R. Fulkerson (*Flows in Networks,* Princeton University Press, Princeton, NJ, 1962). RIP is thus sometimes called a Ford-Fulkerson algorithm or a Bellman-Ford algorithm because R. E. Bellman devised the routing equation (*Dynamic Programming,* Princeton University Press, Princeton, NJ, 1957).

RIP advertises only network addresses and distances (number of hops). It is similar to GGP in that it uses a hop count to compute the route cost, but it uses a maximum value of 16 to indicate that a network is unreachable. GGP uses a value of 255 to designate a network unreachable. Also, RIP needs information on all networks within the autonomous system. Similar to GGP, it exchanges information only with neighbors. Machines that participate in RIP operations are active or passive devices. Active machines (usually gateways) advertise routes to other machines. Passive machines (usually host computers) do not advertise routes but receive messages and update their routing tables.

The hop count is a metric for the cost of the route. Other metrics can be used, such as delay, security, bandwidth, etc., but most implementations use a simple hop count. RIP also uses UDP. UDP port 520 is used by the RIP machines for sending and receiving RIP messages. Each machine that uses RIP must have a routing table. The table contains an entry for each destination serviced by the machine. Each entry in the table must contain at least the following information:

- destination IP address
- a metric (between 1 and 15) of the cost (number of hops) to reach the destination
- IP address of the next gateway in the path to the destination
- indicators to determine if the route has changed recently
- timers associated with the route

RIP timers.   Two timers are associated with each route: a *timeout timer* and a *garbage-collection* timer. The timeout timer is set each time a route is initialized or updated. If 180 seconds elapse before an update is received or if the update contains a distance metric of 16, the route is considered obsolete. The route is not removed, however, until the garbage-collection timer has also expired. This timer is set for another 120 seconds and after it expires the route is removed from the routing table. The route continues to be included in all update messages until the garbage-collection timer expires.

Another timer is used to send updates (called *responses in RIP*) to neighboring machines. Every 30 seconds, these messages are broadcast by active gateways. They contain pairs of values; one value of the pair is an IP address, the other is the hop count to that address from the source of the message. The original versions of RIP broadcasted their entire routing table every 30 seconds, regardless of whether the table has changed—a rather obvious deficiency that has been corrected in newer versions.

Example of RIP operations. Figure 8.22 shows an example of RIP operations. Gateways G5 and G6 are reporting a (D,V) of (1,5) in regard to network 5: they can reach network 5 with a metric cost of 1. This message is relayed to G3, which updates its routing table entry to network 5 with a cost of 2. G3 then sends a message to G1 and G2, which store a cost of 3 to network 5. In turn, G1 and G2 advertise a (D,V) of (3,5) to other gateways, and so on.

Like most route discovery protocols, RIP is based on trust: the router that receives an advertisement trusts that it is accurate and uses it for making routing decisions. Thus, in Figure 8.22, upon G4 receiving the message from G2 that G2 is 3 hops away from network 5, G5 must take the position of, "If you are 3 hops away from network 5, then I must be 4 hops away, and I can reach network 5 through you."

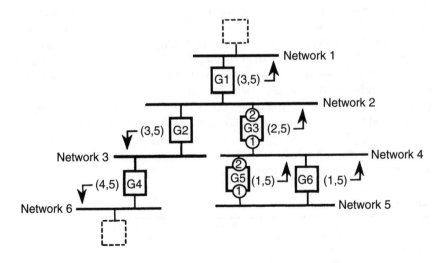

Where: (D,V) = (D) distance to (V) vector (IP address)

(n) = physical port (interface) number

Figure 8.22 Example of RIP Operations.

TABLE 8.6 G5 Routing Table

Destination	Next Hop	Metric	Direct or remote	Local or RIP	Interface
Network 5	0	1	D	L	1

G5's routing table regarding network 5 would appear as shown in Table 8.6. The Destination column is the address of the destination network, as seen by G5 (in TCP/IP based networks, an IP address). Next Hop is the address of the node that is to receive the traffic next. An entry is 0 in this table if no next hop occurs. The Metric column states how many hops are between this machine to the destination network. The Direct or Remote column is either D (directly attached), or R (a remote network, not directly attached). The Local or RIP column is either L (network was discovered because it is local) or R (network was discovered through RIP messages). The Interface column identifies the physical port on G5 on which the discovery was made. Because all gateways are receiving advertisements from each other, reachability to all networks can be computed. As another example, Table 8.7 is the routing table as viewed by G3.

RIP requires that a route, once learned, cannot change until a (D,V) is received that represents a better route to the vector. If a gateway receives a message of the same distance metric to a network (as G3 did by receiving messages from G5 and G6), the gateway uses the first arriving message.

RIP problems. In retrospect, the Internet authorities would most likely have opted for a gateway protocol other than RIP. Indeed, changes have been made to the original version to correct some rather serious deficiencies. One of these problems, called *counting to infinity*, is shown in Figure 8.22. Gateway 5 has lost its connection to network 5. When this event occurs, it sends an RIP message through network 4 to gateway 3 with the (D,V) of (16,5), signifying that it has an infinite distance (16) to network 5.

As noted in event 1, however, gateway 3 understands that it has a distance metric of 2 to gateway 5. Because this value is better than (16,5), it maintains its routing table entry and advertises this value back to G5. G5, upon receiving the message that network 5 can be reached through G3 with

TABLE 8.7 G3 Routing Table

Destination	Next Hop	Metric	Direct or remote	Local or RIP	Interface
Network 1	G1	2	R	R	2
Network 2	0	1	D	L	2
Network 3	G2	2	R	R	2
Network 4	0	1	D	L	1
Network 5	G5	2	R	R	1
Network 6	G2	3	R	R	2

a metric of 2, changes its update table as indicated in event 3 with (D,V) = (3,5). That is, two hops through gateway 3 plus one more hop from gateway 5, for a total of 3 hops. This message is related back to G3, and we see in event 4 that it changes its routing table to (D,V) = (4,5) because it believes that to get to network 5 through G5 it must add one more hop to the value of 3 (which occurred in event 3). Thus, we find the two gateways incrementing their distance metric each time an RIP message is exchanged between them. Moreover, the two gateways continue to send the datagram back and forth until the IP time-to-live value expires. The values are eventually incremented to the RIP infinity value of 16.

To make matters worse, the 30-second rule means it might take a long time for the network to converge (complete the advertisements and build the revised routing tables). For the worst case, 7 minutes is required, which includes propagation delays and processing time. An average of 3.5 minutes expires before the internet converges.

Recent RIP implementations handle this problem with a technique called the *split-horizon* update. This approach requires a gateway to remember the neighbor from which the route was received. The gateway is not allowed to send updates to a neighbor about a route that it learned from that neighbor. A variation to this idea is called the *split horizon with poisoned reverse*. This technique allows the routes to be included in the updates, but their metrics are set to infinity (a value of 16).

Another approach used in conjunction with the poison reverse technique is called a *triggered update*. This technique requires a gateway to send an immediate RIP message when it receives messages indicating problems. The gateway is not allowed to wait for the next ongoing broadcast. In other words, the approach requires that bad news about a connection or another aspect of the network be propagated as quickly as possible.

These techniques ameliorate the routing exchange problems inherent in RIP. The techniques, however, are quite expensive for WANs in which bandwidth is both precious and expensive, and are not used in these types of networks. With smaller, more efficient, and higher-capacity LANs the enhanced approaches discussed in this section offer reasonable compromises. The preferable solution is to not use RIP at all but to migrate to a protocol, such as OSPF, which is discussed later in this chapter.

The RIP message format.   The RIP message format is shown in Figure 8.23. A header contains three fields:

Command: a value of 1 signifies the message is a request and 2 signifies a response.

Version: specifies the version number of the protocol.

Reserved: not used.

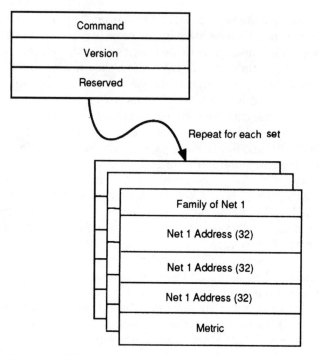

Figure 8.23   RIP Message Format.

Following the header, a set of fields contains the values that identify a specific protocol family. Because RIP is intended to run over systems other than the Internet, the *family of net 1* field identifies the protocol family. For Internet applications, the value is 2. The next 12 octets contain the network ID (*net 1 address*) as reported by RIP. Obviously, an Internet address needs only 4 of these 12 octets. RIP does not distinguish between the type of address in the message; it could be a subnet number, a network number, or a host number. If the message contains a subnet number, the machine must know the mask structure; otherwise, the address is ambiguous.

The *metric* field contains the metric value (usually the hop count) to the identified network.

The request and response.   A request message can be sent from one gateway to another to ask for a routing update. The entries in the request are examined to determine how to respond. For each entry, the machine looks up the metric value in its table and places the value into the metric field in a response message. An entire routing table can be obtained by coding the address family field as 0 and the metric field as 16.

RIP vs. OSPF.   Due to the technical deficiencies and lack of standardization of RIP, the Internet Engineering Task Force developed the OSPF protocol.

It eliminates the routing loops and dead-ends described earlier in this chapter. The OSPF protocol does not broadcast its entire table to other routers. Rather, it sends information only about its own links to each router. Each receiving router must acknowledge this traffic to the transmitting router. After receiving the information, each router builds appropriate entries in its own routing table. OSPF is described in detail later in this chapter.

RIP and IPX. Novell's RIP, known as IPX, was derived from RIP. These two protocols are more similar than they are different. Both are distance-vector-based, however, IPX is proprietary and does not adhere to the Internet RIP RFC. RIP IPX also has a *number-of-ticks* field, which can be used as a measure of delay. IPX advertises every 60 seconds and has a useful mechanism for allowing a router to gracefully close and go offline by informing other routers of this event.

The Hello protocol

In the past, the Hello protocol was widely used throughout TCP/IP-based systems. I mention it here for historical perspective. Digital Equipment Corporation's old LSI/11 minicomputer uses Hello in its "Fuzzball" software. It differs rather significantly from RIP, principally in that the delay is based on time rather than hop counts. A gateway protocol advertising delay requires that the gateways have network clocks reasonably accurate in their alignment with each other. Hello thus periodically provides messages for clock synchronization. In addition to carrying routing information, a Hello message also contains a time-stamp for use in checking time-related events.

The Hello message format. The Hello message format is shown in Figure 8.24. The *checksum* field checks for errors in the message. The *date* field is the value of a local date of the message sender, and the *time* field contains the local time of the sender. The *time-stamp* field is used by the machines to determine the round-trip delay of the message. This field is important for a protocol such as Hello, which uses delay as a metric for computing routes. The *offset* field is a pointer into the delay and offset entries. The *hosts* field specifies the number of entries that follow in the list of hosts. The *delay host* and *offset host* fields contain the delay to reach a host machine and an estimate of the difference (offset) between the sender's clock and the receiver's clock.

If you want more information on Hello, RFC 891 provides a description of the protocol.

Gated

Another "old" protocol is Gated. This internal gateway protocol has also seen considerable use. For example, IBM uses it in its Unix implementation

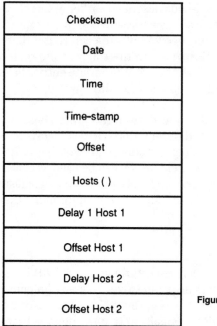

| Checksum |
| Date |
| Time |
| Time-stamp |
| Offset |
| Hosts ( ) |
| Delay 1 Host 1 |
| Offset Host 1 |
| Delay Host 2 |
| Offset Host 2 |

Figure 8.24 Hello Message Format.

on some of its personal computers. Gated combines many of the functions of RIP, Hello, and EGP. The program was developed at Cornell University and operates with Unix. It allows the network manager to establish how Gated can advertise routes to other exterior gateways. It is designed to accept either RIP or Hello messages and modify them for advertising within the Gated framework.

Summary of Distance-Vector Protocols

We can summarize the major features of the distance-vector protocols as follows:

- Neighbor gateways exchange routing information.
- All gateways must participate in the operations, thus creating the potential for large message exchanges.
- Gateways might not know about other gateways beyond their neighbor. They only know that their attached networks are reachable through a neighbor gateway.
- Messages are generally large, containing all routing entries.
- Neighbors periodically test each other's status.
- They adjust slowly to topology changes.

Choosing the Optimum Path with a Shortest Path Algorithm

The Internet Engineering Task Force published RFC 1247, the OSPF protocol. As stated earlier, *SPF* means shortest path first. The term is inaccurate; the protocols described thus far in this chapter are designed to choose the optimum path. A better term is *optimum path*, but the former term is now widely accepted. The OSPF is based on well-tested techniques used in the industry for a number of years. In this section, we describe these techniques. In the next section, we concentrate on the primary features of OSPF. In this discussion, the term *node* is synonymous with *gateway* and *router.*

We have already discussed that data communications networks are designed to route user traffic based on a variety of criteria, generally referred to as least-cost routing or cost metrics. The name does not mean that routing is based solely on obtaining the least-cost route in the literal sense. Other factors are often part of a network routing algorithm:

- capacity of the links

- delay and throughput requirements

- number of datagrams awaiting transmission onto a link

- load leveling through the network

- security requirements for the link

- type of traffic based on the type of link

- number of intermediate links, networks, and gateways between the transmitting and receiving hosts

- ability to reach (connect to) intermediate nodes and, of course, the final receiving host

Although networks vary in their least-cost criteria, three constraints must be considered: (1) delay, (2) throughput, and (3) connectivity. If delay is excessive or if throughput is too little, the network does not meet the needs of the user community. The third constraint is quite obvious: the gateways and networks must be able to reach each other; otherwise, all other least-cost criteria are irrelevant.

As we have learned in this chapter, algorithms that are used to route data through an internet vary. Recently, the attention in the data communications industry has focused on two classes of routing algorithms. The first technique, called *bifurcated routing,* is designed to minimize the average network delay. The second technique, called *shortest path routing,* provides a least-cost path between the communicating pair of users and minimizes the delay to the users. Bifurcated routing is not used much, so I only mention it in passing. For further information, examine *Computer-Communication Network Design and Analysis,* by M. Schwartz (Prentice Hall, 1977).

Several shortest-path algorithms are used in the industry. Most of them are based on what is called *algorithm A*. It is used as the model for the newer internet SPF protocols and has been used for several years to establish optimum designs and network topologies.

One final point is in order before we examine algorithm A. Many vendors have been developing route-discovery protocols for over a decade based on dynamic adjustments to link conditions or the state of a neighbor node. Their research and implementations are impressive. Some of these vendors believe that their proprietary solutions are superior to standardized approaches such as OSPF. While this view has merit, it means that their proprietary solutions are "closed" and their switch (node) does not interwork with a competitor's node. This approach might be attractive to the vendor, especially if the vendor's product has significant market share. It might be attractive to the vendor's clients, if they do not mind a sole-sourced internet. Other clients, however, prefer that these vendors adapt a standardized approach to permit a multivendor operation. While a multivendor operation is technically feasible, it entails a long and complex migration away from the closed solutions deeply embedded in the vendor's architecture.

Figure 8.25 is based on the example used for Figure 8.2 but applies to algorithm A, using node A as the source and node J as the destination (sink). (The topology represented in this figure is for illustrative, not implementation, purposes.) Algorithm A is defined generally as follows:

- Least-cost criteria weights are assigned to the paths in the network (Figure 8.25*a*).

- Each node is labeled (identified) with its least-cost criteria from the source along a known path. Initially, no paths are known, so each node is labeled with infinity. Updates to the values once the weights are established are the same as an initialization.

- Each node is examined in relation to all nodes adjacent to it. The source node is the first node considered and becomes the working node; Figure 8.25*b*. This step is actually a one-time occurrence wherein the source node is initialized with the costs of all its adjacent nodes.

- Least-cost criteria labels are assigned to each of the nodes adjacent to the working node. Labels change if a shorter path is found from this node to the source node. In OSPF, this situation would occur with the sending of link status messages on a broadcast basis to all other nodes.

- After the adjacent nodes are labeled (or relabeled), all other nodes in the network are examined. If one has a smaller value in its label, its label becomes permanent, and it becomes the working node (see Figure 8.25*c*).

- If the sum of the node's label is less than the label on an adjacent node, the adjacent node's label is changed because a shorter path has been found to the source node. In Figure 8.25d, node B is relabeled because node D is a shorter route through node C.

- Another working node is selected, and the process repeats itself until all possibilities have been searched. The final labels reveal the least-cost, end-to-end path between the source and the other nodes. These nodes are considered to be within a set N as it pertains to the source node.

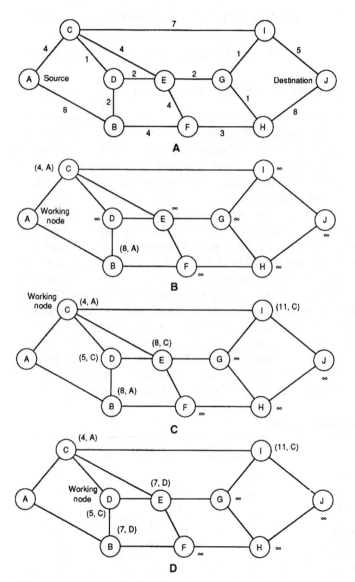

Figure 8.25 Application of Algorithm A.

The following statements describe the preceding discussion:

1. Let $D(v)$ = sum of link weights on a given path.

2. Let $c(i,j)$ = the cost between node i and j.

3. Set $N = \{1\}$.

4. For each node (v) not in N, set $D(v) = C(1,v)$.

5. For each step, find a node w not in N for which $D(w)$ is a minimum; add w to set N.

6. Update $D(v)$ for all nodes still not in N by $D(v) = \min [D(v),D(w) + c(w,v)]$.

7. Repeat steps 4 through 6 until all nodes are in set N.

The algorithm is shown in Table 8.8. The steps are successively performed until all nodes are in N. The process is performed for each node, and a routing table is created for the node's use. Each node's table is constructed in the manner just discussed. The routing topology for node A is shown in Figure 8.26. The numbers in parentheses represent the order of selection as reflected in Table 8.8.

Let us pause momentarily and examine the weighted paths in Figure 8.25a. You might wonder why certain paths are weighted with large or small numbers. As an explanation, consider that node A could have two communication links available for transmission. The link from A to C could be a microwave land link, and the A-to-B link could be a satellite circuit. If an interactive application were being routed through node A, the satellite link would be heavily weighted to discourage its use. As another example, the user data might need a secure link, and the A-to-B link might not use encryption/decryption devices. Networks might not route traffic based on factors such as security or other QOS parameters but rely on performance criteria such as minimum delay.

If the least-cost criteria includes factors other than link and node capacity, a separate capacity analysis is required to determine the ability of

TABLE 8.8 Choosing the Nodes

Step	N	A(B)	A(C)	A(D)	A(E)	A(F)	A(G)	A(H)	A(I)	A(J)
Initial	{A}	8	4	.	.	.	.	.	.	.
1	{A,C}	8	(4)	5	8	.	.	.	11	.
2	{A,C,D}	7	4	(5)	7	.	.	.	11	.
3	{A,C,D,B}	7	4	5	(7)	11	.	.	11	.
4	{A,C,D,B,E}	(7)	4	5	7	11	9	.	11	.
5	{A,C,D,B,E,F}	7	4	5	7	11	(9)	14	11	.
6	{A,C,D,B,E,F,G}	7	4	5	7	11	9	(10)	10	.
7	{A,C,D,B,E,F,G,H}	7	4	5	7	11	9	10	(10)	18
8	{A,C,D,B,E,F,G,H,I}	7	4	5	7	(11)	9	10	10	15
9	{A,C,D,B,E,F,G,H,I,J}	7	4	5	7	11	9	10	10	(15)

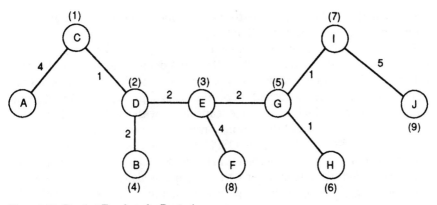

Figure 8.26   Routing Topology for Route A.

the network to handle the traffic. In this regard, the network capacity is like a chain that is no stronger than its weakest link. Likewise, a network has no more capacity than a specific combination of its lowest-capacity resources.

One might argue that network switching provides the means to route traffic around nodes and links that are either saturated or of insufficient capacity to handle the load. Nonetheless, at some point the traffic reaches an *area* within the network that is a bottleneck. This bottleneck limits the throughput of the entire network.

To determine why this limit exists, assume the least-cost weights in Figure 8.25*a* represent the maximum link and node capacities for traffic flow in one direction. A set of nodes and links can be identified that act as the lowest common resource for network capacity. One method to obtain this information is the *cut*. A cut is defined as the removal of connections (paths) between two nodes so that the two nodes are disconnected. In other words, they cannot reach each other. Network designers look for the minimum cut through a network. A minimum cut describes an area with the minimum capacity and thus a potential bottleneck. Each cut is given a capacity that is the *sum* of the weights of the links through the cut. The cut with the lowest sum is the minimum cut.

The Open Shortest Path First Protocol

This section provides an examination of OSPF. This protocol, designed by the OSPF working group of the Internet Engineering Task Force, is an IGP: gateways/routers are all within one autonomous system. Also, as stated earlier, OSPF is a link state or SPF protocol, in contrast to most other protocols that are based on some type of Bellman-Ford approach. The protocol, although it relies on techniques designed outside of the IP environment, is tailored specifically for an IP and includes such capabilities as subnet addressing and TOS routing, the latter being found in the TOS field of the IP datagram header (see Figure 5.2 in Chapter 5).

OSPF bases its routing decisions on two fields in the IP datagram: the destination IP address and the TOS. Once the decision is made on how to route the IP datagram, the datagram is routed without additional headers; that is, no additional encapsulation occurs. This approach is different from many networks in which PDUs are encapsulated with some type of internal network header to control the routing protocol within the subnetwork.

As stated earlier in this chapter, OSPF is classified as a dynamic, adaptive protocol in that it adjusts to problems in the network and provides short convergence periods to stabilize the routing tables. It is also designed to prevent traffic looping, a capability that is quite important in mesh networks or LANs where multiple bridges are available to connect different LANs.

It should also be noted that RFC 1247 uses the term *router* to describe the internetworking unit. We have learned in this book that many vendors use *router* and *gateway* synonymously. In addition, the OSPF PDUs exchanged between routers and networks are called *packets*.

OSPF operations

Each router contains a routing database. The database contains information about operable interfaces at the router, as well as status information about each neighbor to a router. The database is the same for all participating routers.

The routing database information focuses on the topology of the networks using a directed graph. Routers and networks form the vertices of the graph. Periodically, this information is broadcast (flooded) to all routers in the autonomous system (or area). An OSPF router computes the shortest path to the other routers in the autonomous system/area with regard to itself as the working node (the working node is termed the *root* in this protocol). Separate cost metrics can be computed for each TOS. If the calculations reveal that two paths are of equal value, OSPF distributes the traffic equally over these paths.

OSPF can support one to many networks. The networks can be grouped into an *area*, and the protocol allows one area to be hidden from other areas. Indeed, an area can be hidden from the full autonomous system. Because of increasing concerns about security, OSPF includes authentication procedures, and routers must go through a procedure to authenticate the traffic between them. More is said about the authentication aspects of this protocol shortly.

The directed graphs contain values between two points, either networks or gateways. The values represent the weighted shortest path value, with the router as the root. Consequently, the shortest path tree from the router to any point in an internet is determined by the router that performs the calculation. The calculation reveals the next hop to the destination in the hop-to-hop forwarding process. The topological database used in the calculation is derived from the information obtained by advertisements of the routers to their neighbors, with periodic advertisements throughout the autonomous system or area.

Thus far we have discussed in general terms how OSPF performs route discovery within the autonomous system or area. The method to determine routing information outside the autonomous system is referred to as *external routing*. Routing information pertaining to this capability is typically derived from OSPF as well as other protocols, such as the EGP or BGP. Alternately, routing information could be established through static routes between the autonomous systems or even by default routes. This information is also distributed through the autonomous system.

Two types of external routing capabilities exist with OSPF. In type 1 external routing, the external metrics are the same as the internal OSPF link state metric. Type 2 external metrics only use the cost of the router to the external autonomous system. The type 2 method is simple and based on the assumption that routing between autonomous systems is the major cost of routing the packet (which, in some actual operations, is not true). This approach eliminates conversion between internal link state metrics of OSPF and external costs (in which the autonomous system might have little influence).

The OSPF working group also adapted a very sound concept of autonomous system *areas* in which contiguous networks and hosts can be grouped together. In this situation, each area runs its own SPF algorithm and has its own topological database that differs from other areas. The purpose of the area concept is to isolate and partition portions of the autonomous system and thus reduce the amount of information a router must maintain about the full autonomous system. Having such an area also means that the overhead information transmitted between routers to maintain OSPF routing tables is reduced.

OSPF uses the term *backbone* to define that part of an autonomous system that conveys packets between areas. For example, in Figure 8.27 the routers R4 and R2 and their links serve as the backbone between the areas. The full path of a packet proceeds as follows: (1) intra-area path to a router attached to the backbone; (2) the backbone path to the destination area router; and (3) the destination intra-area path to the destination network.

The resources (links, routers) of a backbone need not be contiguous. For example, R2 in Figure 8.27 has network N1 between it and backbone router R4. This configuration is permissible; the intervening networks simply become *virtual links* within the backbone when constructing the topological database.

OSPF utilizes a Hello protocol for advertising state information between neighbors. Hello packets are used to confirm agreements among routers in a common network about a network mask and certain timers (dead interval,

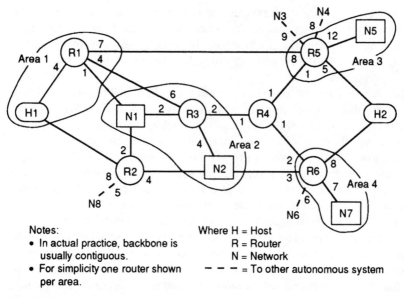

Notes:
- In actual practice, backbone is usually contiguous.
- For simplicity one router shown per area.

Where H = Host
      R = Router
      N = Network
      − − − = To other autonomous system

Figure 8.27 OSPF Concepts and Terms.

Hello interval). In effect, the Hello protocol is used to ensure that neighbor relationships make sense.

Classification of routers

The OSPF routers are classified according to the functions they perform:

Internal router: all networks directly connected to this router belong to the same area; all routers with only backbone interfaces are internal routers.

Border router: any router that is not an internal router.

Backbone router: any router that has an interface to the backbone.

Boundary router: a router that exchanges information with another autonomous system.

Types of advertisements

The purpose of OSPF is for routers to inform each other about internet paths via advertisements. These advertisements are sent to routers by update packets. Four types of advertisements are used:

Router links advertisement: contains information on a router's interfaces into an area. It is used by all routers and flooded throughout an area.

Network links advertisement: contains a list of routers connected to a network. It is used by a broadcast network and flooded throughout an area.

Summary links advertisement: contains information on routes outside an area. It is used by border routers and flooded to the border routers' areas (but inside the autonomous system).

Autonomous systems (AS) extended links advertisement: contains information on routes in other autonomous systems. It is used by a boundary router and flooded through the autonomous system.

Example of the OSPF shortest path tree

This discussion expands earlier discussions of how OSPF uses least-cost-path logic to obtain a directed graph and the pruned tree. The example is a very simple topology for this general overview. RFC 1131 has an excellent and detailed example if you need more information. Figure 8.27 is based on the previous examination of algorithm A. In this example, the labels have been changed to identify hosts, networks, and routers (gateways). The autonomous system consists of areas 1, 2, 3, and 4. Routers 2, 5, and 6 provide connections to other autonomous systems with the EGP or BGP software.

The numbers have been rearranged from the previous examples for this illustration. These numbers represent costs determined by the network administrator for each output port at each router. In this example, a lower-cost value determines a better route. Two numbers can be shown on a link in which two routers are directly connected. The numbers reflect the cost at each router's output port. For example, a connection between routers R3 and R4 indicates that the cost of moving traffic from R3 to R4 is 2 and the cost from R4 to R3 is 1. The reason that this cost can vary could be the different traffic loads and queue sizes at the routers, which result in different delays at the links of these machines (assuming delay is part of the cost metric). In addition, the metric values vary if frequency division multiplexers/modems divide the bandwidth on the link unevenly in the two directions. For example, the bandwidth from R3 to R4 could be 64 kbit/s and the bandwidth from R4 to R3 could be 128 kbit/s.

Also note that no costs are associated with the ports emanating from the networks to the routers, nor are there costs associated with the hosts' interfaces to the routers. OSPF does not assume that a network or host computer is capable of participating in the shortest path operations. Notwithstanding, a network or host can participate in the operations by the same methods used by the routers (if the network administration allows a network or host to become involved in the operation). In this context, a convenient way to view the directed graph (visually) is to remove the network from the picture and then view the arrows between the two routers.

Figure 8.28 depicts the directed graph of our hypothetical network. The direction of the arrows represents the cost of the path from a router to another router. The arcs with no value were explained in the previous paragraph. You might notice that only one directional arrow is drawn from the

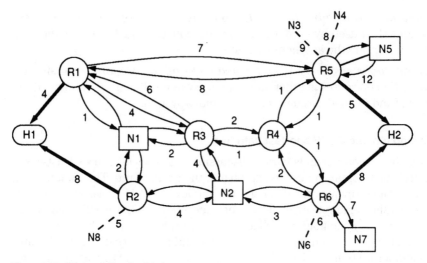

Figure 8.28 Directed Graph with Arcs.

routers to the hosts. In accordance with the rules of OSPF directed graphs, the figure shows what are known as *point-to-point networks,* in which a network is joined by a single router or a single pair of routers. This situation is depicted by the connection having one arrow in the direction of the host.

Based on the values obtained with the directed graph, OSPF creates a pruned tree representing the shortest (best) path between a router and all other nodes. Each router develops its own tree, and the router acts as the root in performing these calculations. Eventually, after messages have been exchanged between the routers and the topological database has been built, the tree provides the destination to any network or host within the autonomous system.

In these examples, routers R2, R6, and R5 are responsible for providing connections to other autonomous systems. As explained earlier, these routers make their connections known to the other routers in the autonomous system through type 1 or type 2 metrics.

Finally, Figure 8.29 shows the pruned tree as viewed by R1. It is quite similar to the tree developed in the previous discussion of algorithm A, except that the nodes have been relabeled as routers, networks, and hosts, and no costs are associated with the output ports of the networks and hosts.

The tree and an accompanying topological database provide R1 with a route to all hosts and routers in the autonomous system. Once again, emphasis is on the arcs from N1 to R2 and N1 to R3. No values are associated with these arcs because OSPF is designed as a gateway protocol. The direction of these arcs shows that the network does not furnish information to the routers. In a sense, the routers establish virtual connections between themselves across transit networks. In this example, N1 is a transit network. Certainly, these connections are significant as far as the least-cost-path value is concerned. In such a situation, the link state advertisement for a network (N1) must be generated by one of its attached routers, which is identified as the designated router for that network.

Based on this discussion, imagine the topological database that is built by R4. Indeed, you may wish to experiment with Figure 8.27 and draw the pruned tree as viewed by R4. To assist you in this exercise, the routing table for R4, based on Figure 8.27, is shown in Table 8.9. (The host entries, H1 and H2, are usually not stored at a remote router.)

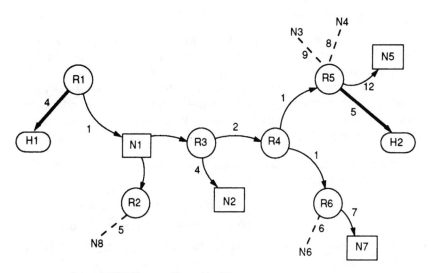

Figure 8.29 Pruned OSPF Tree, as Viewed by R1.

TABLE 8.9   R4 Routing Table

Destination	Next hop	Distance metric
H1	R3	7
H2	R5	6
N1	R3	3
N2	R6	4
N3	R5	10
N4	R5	9
N5	R5	13
N6	R6	7
N7	R6	8
N8	R3	8
R1	R3	3
R2	R3	3
R3	R3	1
R5	R5	1
R6	R5	1

OSPF data structures

OSPF operates with five data structures. These data structures contain the information needed by OSPF to perform its operations. The data structures discussed in this section are

- protocol data structures
- area data structures (and backbone data structures)
- interface data structures
- neighbor data structures
- routing table structures

A useful way to view these data structures is depicted in Figure 8.30. The *protocol data structure* consists of high-level data structures used in the autonomous system. Next are the *area data structures,* which contain information about the area. Following are the *interface* and *neighbor data structures,* which contain information on the router-to-network and router-to-router operations, respectively. Last is the *routing table structure* stored at the routers and containing information for routing an IP packet.

Protocol data structure. This high-level OSPF data structure provides the following information and services:

Router ID: the 32-bit identifier of the autonomous system router.

Area structure pointers: ID to each area with which the router is concerned.

Backbone structures pointer: ID to the backbone structure, which is the same as an area structure.

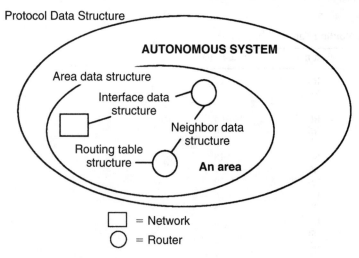

Figure 8.30 OSPF Data Structures.

Virtual links configured: ID of the router at the other end of virtual circuits.

External routes list: list of routes external to this autonomous system.

Routing table: contains an entry for each destination to which the router can forward traffic.

Area data structure. This data structure provides the following information and services:

Area ID: the identifier of the area.

Address ranges: a list of IP addresses that define the area. A network is associated with an area depending on its IP address value.

Router interfaces: the ID of those router interfaces that belong to the area.

Advertisements lists: Description of the following information:
Network links: advertisements of each router connected to a network.
Summary links: advertisements from border routers of routes with the autonomous system.
Router links: advertisements to routers in the area.

Shortest path tree: the pruned tree, with this router as the root, based on the Dijkstra method described earlier in this chapter.

Authentication type: The type of authentication (none, simple password) used in this area.

Interface data structures. This data structure describes the router and network connection. The interface belongs to the area in which the network resides. The following information and services are provided by the interface data structure:

Interface type: type of attached network—broadcast, multiaccess (such as a packet-switched network with two or more routers), point-to-point, or virtual.

State: current state of the interface (down, waiting, etc.). (OSPF works with states and state transition diagrams.)

IP address: IP address for this interface.

IP mask: subnet mask for this interface.

Area ID: area associated with the network.

HelloInterval: time between a router issuing Hello packets on this interface.

DeadInterval: time at which the machine considers a router down and will not accept Hello packets.

InfTransDelay: estimated time to send an update packet on this interface.

Router priority: priority of the router on this interface (highest priority becomes the designated router for this network).

Hello timer: interval at which the Hello packet is launched (every HelloInterval seconds).

Wait timer: interval at which this interface looks for a designated router (every DeadInterval seconds).

Neighboring routers: list of all routers attached to this network.

Routers: IDs of designated router and backup router.

Output cost(s): metric cost of sending traffic on this interface, possibly based on each IP TOS.

RxmInterval: timer of issuing link state advertisement retransmissions.

Authentication key: value to verify an authentication field in the OSPF header.

Neighbor data structure. This data structure is used between neighboring routers to control router roles and backup operations. The following information and services are provided by the neighbor data structure:

State: states of the neighbor communications process (down, exchange, etc.). (Neighbor routers operate with states and state transitions machines.)

Inactivity timer: reveals that a Hello packet has not been received from this neighbor.

Master/slave: relationship of the neighbor routers.

Sequence number: values used to coordinate exchange of packets between neighbors.

Neighbor ID: neighbor router ID.

Neighbor priority (PRI): router priority used to select a designated router and its backup router.

IP address: neighbor router's IP address.

Routers: IDs of neighbor's designated router and designated backup router.

Lists: three lists are used to manage link state advertisements:
   Link state retransmission: advertisements not yet ACKed.
   Database summary: list of advertisements that constitute the area's database.
   Link state requests: advertisements still needed from a neighbor to synchronize the database.

Routing table structure. The OSPF routing table structure is used by IP packet forwarding. It contains the entries in our previous example (Table 8.9) along with other values. The entries in the table are as follows:

Destination: the destination's IP address (and mask).

Destination type: a network, border, or boundary router.

Type of service: possibly a separate set of routers for each TOS.

Area: area whose link information led to this entry in the table. Multiple entries are possible if two border routers share common areas.

Path type: intra-area, inter-area, or external-to-autonomous systems.

Cost: full cost to the destination.

Next hop: next hop (router) for the datagram.

Advertising router: used for inter-area and autonomous system links.

The OSPF packets. This section describes the formats of the OSPF packets. OSPF runs over IP and relies on IP for fragmentation services for large OSPF packets. In addition, some OSPF packets are multicast. OSPF requires the reservation of two multicast addresses:

ALLSPFrouters: multicast address reserved for all routers that support OSPF. Its value is 224.0.0.5.

ALLrouters: address reserved for the designated router and a designated backup router. The address value is 224.0.0.6.

RFC1010 identifies the OSPF with IP protocol number 89. The OSPF routing protocol packets are always sent in an IP datagram with the IP TOS value equal to zero. It is recommended that OSPF packets be treated as high-priority traffic and given precedence over regular IP traffic. The IP precedence field is useful in this situation.

The OSPF packet header. Figure 8.31 illustrates the 24-octet OSPF packet header. Each OSPF packet is appended with this header. The *version* number describes which version of the protocol is currently used (currently version 2). The *type* field identifies the type of packet. It can contain one of the following values:

1 = Hello

2 = database description

3 = link state request

4 = link state update

5 = link state ACK

The *packet-length* field indicates the length of the field in octets, including the OSPF header.

The *router ID* field contains the identification of the source of the packet. The *area ID* identifies the area from which the packet is transmit-

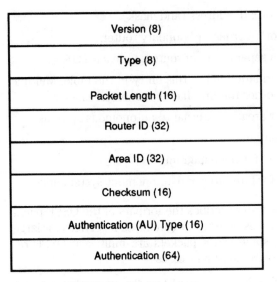

Version (8)
Type (8)
Packet Length (16)
Router ID (32)
Area ID (32)
Checksum (16)
Authentication (AU) Type (16)
Authentication (64)

Figure 8.31 OSPF Packet Header.

ted. The *checksum* field performs an IP-type checksum on the entire packet, including the authentication field.

The *authentication type (AUType)* identifies the type of authentication that is used. Presently, two authentication types are used: 0 for none and 1 for a simple password. Finally, the *authentication* field contains the value used by the authentication scheme. The authentication field can be established on a per-area basis.

The link state advertisement header. OSPF uses one other header type: the link state advertisement header. This header constitutes the topological database. Its purpose is to identify each advertisement between the routers. The format for the header is shown in Figure 8.32. All link state advertisements must use this header, which consists of 20 octets.

The *LS age* field contains (in seconds) the time since the link state advertisement originated. The options field contains IP TOS values supported by the sender. The *LS type* describes the type of link advertisement, which further defines a format for the advertisement (discussed shortly). This field can be set to the following values:

1 = router links (data on router-to-area interfaces)

2 = network links (data on router-to-network interfaces)

3 = summary link (data IP network)

4 = summary link (data on autonomous system border router)

5 = AS external link (data on destinations external-to-autonomous system)

The *link state ID* field identifies that portion of the internet being described in the advertisement. Its contents can take values to depict router IDs and IP network numbers; the value depends on the LS type field.

The *advertising-router* field is the identifier of the originating router for the link state advertisement. The *LS sequence number* is used to sequence the advertisements to detect duplicate or old packets. The *LS checksum* field is used to perform an error check on the contents of the packet. Finally, the *length* field contains the size of the advertisement in octets, including the 20-octet header.

The Hello packet. The Hello packet is used in OSPF to perform operations between adjacent neighbors. Parameters in the Hello packet allow the router neighbors to agree upon operating parameters, such as common network mask, Hello interval, and dead interval.

The contents of the Hello packet are depicted in Figure 8.33. The *OSPF header* is required for the packet. The next field is the *network mask* that is associated with the interface. The *Hello interval (HelloInt)* field contains a value representing the number of seconds before the router sends another Hello packet. The options field contains the IP TOS values supplied by the sender. The *dead interval (DeadInt)* field contains a value that describes the number of seconds before a router is declared down. The *router priority (Rtr Pri)* field defines if a router is designated as a backup. If this field is set to zero, the router is not allowed to become a designated backup router. The *designated router* field contains the identity of the router for the network in question. If this value is set to zero, there is no designated

LS Age (16)
Options (8)
LS Type (8)
Link State ID (32)
Advertising Router (32)
LS Sequence Number (32)
LS Checksum (16)
Length (16)

Figure 8.32 Link State Advertisement Header.

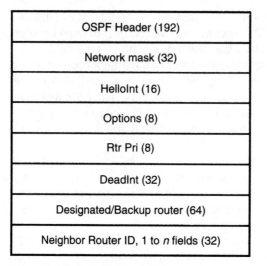

OSPF Header (192)
Network mask (32)
HelloInt (16)
Options (8)
Rtr Pri (8)
DeadInt (32)
Designated/Backup router (64)
Neighbor Router ID, 1 to *n* fields (32)

Figure 8.33   Hello Packet for OSPF.

router. The *backup router* field contains the identity of the designated backup router for the network in regard to the advertising router. Finally, the repeating fields designated *neighbor router ID* contain the IDs of each router that have recently sent Hello packets on the network. *Recently* is defined by the value in the DeadInt field.

Figure 8.34 illustrates the operations when a router has received a Hello packet. Upon receiving this packet, the OSPF logic performs editing checks on the IP and OSPF headers. If any errors occur, the packet is discarded and processing stops. If no errors occur, OSPF checks the network mask, Hello interval, and DeadInt fields for proper matches with the configuration at this interface.

If the "no mismatches" occur, OSPF checks for the source of the Hello packet. If the source is not currently contained in its neighbor data structure, it creates a skeleton neighbor data structure for this source. The creation of the neighbor structure at this point consists of the insertion of the neighbor ID, the state of the interface, and the neighbor IP address. If there is a "match in neighbor data structure (NDS)," OSPF examines and stores the list of neighbors contained in the Hello packet. OSPF then examines the router priority field in the Hello packet and stores this information in the neighbor data structure. Additionally, it notes the designated router and backup router and stores this information in the neighbor data structure.

Once the Hello packet has been processed, OSPF then executes logic to establish or reestablish designated routers (DRs) and designated backup routers (DBURs). This process is shown in Figure 8.35. First, OSPF discards any ineligible routers (those routers that have a priority value of 0). Next, all attached routers are examined in relation to the information received in the Hello packets. Two major steps are involved in establishing routers and backup routers. In step 1 of Figure 8.35, the designated backup router is chosen by examining the priority field relating to that router. In step 2, the designated router is established. Note that if no router has de-

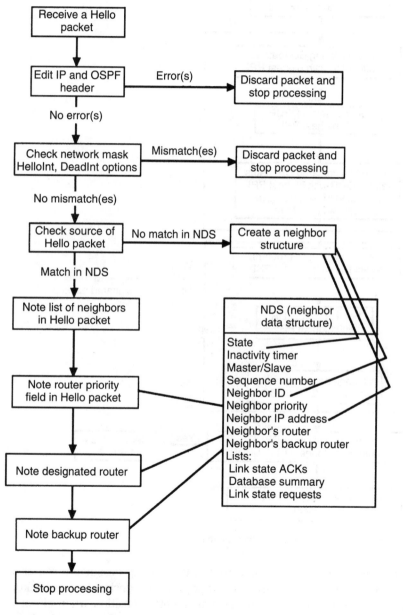

Figure 8.34 Processing Hello Packet.

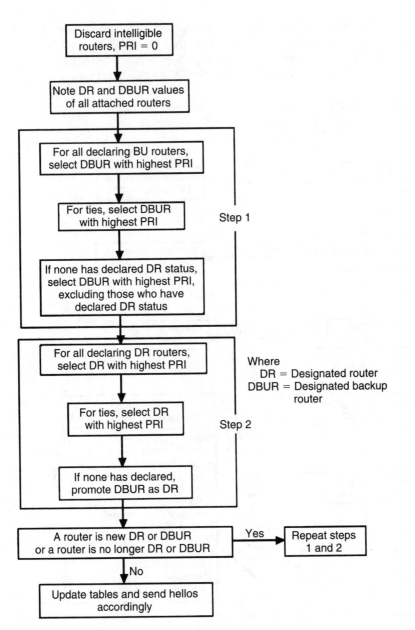

Figure 8.35 Establishing Routers and Backup Routers.

clared itself to be the designated router, the backup designated router is promoted. Steps 1 and 2 are then repeated to redesignate the backup router. The logic is designed to allow a smooth transition when either a backup or designated backup router fails in an internet. It is possible that a router could, for a time, be designated as both a router and a backup router. Once this router detects that the primary router is inoperable, however, the logic requires that it remove itself as a designated router.

The database description packet. The purpose of the database description packet is to initialize a database at a router. The database packet can contain information on part of the pieces of the topological database or the entire topology. These packets are managed through a master/slave relationship. One of the routers is designated as a master and the other becomes a slave. The master sends polls in the database description packets, which must be acknowledged by database description responses.

The format of the database description packet is illustrated in Figure 8.36. The *OSPF header* is required for this packet. The options field was described earlier, and the next two octets are reserved and set to zero.

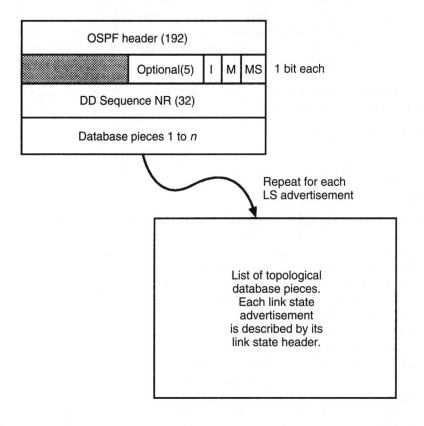

= Reserved and set to 0

Figure 8.36 Database Description Packet.

Three bits are used in the next octet, labeled the *I bit*, the *M bit*, and the *MS bit*. The *I bit*, when set to 0, indicates that the packet is the first in a sequence of packets to follow. The *M bit* is the more-data bit. When set to 1 it means that more database description packets follow. The *MS bit* designates the master/slave. When set to 1 it indicates that the originating router of the packet is the master. When set to 0, the originating router is the slave.

The *DD sequence number (NR)* is used to sequence the packets between the master and the slave. The number is incremented by 1 with each transmission of a packet. The remainder of the packet field repeats the number of advertisements for each piece of the topological database. The *link state type*, *link state ID*, the *advertising router*, *LS sequence number*, *LS checksum*, and *LS age* have been described previously in this chapter.

The link state request packet. The purpose of the link state request packet is to request additional information about a topological database from a neighbor (see Figure 8.37). Typically, this packet is exchanged when it is discovered that pieces of the database are missing or out of date. The contents of this packet are the *OSPF header* and repeating fields for *LS type*, *link state ID*, and *advertising router*.

The link state update packets. The link state update packets are used to provide four types of updates:

- router links
- network links
- summary links
- AS external links

Each of these four types of update packets contains different formats. To provide an example of the use of these packets, Figure 8.38 depicts a router that has three links in an internet, labeled link 1, link 2, and link 3. Additionally, each link is labeled with the TOS required. Link 1's TOS requires low delay and high reliability. Link 2 requires high throughput. Link 3 has no additional TOS beyond the default value of 0.

When a link-state refresh timer expires or when a link state changes, the router advertises this information to its neighbors through these four types of packets. The advertisement is sent to the neighbors, which are then sent to the next neighbors. Eventually, all advertisements are flooded throughout the area. Figure 8.39 shows the principal advertisement packet of OSPF designated as the router links advertisement packet. It is drawn in this figure to illustrate how information is repeated for each link of the router and each TOS feature on each link.

The *OSPF header* is placed in front of the packet, as are the number of advertisements. Each router in an area originates this advertisement to describe the state and cost of the router's links in its respective area.

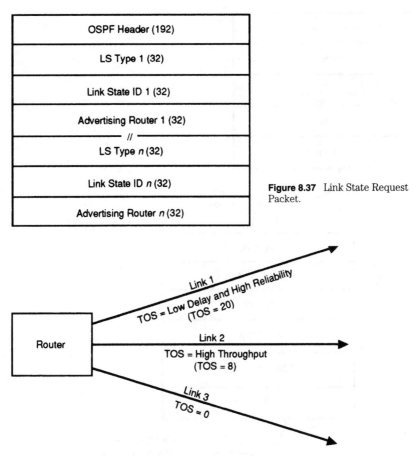

OSPF Header (192)
LS Type 1 (32)
Link State ID 1 (32)
Advertising Router 1 (32)
//
LS Type n (32)
Link State ID n (32)
Advertising Router n (32)

Figure 8.37 Link State Request Packet.

Figure 8.38 Example of Link State Update.

The E bit set to 1 identifies the router as an area boundary router. The B bit set to 0 identifies the router as a border router. The NR links depicts how many links are advertised in this packet. The link ID describes the object that the link connects, and its value depends upon the link's type. The link data field value also depends upon the link's type field. The type field can be any of the following:

- point-to-point interface with another router
- interface to a transit network
- interface to a subnetwork
- interface to a virtual link

The NR TOS field contains the number of TOS metrics for the link. The TOS 0 metric field is the cost of using this link for TOS 0, which must always be included.

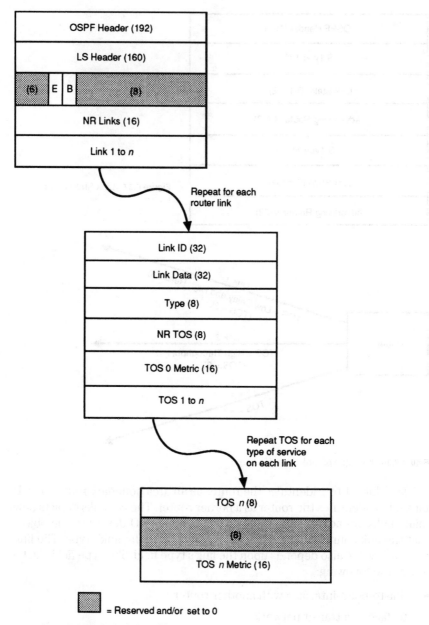

Figure 8.39 Router Links Advertisement Packet.

Finally, the figure shows repeating sets of fields designated as *TOS n* and *TOS n metric*, which are contained in the packet for each TOS value for each link. In our example, two sets of these fields would exist for link 1, one set for link 2, and none for link 3.

Figure 8.40 depicts the remaining three formats for the link state update packets. These three formats (starting at the top of the figure) are used to advertise network links, summary links, and AS external links, respectively.

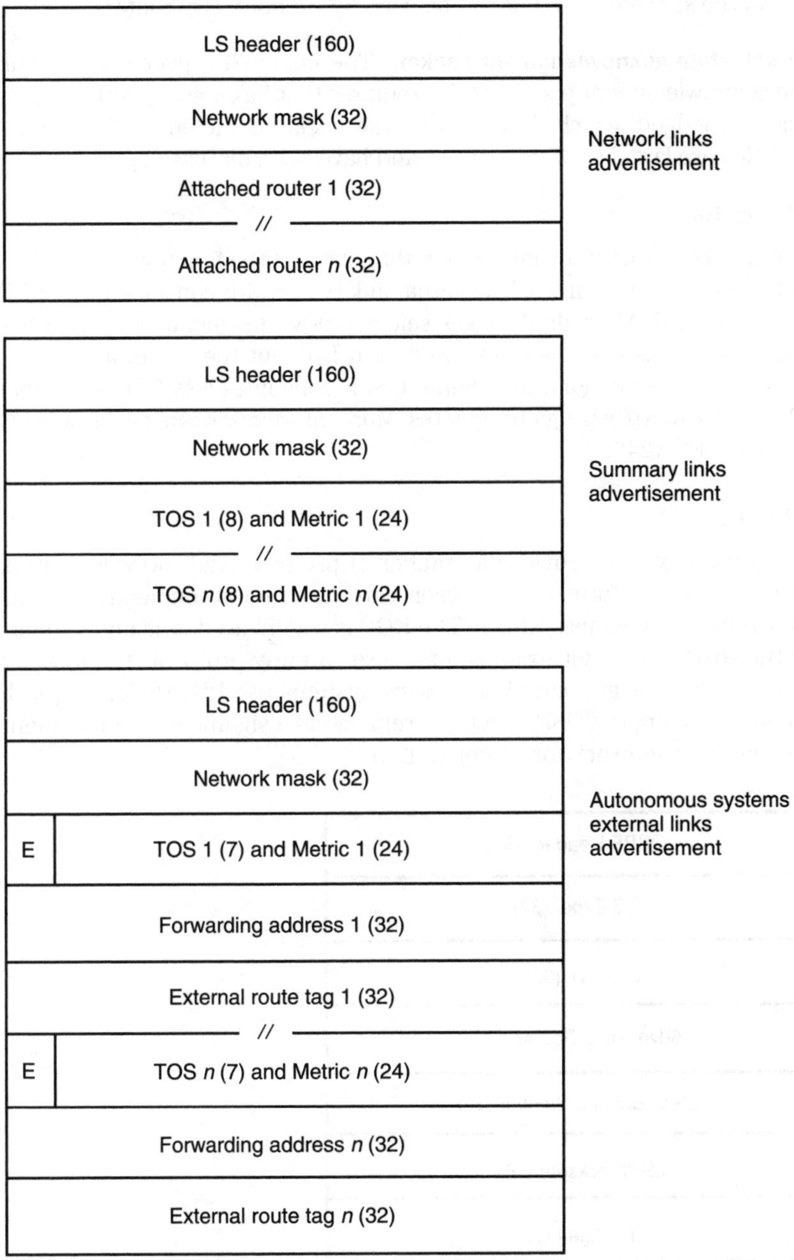

LS header (160)	
Network mask (32)	Network links advertisement
Attached router 1 (32)	
—— // ——	
Attached router n (32)	

LS header (160)	
Network mask (32)	Summary links advertisement
TOS 1 (8) and Metric 1 (24)	
—— // ——	
TOS n (8) and Metric n (24)	

	LS header (160)	Autonomous systems external links advertisement
	Network mask (32)	
E	TOS 1 (7) and Metric 1 (24)	
	Forwarding address 1 (32)	
	External route tag 1 (32)	
	—— // ——	
E	TOS n (7) and Metric n (24)	
	Forwarding address n (32)	
	External route tag n (32)	

Figure 8.40 Link State Update Packets.

Most fields in these three formats have been discussed previously in this chapter. The forwarding address field identifies the address that receives data traffic for the advertised destination. The external route tag is not defined in the specification, but can be used by AS boundary routers.

The link state acknowledgment packet. The final OSPF packet is the link state acknowledgment packet. OSPF requires that link state advertisements be acknowledged, which they are with the packet depicted in Figure 8.41. The fields are largely self-descriptive and have been discussed previously.

OSPF vs. RIP

You might be left with the impression that, with all the functions of OSPF, it must use a lot of resources. The actual link bandwidth consumed by OSPF is less than RIP. After all, it makes selected advertisements. On the other hand, OSPF consumes more memory than RIP, but the use of area partitioning can save memory. In general, OSPF consumes less CPU time than RIP, because of RIP's frequent updates. More information is available in RFC 1245 and RFC 1246.

Summary

The Internet system provides a number of protocols that provide routing and reachability information between gateways and autonomous systems and within autonomous systems. The EGP is widely used in many systems, and the GGP is an older example of a core gateway protocol. The internal gateway protocols are varied, and many systems use RIP, Hello, or gated. Without question, the OSPF protocol represents a significant improvement in the Internet internetworking operations.

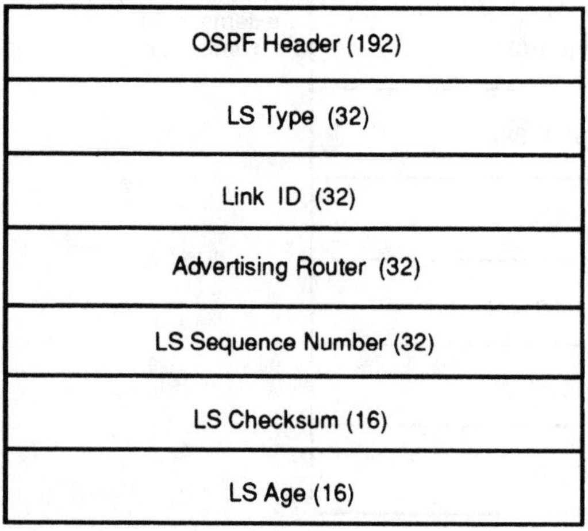

OSPF Header (192)
LS Type (32)
Link ID (32)
Advertising Router (32)
LS Sequence Number (32)
LS Checksum (16)
LS Age (16)

Figure 8.41 Link State Acknowledgment Packet.

The Major
Application-Layer Protocols

This chapter examines the application-layer protocols that are used by many internet installations. Some of these protocols are very rich in function, and a full explanation of their operations would require an extensive discourse. Our goal here is to provide a general overview of the major services they offer to an end user. The protocols covered in this chapter are the following:

TELNET: for terminal services

trivial file transfer protocol (TFTP): for simple file transfer services

file transfer protocol (FTP): for more elaborate file transfer services

simple mail transfer protocol (SMTP): for message transfer services (electronic mail)

In most vendor products, the execution of these protocols is easy, usually no more complex than entering one or a few terminal commands or clicking on an icon on the computer screen. This part of the description is best left to the vendor-specific user manuals. This chapter concentrates on the architectures of these protocols, rather than their execution.

The TELNET Protocol

To begin this discussion, imagine that a manager is responsible for a computer operations center. A host computer in the operations center is tasked with supporting the communications operations among many terminals that have different characteristics. For example, a user at a DEC terminal needs to communicate with a user at a Hewlett-Packard terminal. Communication is not so easy. Both devices use different screen and keyboard control characters, and both use different line protocols for managing traffic on the communications link.

If the host computer needs to support a wide variety of terminals, precious resources are consumed in machine CPU cycles to resolve protocol differences, and the design and coding of supporting software to translate the protocols is an expensive undertaking. The manager of the computer operations center must spend a great deal of time and expend considerable resources developing or acquiring systems that provide translation facilities between the different machines.

TELNET provides solutions to these problems. For example, it defines a procedure that permits host computers to learn about the characteristics of terminals attached to other hosts with which they communicate. Equally important, TELNET provides conventions for the negotiation of a number of functions and services for a terminal-based session between two machines. This approach ameliorates the protocol conversion problem because the negotiating machines have the option of not using a service that cannot be supported by both machines. TELNET does not perform any protocol conversion between different machines. Rather, it provides a mechanism that determines the characteristics of the machines and a means to negotiate the interworking of the machines to exchange data.

The TELNET protocol allows a program on a host machine (called the *TELNET client*) to access the resources of another machine (called the *TELNET server*) as if the client were attached locally to the server (see Figure 9.1). Although TELNET provides a variety of features, some people call the standard a *remote login* protocol because it supports a remote device's login with a host machine. Be aware that other "remote login" protocols exist besides TELNET. For example, the SUN workstation has a remote login (R login) procedure.

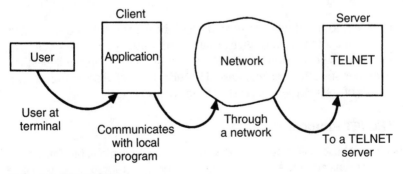

Figure 9.1 TELNET Model.

Network virtual terminal

The TELNET standard is based on the idea of a network virtual terminal (NVT). The term *virtual* is used because an NVT does not actually exist; it is an imagined device that provides a standard means of representing a terminal's characteristics. The idea is to relieve the host computers from the tasks of maintaining characteristics about every terminal with which they are communicating. With the TELNET standard, both the user and server devices are required to map their terminal characteristics into the virtual terminal description. The end result is that the devices appear to be communicating with the NVT because both parties are providing a complementary mapping.

Negotiations. The TELNET protocol, similar to other virtual terminal protocols, allows the communicating machines to *negotiate* a variety of options to be used during the session. The server and client are required to use a standard set of procedures to establish these options. These options are examined during the analysis of the TELNET protocol.

The use of negotiated options considers the possibility that host machines can provide services beyond those provided by the virtual terminal. Moreover, the TELNET model does not restrict the negotiated options solely to those stipulated in the protocols. Rather, TELNET allows the negotiation of different conventions beyond the TELNET specifications.

TELNET RFCs

The Internet standards include several Requests for Comments (RFCs) that describe the TELNET options that can be negotiated. Table 9.1 provides a list of TELNET option codes, along with their number and the relevant RFCs, if available. Do not assume that all these options are provided in each vendor product; many TELNET products do not support all available options.

TABLE 9.1   TELNET Option Codes

Number	Name	RFC
0	Binary transmission	856
1	Echo	857
2	Reconnection	NIC 15391
3	Suppress go ahead	858
4	Approximate message size negotiation	NIC 15393
5	Status	859
6	Timing mark	860
7	Remote controlled trans and echo	726
8	Output line width	NIC 20196
9	Output page size	NIC 20197
10	Output carriage-return disposition	652

TABLE 9.1   TELNET Option Codes (Continued)

Number	Name	RFC
11	Output horizontal tabstops	653
12	Output horizontal tab disposition	654
13	Output form feed disposition	655
14	Output vertical tabstops	656
15	Output vertical tab disposition	657
16	Output line feed disposition	658
17	Extended ASCII	698
18	Logout	727
19	Byte macro	735
20	Data entry terminal	732
21	SUPDUP	736
22	SUPDUP output	749
23	Send location	779
24	Terminal type	930
25	End of record	885
26	TACACS user identification	927
27	Output marking	933
28	Terminal location number	946
29	3270 regime	1041
30	X.3 PAD	1053
31	Window size	1073

Figure 9.2 shows how the options can be negotiated between two parties. One party can begin the negotiation by inquiring to another party about a particular option (function x in the figure). The response in this figure says that the responding party can support the option. Next, the initiating party asks for the characteristics of the option from the responding party. The responding party then sends its information about the option. This information describes characteristics of the responding party's terminal or other operating requirements.

The messages flowing between the two parties must adhere to a TELNET message format (called the *command structure*). For example, the initial signal of "do you support" or "will you support" is established by the special TELNET codes *do* or *will*. In turn, the responder must return a TELNET code (in this example, the responder returns the *will* code).

Table 9.2 lists the names of the codes, their numeric values placed in the TELNET message, and a brief description of their meaning. The table includes six line entries describing the six TELNET functions. These functions are common across almost all terminal-based applications; therefore, the TELNET standard defines a standard means of representing them.

The *interrupt process* function allows a system to suspend, interrupt, abort, or terminate a user process. For example, it allows a user to terminate an operation to get out of an endless loop.

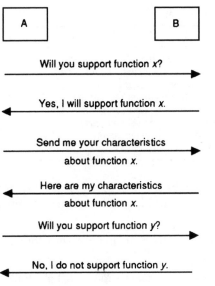

Will you support function *x*?

Yes, I will support function *x*.

Send me your characteristics about function *x*.

Here are my characteristics about function *x*.

Will you support function *y*?

No, I do not support function *y*.

Figure 9.2   TELNET Negotiations.

The *abort output (AO)* function allows an application to run to completion but not send the output to the user's workstation. This function also clears output stored but not yet displayed.

The *are you there (AYT)* function is a useful operation invoked when a user wishes to know that the application is executing. Typically, the AYT function is invoked if a user has not received messages for an extended time.

TABLE 9.2   TELNET Command Codes

Code name	Value	Meaning
SE	240	End of subnegotiation parameters
NOP	241	No operation
Data mark	242	The data stream portion of a sync
Break	243	BRK character
Interrupt process	244	The IP function
Abort output	245	The AO function
Are you there	246	The AYT function
Erase character	247	The EC function
Erase line	248	The EL function
Go ahead	249	The GA function
SB	250	Subnegotiation of the indicated option
Will (option code)	251	Begin performing, or confirmation that device is now performing the indicated option
Won't (option code)	252	Refusal to perform or continue to perform the indicated option

TABLE 9.2 TELNET Command Codes (Continued)

Code name	Value	Meaning
Do (option code)	253	The request that the other party perform, or confirm that you expect the other party to perform, the indicated option
Don't (option code)	254	Demands that the other party stop performing, or confirm that party is no longer expecting the other party to perform, the indicated option
IAC	255	Interpret as command

The *erase character (EC)* function enables the user to delete a character in a stream of data. In its simplest form, it is used to edit data on a screen if input mistakes are made.

The *erase line (EL)* function allows a user to delete an entire line for editing purposes.

The *go ahead (GA)* function allows the session to follow a half-duplex transmission sequence.

In addition to the codes described in Table 9.2, TELNET has a number of codes for manipulating hard copy output on a printer. The codes are quite similar to their virtual terminal protocols, such as the ITU-T X.3 PAD Recommendation. These codes perform operations such as horizontal tab (HT), vertical tab (VT), form feed (FF), back space (BS), Bell (BEL), line feed (LF), carriage return (CR), etc.

TELNET commands

The TELNET data unit is called a *command,* and the format is depicted in Figure 9.3 (the different commands were already described in Table 9.2; options in Table 9.1). If three bytes are used, the first byte is the *interpret as command (IAC)* byte, which is a reserved code in TELNET. It is also an escape character because it is used by the receiver to detect if the incoming traffic is not data but a TELNET command. The next byte is the *command code*, used in conjunction with the IAC byte to describe the type of command. The third byte is called the *option negotiation* code. It is used to define a number of options to be used during the session.

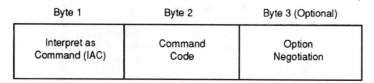

Byte 1	Byte 2	Byte 3 (Optional)
Interpret as Command (IAC)	Command Code	Option Negotiation

Figure 9.3 TELNET Command Format.

Example of TELNET commands

The RFCs listed in Table 9.1 should be studied if you wish to gain an in-depth understanding of the many functions of TELNET terminals. This section provides an example of one of these functions: the echo service.

Echoes are used in practically all workstation environments to allow the data entered on the keyboard to be placed (echoed) onto the screen. In some situations, the echo occurs only locally. In others, the echo is sent to the receiving machine and then echoed back to the transmitting machine. The particular implementation of the echo depends on the type of hardware and software that exists on the workstations.

The TELNET echo option allows two users to determine how echoing will occur during the session. The command format for the echo is as follows (the values in parentheses represent the IAC, command code, and option negotiation parameter explained in Figure 9.3 and Table 9.1):

```
IAC WILL ECHO (255 251 1)
```

This command allows a user to begin echoing the characters it receives over the connection back to the sender of the data characters. Conversely, the command:

```
IAC WON'T ECHO (255 252 1)
```

specifies that the sender of this command will not echo, or wishes to stop echoing, the data characters it receives back to the sender.

Another command is used to request that the receiver of the command begin echoing. This command takes the form:

```
IAC DO ECHO (255 253 1)
```

The last TELNET echo command is used by the sender to require the receiver of the command either to stop or not start echoing characters it receives over the connection. This is formatted as:

```
IAC DON'T ECHO (255 254 1)
```

The TELNET echo option defaults to *won't echo* and *don't echo*. That is, no echoing is done over the connection.

Another commonly used option is the transmit binary, in which the data stream is interpreted as 8-bit binary images. To request permission to use this service, the sender issues:

```
IAC WILL TRANSMIT-BINARY (255 251 0)
```

The sender of the next command, if it does not want the connection to be operated with the transmit binary option, issues:

```
IAC DON'T TRANSMIT-BINARY (255 254 0)
```

All the TELNET operations are conducted in a manner similar to these examples. Thus, the protocol is simple and easy to implement.

Trivial File Transfer Protocol

TFTP is appropriately named; it is a simple file transfer protocol. It is not as complex as FTP, nor does it have as many functions. It does not consist of much code, nor does it consume much memory; consequently, it can be used on small machines.

TFTP has no security provisions or user authentication provisions. Indeed, it has very little end-to-end reliability because it rests on the user datagram protocol (UDP). It does not use TCP. TFTP does have integrity checks, timer support, and retransmission capabilities.

Typically, the transmitter sends a fixed block of data (512 bytes) and waits for an acknowledgment from the receiver before sending the next block. This type of operation is known as a *flip-flop protocol*, because the transmitter must wait for an acknowledgment from the receiver before it sends the next block of data.

Each block is numbered sequentially, and the acknowledgment field contains the number of the block that has been acknowledged. The end of a message is detected by sending a fragmented block that consists of less than 512 bytes.

This protocol is not designed to be robust. Almost any type of problem causes a termination of the connection. TFTP does, however, provide some error messages, and it also supports timeouts to detect when messages have been lost.

Generally, errors occur in the following situations:

- one party is unable to satisfy a request (for example, the format of the request is ill-formed, a file cannot be located, etc.)
- a file can be found but the request cannot be fulfilled because the servicing party does not have sufficient resources
- other errors have occurred (such as duplication of a request)

TFTP is not used extensively today, although some vendors have brought it into their product line to ease compatibility problems. For example, IBM's TCP/IP product line for its personal computers implements the TFTP product to allow interaction between AIX and PC DOS machines.

TFTP and other protocols

As discussed earlier, TFTP runs over UDP. Because a user datagram header is encapsulated into an IP PDU, TFTP can rely on these lower-layer protocols to provide their services. For example, TFTP uses the UDP source and destination ports to map the two TFTP users onto the file transfer session. This operation is accomplished by the use of TFTP transfer identifiers (TIDs). They are created by TFTP and passed to the UDP, which places them in the port identifier fields in the datagram.

TFTP uses the concept of port binding (discussed in Chapters 1 and 7). To review, the initiator of the file transfer (say, host A) selects a value for the source TID. The source TID is set to any value, as determined by source A. The destination TID is the well-known port number 69 permanently assigned to TFTP. When host B returns an acknowledgment to the TFTP connection request, its source TID is 69, and its destination TID is the same identifier as host A's source TID.

TFTP packets

TFTP supports five types of PDUs, which are called *packets* in the standard:

- read request
- write request
- data
- acknowledgment
- error

The names of the packets describe their functions. The *read request (RRQ) packet* is transmitted to request a read operation on a foreign file. Conversely, the *write request (WRQ)* requests modification to a file. After receiving one of these requests, the foreign system returns an *acknowledgment data unit (ACK)*. This contains the block number 0. After these handshaking operations have occurred, the data packets *(DATA)* are transmitted. They contain sequence numbers that identify each block of data. The block numbers are sequentially numbered from a value of 1. The *error packet (ERROR)* contains information about problems that occurred during the operation.

The structure of these control packets is shown in Figure 9.4. The *opcode (operation code)* contains the values used to identify the type of packet. In the RRQ and WRQ packets, the opcode field is followed by the *filename* field. It identifies the file to be retrieved (typically performed with GET <remote filename> {<local filename>}) or the name of the file that is to receive the data using PUT <remote filename> {<local filename>}.

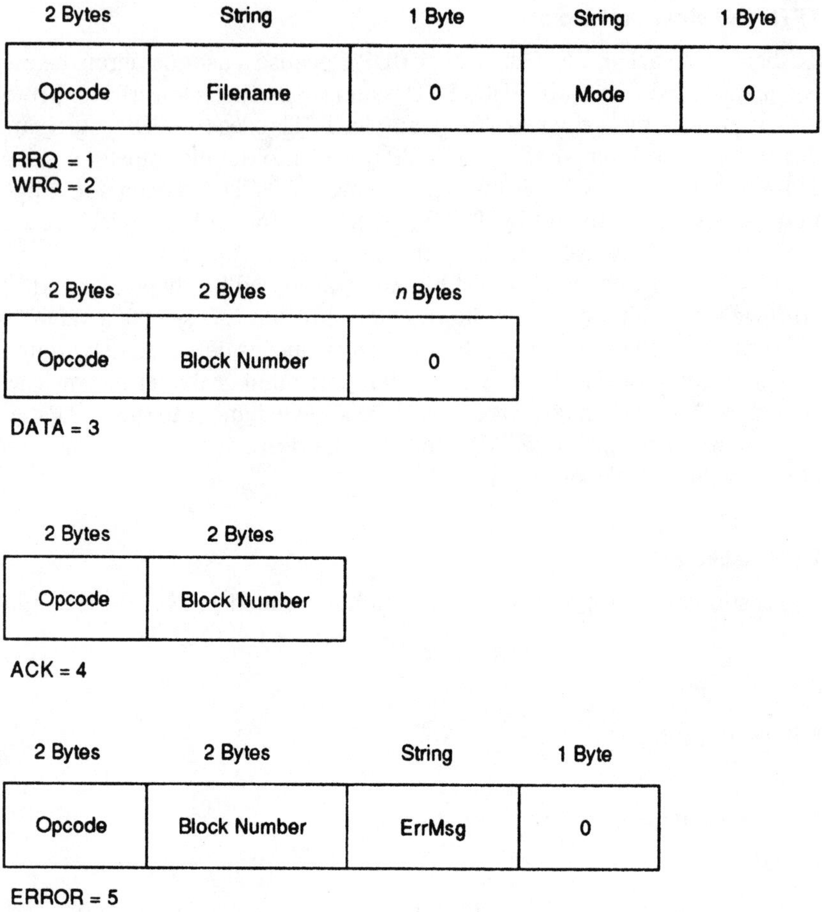

2 Bytes	String	1 Byte	String	1 Byte
Opcode	Filename	0	Mode	0

RRQ = 1
WRQ = 2

2 Bytes	2 Bytes	n Bytes
Opcode	Block Number	0

DATA = 3

2 Bytes	2 Bytes
Opcode	Block Number

ACK = 4

2 Bytes	2 Bytes	String	1 Byte
Opcode	Block Number	ErrMsg	0

ERROR = 5

Figure 9.4   TFTP Packets.

The *mode* field signifies the mode of transfer that is to take place during the operation. As established in RFC 783, three modes are supported in TFTP:

NetASCII: U.S. standard code for information interchange

Byte: 8-bit bytes or binary data

Mail: Traffic goes to a user rather than to a file, but code is still NetASCII

The block number (*block number*) in the *data packet* begins with the value 1 and is incremented by 1 with each succeeding packet transmittal. The *data field* is a fixed-length block of 512 bytes. The last block in the file transfer contains between 0 and 511 bytes of data (labeled 0 in the figure).

The *acknowledgment (ACK) packet* also contains a block number field. This field acknowledges the transmitted data. It uses the same value that was received in the block number in the data packet.

The *error packet* contains an *ErrMsg* field to describe six types of errors:

0 = not defined

1 = file not found

2 = access violation

3 = disk full or allocation exceeded

4 = illegal TFTP operation

5 = unknown transfer ID

Figure 9.5 shows the handshake and transfer operations between two machines using the TFTP standard. The initial handshaking activities are

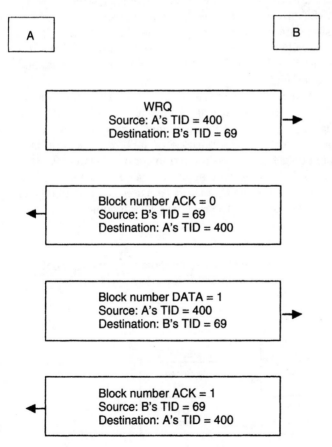

Figure 9.5   TFTP Operations.

accomplished with the WRQ and ACK transactions. Data are then sent and acknowledged as depicted in the third and fourth boxes of the figure.

File Transfer Protocol

The Internet standards include a more powerful and widely used file transfer protocol called the *file transfer protocol (FTP)*. FTP defines procedures for the transfer of files between two machines.

FTP is rather unusual in that it maintains two logical connections between the machines. One connection is used for the login between machines and uses the TELNET protocol. The other connection is used for data transfer. The concept is shown in Figure 9.6. The end *user* communicates with a *protocol interpreter (PI)*, which governs the control connection. The PI must transfer information between the user and the PI's *file system*. Commands and replies are transmitted between the user-PI and server-PI. As depicted in the figure, the other machine's (server's) PI responds to the TELNET protocol in managing connections.

During file transfer, data management is performed by the other logical connection, which is called the *data transfer process (DTP)*. Once the DTP has performed its functions and the user's request has been satisfied, the PI closes the connection.

FTP also permits transfers between a device other than the original server and client. This operation is typically known as a *third-party transfer*. As shown in Figure 9.7, a client opens a connection to two remote machines that both act as servers. The purpose of such a connection is to request that the client be given permission to transfer files between the two servers' file systems. If the requests are approved, one server forms a TCP connection with the other server and transfers data across the sending FTP module, the TCP modules, and into the receiving FTP module.

Data types

FTP is somewhat limited in its capability to support different *types* of data representation and the negotiation of the use of these types between ma-

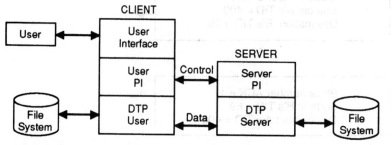

Figure 9.6 FTP Model.

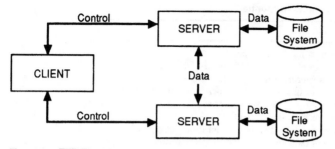

Figure 9.7 FTP Third-Party Transfer.

chines. The FTP user can specify a type that is to be used in the transfer (for example, ASCII, EBCDIC, etc.). ASCII is the default, and FTP requires that all implementations support ASCII code. EBCDIC is also supported and is used rather extensively in data transfer between mainframe host computers.

Both ASCII and EBCDIC use a second parameter to indicate if the characters will be used for format control purposes. For example, the carriage return (CR), line feed (LF), vertical tab (VT), and form feed (FF) can be defined as control characters during the FTP session.

FTP also supports the transfer of bit streams, which it calls *image types*. With this operation, the data are sent in continuous bit streams. For the actual transfer, they are packed into 8-bit bytes. Most operations use image types for transmitting binary images, and therefore most FTP implementations support the image type.

A local type is also supported. This type is transferred in bytes whose size are determined by a parameter called *byte size*. FTP requires that the byte size value be a decimal integer.

FTP commands and replies

FTP uses a number of *commands* for preliminary identification, password authentication, and file transfer operations. Table 9.3 lists the acronyms for these commands and a brief description of their functions.

TABLE 9.3 FTP Commands

Commands	Function
USER	Identifies the user; required by the server
PASS	User password; preceded by USER
ACCT	User account ID
CWD	Change working directory
CDUP	Change to parent directory
SMNT	Mount a different file system data structure
QUIT	Terminate connection
REIN	Terminate connection and start another
PORT	Port address

TABLE 9.3   FTP Commands (Continued)

Commands	Function
PASV	Request for passive-open
TYPE	Representation type (ASCII, EBCDIC, etc).
STRU	File structure = file, record, or page
MODE	Transfer mode = stream, block, or compressed
RETR	Transfer copy of file to other party
STOR	Accept data and store it
STOU	Accept data and store it under different name
APPE	Accept data and append it to another file
ALLO	Allocate (reserve) storage for operation
REST	Restart marker (checkpoint) at which transfer restarts
RNFR	Old pathname of file to be renamed
RNTO	New pathname of file to be renamed
ABOR	Abort previous FTP command and associated data transfer
DELE	Delete specified file at the server site
RMD	Remove directory
MKD	Create (make) a directory
PWD	Return (print) name of current working directory
LIST	Transfer list of directories, files, etc., to DTP
NLST	Transfer a directory listing to user site
SITE	Provide services specific to user site
SYST	Query to determine type of operating system at server
STAT	Return a status over the control connection
HELP	Retrieve helpful information from the server
NOOP	No operation

TABLE 9.4   FTP Reply Codes

Value code	Function
1yz	A positive preliminary reply that means the command action is being initiated. The invoker of the command can expect another reply before proceeding to a new command.
2yz	A positive completion reply that informs the invoker that the command action has been completed successfully, and a new request can be initiated.
3yz	A positive intermediate reply signifying that the command has been accepted, but the action is in a hold state because the performer needs additional information.
4yz	A transit negative completion reply signifying that the command is not accepted and an action did not take place. It also signifies a temporary error condition, and the action can be requested again.
5yz	A permanent negative completion reply stating that the action did not occur, the command is not accepted, and it is not expected that the reinitiation of the command will have any better success.

FTP also describes a number of *replies* used for the correct file transfer between the two processes. As the name suggests, these replies are invoked as a result of the FTP commands. The replies consist of a three-digit number followed by descriptive text. The first digit of the replies can take values from 0 to 5. This value is used to identify the five major types of replies. Table 9.4 lists the major types of replies and a brief description of their functions.

The y value of the reply codes can be coded to contain additional information about the nature of the reply. The type of reply in this code is identified by five values, 0 through 5, to define replies relating to status commands, syntax errors, authentication commands, control, data connection commands, etc. Table 9.5 lists and describes these codes.

The third digit defines an even finer level of detail about the meaning of the reply. These codes are numerous and beyond the scope of this book, but an example of their use is provided shortly. Refer to RFC 959 for more information on this level of detail about the FTP reply codes.

Sequence of operations in an FTP session

FTP follows several well-ordered steps to effect a data transfer between two users. These steps are discussed in this section in the order in which they occur.

Remote host login. Before data transfer can occur between two users, the login operation must be completed. One of the functions of this login is to ensure that passwords, authorization codes, and other security features have been satisfied. At a minimum, a user must have an acceptable user name and password available for the other host machine.

During the login process, it is possible to change some tables used to control the data transfer. This is a very useful function if a user wants different support services for different connections.

TABLE 9.5 FTP Reply Codes

Value code	Function
x0z	Identifies a syntax error; syntax is correct but the command makes no sense
x1z	Replies to requests for information, such as status
x2z	Replies that refer to connection management
x3z	Replies for authentication and accounting commands
x4z	Not specified
x5z	Replies on the status of file server system

Directory definition. This feature might or might not be needed, but once the control connection is available, it might be necessary to change a directory to manage the space in which the data will reside.

File transfer definition. Using the directory, this third operation defines the file to be transferred through a list of subcommands. FTP supports a very wide repertoire of subcommands. The most common are GET and PUT, which allow copying of the file from the remote host to a local file system, or from the local file system to the remote host.

Mode transfer definition. The next step in the FTP file transfer process involves defining the type of mode to be used during the transfer. Basically, this step entails defining how the data are to be represented and how the bits are to be transferred. FTP supports several subcommands to support these operations:

Block: This parameter preserves the logical record within the file. It transfers the file in the same format as input to the transmitting module.

Stream: This mode is a default mode for the transfer. It is quite efficient, sending no block control information. Stream mode does not care what type of data is transmitted, so it is code and block transparent.

TYPE: This mode is used with IMAGE, ASCII, or EBCDIC parameters.

ASCII: This mode is the default transfer mode for TYPE.

EBCDIC: EBCDIC is used frequently between hosts that use EBCDIC characters, such as IBM type machines.

IMAGE: This mode supports the transfer of contiguous binary bits packed in 8-bit bytes. It is the most widely used method for transferring straight binary data.

Starting the data transfer. This sequence of operations can begin with many of the FTP commands. For example, the retrieve command can be used to begin operations or the append command can be used to add records to an existing file.

Stopping the data transfer. This rather simple procedure involves the use of an FTP QUIT subcommand. This subcommand disconnects the host running the FTP operations. It might be preferable to issue the CLOSE subcommand, which does not cause a disconnection. If you use CLOSE, FTP stays active and another user can begin a new FTP session with the OPEN subcommand.

Examples of FTP operations

In this section, examples of the FTP protocol are provided to summarize the operations and piece together the FTP overview information provided so far.

FTP, similar to several other internet protocols, is state-driven. Consequently, it is useful to illustrate and explain several state diagrams with examples. Use the following definitions for all the examples:

B: The operations begin.

W: The protocol machine is waiting for a reply.

E: The operation was created in error.

S: The operation was a success.

F: The operation was a failure.

Each operation is depicted with the reply codes emanating from the function boxes. The reply codes are coded as $1yz$, $2yz$, $3yz$, $4yz$, and $5yz$, which were discussed earlier. Remember that the yz values give more specific information about the replies.

The general notation for these figures can be seen in Figure 9.8. The figure shows a code labeled CMD that begins the operation. This command creates a wait state, after which reply codes signify the success or failure of the operation. With this in mind, let us move to a discussion of several operations of FTP.

Refer again to Figure 9.8. This figure illustrates a state diagram modeled for many of the FTP operations. The model in Figure 9.8 supports the following commands: ABOR, DELE, CWD, CDUP, SMNT, HELP, MODE, NOOP, PASV, QUIT, SITE, PORT, SYST, STAT, RMD, MKD, PWD, STRU, and TYPE. (Refer back to Table 9.3 for a brief description of these commands.) You can simply insert one of these commands into the command notation (CMD) in the figure and follow the remainder of the flow chart to determine possible outcomes.

Figure 9.9 shows a similar state diagram, with the exception that reply code 1 entails the protocol machine returning back to a wait-to-reply state.

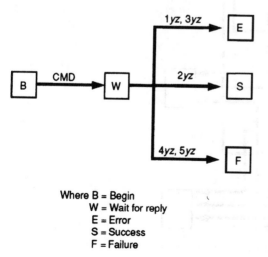

Where B = Begin
W = Wait for reply
E = Error
S = Success
F = Failure

Figure 9.8 FTP State Diagram for Elementary Operations.

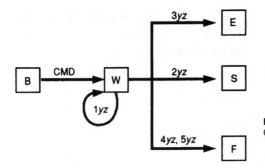

Figure 9.9 FTP State Diagram for Other Options.

This diagram supports the following commands: APPE, LIST, NLST, REIN, RETR, STOR, and STOU.

The last example, Figure 9.10, shows a rather complex state diagram. Figure 9.10 depicts the operations in state transitions for the login procedure. As depicted in the figure, the operation begins with the issuance of a USER message. Subsequently, the password (PASS) and accounting (ACCT) messages are issued to determine if the login is a success, failure, or error.

Example of a file retrieval

Figure 9.11 shows an example of a file retrieval. The top part of the figure depicts the permissible replies that can be returned from a retrieve (RETR) command. The bottom part of the figure shows the sequence of the replies. RFC 959 uses the following convention for documenting reply sequences: prelimi-

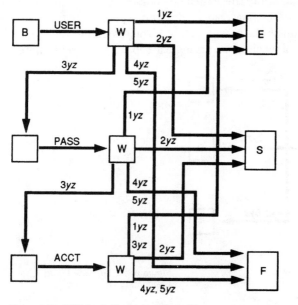

Figure 9.10 FTP Login Procedure State Diagram.

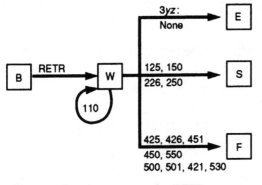

Command-reply sequence for RETR:

```
RETR
  125, 150

  (110)
  226, 250
  425, 426, 451
  450, 550
  500, 501, 421, 530
```

Figure 9.11 Example of Retrieve Operations.

nary replies are listed first, followed by succeeding replies (indented under the preliminary replies). Next are the positive and negative completion replies. To help analyze Figure 9.11, the reply codes for RETR are listed in Table 9.6. Remember that many other reply codes are also defined in the FTP standard.

Minimum implementation of FTP

All FTP implementations must support the minimum services and commands depicted in Box 9.1.

TABLE 9.6   Codes Relevant to Figure 9.11

Code	Meaning
125	Data connection already open; beginning the transfer
150	File status correct; about to open data connection
110	Remark marker reply
226	Closing data connection; action was successful
250	Request action successfully completed
425	Cannot open data connection
426	Connection closed; action aborted
451	Local error; action aborted
450	Requested action not taken; file unavailable (e.g., busy)
550	Requested action not taken; file unavailable (e.g., not found)
500	Syntax error; command cannot be interpreted
501	Syntax error; parameters cannot be interpreted
421	Service not available; closing control connection
530	Not logged in

Type:	ASCII, Nonprint
Mode:	Stream
Structure:	File, record
Commands:	USER, QUIT, PORT, TYPE, MODE, STRU, RETR, STRO, NOOP

Default values as follows:
TYPE:	ASCII, Nonprint
MODE:	Stream
STRU:	File

Box 9.1   Minimum implementation of FTP.

Simple Mail Transfer Protocol

The SMTP standard is one of the most widely used upper-layer protocols in the Internet Protocol stack. As its name implies, it defines how to transmit messages (mail) between two users.

SMTP uses the concept of *spooling*. The idea of spooling is to allow mail to be sent from a local application to the SMTP application, which stores the mail in a device or memory. Typically, once the mail has arrived at the spool, it has been queued. A server checks to see if any messages are available and then attempts to deliver them. If the user is not available for delivery, the server might try later. Eventually, if the mail cannot be delivered, it is discarded or returned to the sender. This concept is known as an *end-to-end delivery system* because the server attempts to contact the destination to deliver the mail, and it keeps the mail in the spool for a period of time until it has been delivered.

SMTP is found in two RFCs. RFC 822 describes the structure for the message, which includes the envelope as well. RFC 821 specifies the protocol that controls the exchange of mail between two machines.

SMTP model

Figure 9.12 illustrates a general model of SMTP. The operations begin with the sender-SMTP establishing communications with the receiver-SMTP. Before the transmission of the mail, the two SMTP entities might exchange passwords or other authentication signals. Next, the sender transmits a special command called "MAIL," which gives the sender's identification and other information for the mail exchange. The receiver must then return an acknowledgment to the MAIL command. In SMTP, this acknowledgment is written as 250, or in some documents as 250 OK. Regardless of the format, the acknowledgment means that the requested mail action was completed.

The next step in the procedure is the transmission of an RCPT command. Its purpose is to identify the destinations of the message. Again, an acknowledgment is required from each potential receiver.

The third step in the process is issuing the DATA command. This message is sent by the sender-SMTP to alert the receiver(s) that a message is forthcoming. The data are then transmitted, line by line, until the sender sends a special sequence of control characters to signal the end of the message. At this time, the server can choose to terminate the process with a *QUIT* command.

Address field format

The sender-SMTP uses a standard format for its sending address and receiving address fields. They take the form

```
local-part@domain-name
```

An SMTP name thus follows the domain name system (DNS) concept, and some systems use the same server facility to derive an IP address from this name.

In practice, this format scheme could appear as

```
Jones@beta.aus.edu
```

where the local person's name is Jones and `beta.aus.edu` is the domain identifier for the person.

The local-part@domain-name can take other forms to designate the following:

- a direct connection: user@host

- a mail receiver located at a non-SMTP host via a mail gateway: user%remote-host@gateway-host

- a relay between more than two hosts: @host-b@host-c@host-d

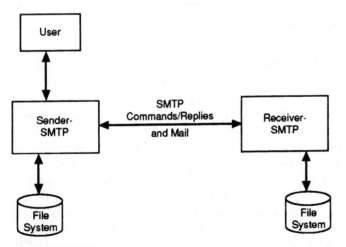

Figure 9.12 SMPT Model.

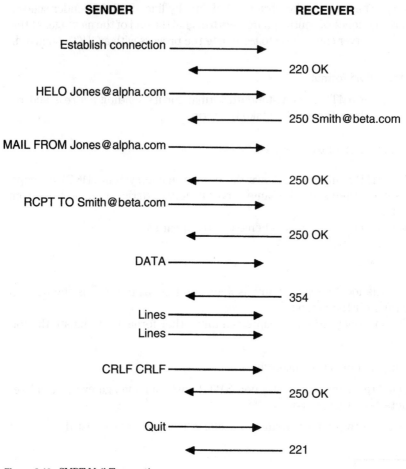

SENDER   RECEIVER

Establish connection ──────────▶

                    ◀──────────── 220 OK

HELO Jones@alpha.com ──────────▶

                    ◀──────────── 250 Smith@beta.com

MAIL FROM Jones@alpha.com ──────────▶

                    ◀──────────── 250 OK

RCPT TO Smith@beta.com ──────────▶

                    ◀──────────── 250 OK

DATA ──────────▶

                    ◀──────────── 354

Lines ──────────▶
Lines ──────────▶

CRLF CRLF ──────────▶

                    ◀──────────── 250 OK

Quit ──────────▶

                    ◀──────────── 221

Figure 9.13 SMPT Mail Transaction.

Examples of SMTP operations

Figure 9.13 shows a simple operation of two SMTP users exchanging mail. The left side of the figure shows the sender establishing the connection. The receiver responds with 220 OK. The HELLO command is used as an identifier exchange between the two machines. The MAIL FROM command tells Smith@beta.com that a new mail transaction is beginning. The receiver uses this command to clear its buffers, reset state tables, and prepare for the message. Next, the RCPT command gives the forward path address of the receiver. In this example, it is Smith@beta.com, which replies with 250 OK. The DATA command informs the receiver that message contents follow. The response is 354, which means start mail input and end it with CRLF CRLF.

The data are transmitted, and the end-of-transmission is signaled with CRLF CRLF. The receiver responds with 250 OK, and the connection is taken down with QUIT and the responding 221, which means the server is closing the connection.

Figure 9.14 shows examples of other types of SMTP mail exchanges. The top part of the figure illustrates the use of the verification command (VRFY). Its purpose is to confirm the name of the receiver. In this example, JSmith should return a full name and a fully specified mailbox. The second operation in Figure 9.14 depicts how SMTP can be used to confirm an identity in a mailing list. The respondents should return full names and fully specified mailboxes.

These figures provide only a few examples of the many features of SMTP. As stated before, study the relevant RFC if more detailed information is needed.

SMTP and the Domain Name System

If an installation runs DNS and SMTP, a name server must store the mail exchange (MX) reserve records (RRs). RFC 974 states that a sending SMTP should query the host to determine if a well-known (WKS) entry indicates that SMTP is supported.

An example of RRs supporting an SMTP mailbox was provided in Chapter 3. Another example follows:

```
RD.ACME.COM. IN MX 1 0        RD.ACME.COM.
RD.ACME.COM  IN MX 2 0        MKT.ACME.COM.
RD.ACME.COM  IN WKS 12.14.1.1 TFCP (SMTP)
```

In this example, the mail for RD.ACME.COM. is delivered to the host. If RD.ACME.COM. is not available, mail is delivered to MKT.ACME.COM.

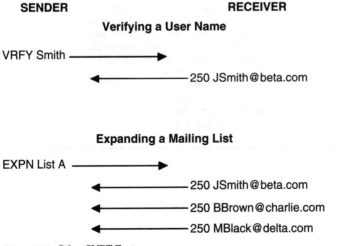

SENDER   **RECEIVER**

Verifying a User Name

VRFY Smith ─────────▶

◀───────── 250 JSmith@beta.com

Expanding a Mailing List

EXPN List A ─────────▶

◀───────── 250 JSmith@beta.com

◀───────── 250 BBrown@charlie.com

◀───────── 250 MBlack@delta.com

Figure 9.14 Other SMPT Features.

Obtaining Internet Services

In addition to SMTP, the Internet supports other messaging systems. The post office protocol (POP) provides remote access to a mail box. POP stores messages until a POP user agent accepts delivery of the traffic. Two POP agents (a user agent and a message-transfer agent) can be remotely located from each other. The POP port is 109. POP services are available from several Internet access providers through either dial-up or leased line connections.

The network news transfer protocol (NNTP) is another messaging store-and-forward service. NNTP identifies news groups and transfers news articles between the news groups. The NNTP port is 119.

Table 9.7 summarizes the more prevalent systems available to find and retrieve resources in the Internet. You might have some of these systems available through your local Internet access provider. Check with your network administrator. For more information about these systems, refer to page 8 of the September 1993 issue of *Computer Magazine.*

Summary

The Internet application-layer protocols are the most widely used standards in the industry. They provide the user with relatively simple yet functionally rich services and can be run on large or small machines. Some of them are provided as part of a vendor's network product. Their long-range future is questioned by some people who think the OSI application-layer protocols will supplant them. For the near future, they remain the preferred approach for the majority of users in the industry.

TABLE 9.7 Resource Discovery Services

Wide Area Information Servers (WAIS)	Clients and servers use ISO's Z39.50 Developed by several companies to provide an information discovery-and-retrieval system
Archie	Locates files in Internet public archive sites *Filenames*: contains names of files (FTP) *What is*: names and descriptions of software, documents, and other information
Prospero	Tool for organizing and viewing information
Gopher	Search-and-browse system
World-Wide Web (WWW)	Another search-and-discovery system
Indie	Another discovery-and-retrieval system

10

Other Protocols

An internet uses numerous protocols. The focus in this book has been on TCP, IP, route discovery protocols, naming/addressing protocols, and internet operations. This chapter provides an overview of several other important protocols used in many internet systems.

X Windows

X Windows (also known simply as *X*) was developed at the Massachusetts Institute of Technology as a windowing system for bitmap display computers. It has the term *windows* in its title because it allows a user to display several programs on the screen at one time without having multiple screens to control the multiple sessions. If necessary, X Windows and other software can support multiple applications running on separate terminals, with the icons representing executions displayed on the primary screen. You might recognize this feature in IBM's OS/2 Presentation Manager software.

X Windows can be run on different CPUs or different networks (as long as the CPU operating system supports X). As we shall see shortly, an X message can be coded to stipulate the type of network communication needed (TCP, DECnet, etc.). Another attractive feature of the X Windows protocol is that it can be used with byte-oriented systems by using a block protocol on top of a stream protocol.

Both local and remote windows can be managed with X Windows. Remote windows are established by going through the TCP/IP protocols. Local windows are established with Berkeley UNIX sockets.

X Windows consists of two major modules: *xlib* and *X-server.* As indicated in Figure 10.1, xlib rests in front of the client application. xlib is a C

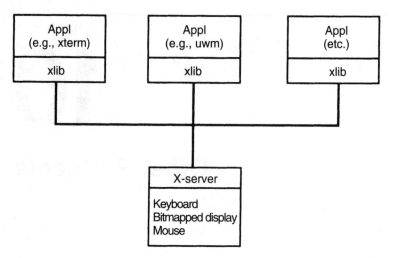

Figure 10.1   X Windows.

language module that accepts input from the user. The module is responsible for sending data back and forth to the user terminal. The user is also called the X-client. The X-server rests in the user's terminal and is nothing more than the display software that receives data and sends the data to and from the client application.

To further understand X Windows, it is useful to outline some of the principal rules and functions of the system:

- One X-server is installed per terminal, although more than one X-client can communicate with the X-server. As discussed earlier, the X-server then displays the application windows from the clients and, of course, sends input to the appropriate X-client interface.

- The X-server does not maintain the windows, which is the responsibility of the X-client. The X-client is notified, via transactions called *events*, by the X-server when something has changed on the display. The X-server must keep track of the window visibility, however.

- Windows are managed through a concept called *stacks*, as well as parent and child windows. This approach is hierarchical in nature in that a child window rests beneath a parent window. In turn, a child window can be a parent window above other child windows. The rationale for this approach is to provide a means for subwindows to be visible on the screen when their parent is on top of the child's stack.

The xlib module is not the only available interface to X. A number of tool kits are available to mask the application from xlib, and they never use xlib directly.

The X Window system protocol

Client applications and the server communicate with each other through the X Window system protocol. Four types of messages are used:

Request: an instruction to the workstation server to perform an action, such as draw a line.

Reply: sent from the server in response to a request (or for requests).

Event: used by the server to inform the application of changes that affect the application (e.g., a user clicking a mouse, a foreign application changing a window).

Error: sent to the client application by the server if something is wrong (e.g., the user selects execution of a program that consumes more memory than available).

The formats for these messages are shown in Figure 10.2. The request format contains *major* and *minor opcodes* of one octet each. The *length* field is two octets, and the *data* field is variable. The reply, error, and event formats contain one octet for the *type* field and a 31-octet *data* field.

Many messages on X do not warrant a reply. For example, a "move mouse" message is a one-way request. Additionally, these one-way messages are often buffered and sent in a *batch stream*. This approach allows a user to issue an xlib request and go on to other operations. On the other hand, a round-trip transaction with a returned request requires that the application wait for the reply.

An event message is sent only if an application has *solicited* the type of event being sent. This approach is quite important in that it allows an application to receive only relevant events.

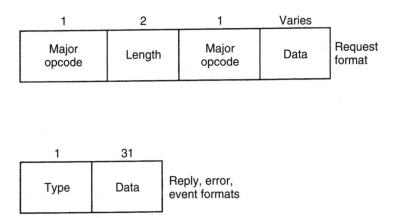

Figure 10.2 X Window System Protocol Message Formats.

The display connection

X Window applications must establish a display connection before they can communicate. The application uses an X request called *XOpenDisplay* from the xlib library to establish a connection with a workstation. The workstation and xlib exchange information with each other while establishing the connection. xlib then creates a *display structure* that contains the necessary configuration data for proper communication between the application and the workstation. A reply to XOpenDisplay returns a pointer to the display structure.

After a *display connection* has been established, the application and workstation are ready to work. Of course, the nature of the work depends on the application. For example, if the application wants to know what window the mouse pointer is in, it issues the *XQueryPointer* call to xlib. The position is returned in a reply.

As another example, suppose the application wishes to move the screen cursor (in contrast to it being moved by the mouse user). Issuing the *XWarpPointer* moves the cursor pointer in accordance with the arguments supplied to the call by the application.

While these are specific examples of X operations, on a more general level applications use standard X requests to operate on the following objects (resources):

Windows: The rectangular image on a screen that identifies the manipulated resource (user applications, database, file, etc.).

Graphic contexts: control the look of objects (line size, boldness, etc.).

Color: translates application commands to colors on the screen.

Fonts: support shape, size, style of text.

Pixmaps: hide displays for later use (a cut and later paste, for example).

Cursors: control the look of the cursor and its movement.

It should be helpful to examine a few examples of X events generated to inform an application about something that happened. These examples are far from being all inclusive and show only mouse-related events.

A *ButtonPress* event is generated each time a mouse user presses a button (or buttons) on the mouse (when the pointer is within a specified window). The opposite holds true for the generation of a *ButtonRelease* event. The *MotionNotify* event is generated when the pointer moves within a specified window. It can be generated by manipulating the mouse or through program control.

We have only touched the surface of the capabilities of the X Window system. Many books and articles are available on the system, and RFC 1198 (FYI:6) provides more information and contact points within the Internet.

Remote Procedure Call

Remote procedure call (RPC) is a widely used software module developed by Sun Microsystems, Inc., used on almost all UNIX-based systems. It greatly facilitates the distribution of applications to multiple machines. The RPC is published in RFC 1057.

RPC is a remote subroutine call program. It allows a caller program, referred to as a *client*, to send a message to a server. The caller program then waits for a reply message. This call message includes parameters defining what is to be performed at the remote site. In turn, the reply message contains the result of the procedure call.

RPC can be implemented on either a TCP or a UDP transport layer. We know that UDP does not provide reliability; therefore, it is up to the end-user application to provide for retransmissions, timeouts, and other transport-layer mechanisms. The RPC call message contains only three fields: remote program number, remote program version number, and remote procedure number.

The purpose of the *remote program number* is to identify a group of procedures, such as a database system, a file system, etc. Sun Microsystems administers numbers in the range of *0_1fffffff*. They are intended to be identical for all installations. The procedures are actually macros or catalogued procedures, such as a read or write and are identified with *remote procedure numbers*. Within the procedures, it might be necessary to change the system, in which case the *remote version number* is assigned as different releases are placed into production.

The RPC reply message is also quite simple. It provides the status of a procedure call with the replies shown in Figure 10.3.

Network File System

The network file system (NFS) was also developed by Sun Microsystems, Inc., to allow computers to share files across a network or networks. It is published in RFC 1094. NFS is computer-independent and is also independent of lower layers, such as the transport layer, because it rests above the RPC.

NFS consists of two other protocols called the *mount protocol* and the *NFS protocol*. The purpose of the mount protocol is to identify a file system and the remote host to be accessed. The NFS protocol is responsible for performing the file transfer operations.

The NFS server procedures

An NFS server performs its operations through several procedures. These procedures are *stateless*, in that no state tables are maintained to track the progress of the procedures' operations. This approach might seem a bit strange. After all, file reading, and especially writing, is inherently state ori-

Possible RPC replies

— MSG_ACCEPTED

    — Success (RPC execution was successful)

    — PROG_UNAVAIL (Program is not available)

    — PROG_MISMATCH (Version not supported)

    — PROC_UNAVAIL (Procedure is not supported)

    — GARBAGE_ARGS (Parameters cannot be decoded)

— MSG_DENIED

    — RPC_MISMATCH (RPC version problem)

    — AUTH_ERROR (Authentication problem)

        — AUT_BADCRED (Bad credentials)

        — AUTH_REJECTEDCRED (Client must start again)

        — AUTH_BADVERF (Bad verifier)

        — AUTH_REJECTEDVERF (Verifier expired)

        — AUTH_TOOWEAK (Security problems)

Figure 10.3 Possible Replies to Remote Procedure Call.

ented (sometimes called "stateful") because these operations must be tracked. NFS solves the problem by assuming that any required state-oriented services are implemented in other protocols. A user application could therefore contain the state-oriented logic (file locks, write positions, etc.) and call NFS for the use of its procedures.

The procedures of NFS are similar to other network transfer or management protocols. A user can invoke procedures to perform the following:

- create, rename, remove a file
- get attributes of files
- create, read, and remove a file directory
- read and write to a file
- perform other procedures

The user application is responsible for keeping track of the position in the file where reading and writing is to occur. For example, the NFS read file procedure, NFSPROC_READ, requires the application to furnish the position in the file where the reading is to begin, as well as the number of bytes to be returned in the reply.

Remote Exec Daemon

The remote exec daemon (REXECD) allows the execution of the REXECD command on a remote host through a TCP/IP-based network. The client is required to perform the REXECD processing. REXECD is designed to handle commands issued by host machines and to delegate these commands to slave machines for job execution. REXECD is responsible for authenticating the user (if a user ID/password is used). It also performs automatic login functions to the host. The protocol rests above TCP in the IP suite.

IBM systems extensively use REXECD. IBM's VM, AIX, and DOS machines can run this protocol.

PING

PING is a very simple protocol that uses the user datagram protocol (UDP) segment. Its principal operation is to send a message and simply wait for it to come back.

PING is so named because it is an echo protocol and uses the ICMP echo and echo-reply messages. Each machine is operating with a PING server whenever IP is active on the machine. PING is used principally by systems programmers for diagnostic and debugging purposes. It is very useful because it provides the following functions:

- The *loopback ping* is used to verify the operation of the TCP/IP software.

- The *ping address* determines if a physical network device can be addressed.

- The *ping remote IP address* verifies whether the network can be addressed.

- The *ping remote host name* verifies the operation of a server on a host.

Refer to Chapter 6 for more information on this protocol.

Host Monitoring Protocol

The host monitoring protocol (HMP) is used to collect information from host computers in an internet. Typically, the information is used by a network control center (NCC) to determine the performance and status of hosts. HMP uses the term *monitoring entity* to describe a monitored host and *monitoring host* to describe what would typically be the NCC. One host is able to monitor another.

Earlier implementations of HMP were used by NCCs to collect network information from gateways, cluster controllers, and other network entities. Some implementations have been used simply to exchange information between host machines.

HMP is a connectionless protocol. It operates at the transport layer over IP and ICMP. This approach does not preclude other layer suites; for example, HMP could rest over logical link control (LLC) Type 1, 2, or 3 in a LAN. The idea of HMP is based on the realization that the following information needs to be exchanged between hosts and hosts and NCCs. First, the monitored entity might need to send unsolicited traffic to a monitoring center. One action that comes to mind is the sending of alarms from a monitored host. Second, the monitoring host (the control of the NCC) might need to gather information from the monitored entity for log control management. Finally, the NCC might need to set certain control parameters at the monitored host and ascertain if these control parameters have been set and carried out successfully.

To meet these needs, HMP is designed to collect three classes of data:

1. *Spontaneous events* are captured by the monitoring entity. These events are called *traps* in the Internet. Typically, a trap would be on something deemed important enough to warrant the NCC's attention. The trap messages must contain identifiers to indicate the report, time, host, and, of course, any data relevant to the trapped message.

2. The second type of data collected by HMP deals with the current status of a host machine. *Status information* is topical, and not necessarily collected over a long period of time. HMP accomplishes this action by sending a typical poll message to a host. The poll requires the host to respond with its latest status information.

3. The third type of data collected by HMP is longer-range data, such as performance data over a period of time. Unlike status information, all this data is important because it is used for the analysis of the performance of the network and the host.

Discard Protocol

This protocol is also useful as a diagnostic tool. As its name implies, it discards any data it received. The usefulness of this protocol might initially escape you. Typically, it is used by the receiver to analyze received data. The data likely is not actual end-user data, but data introduced at the transmitting entity for network tuning considerations. Therefore, instead of passing this data up to an upper layer, the discard protocol discards it.

The discard protocol is used with TCP in which the discard server listens for the connections on TCP port 9. After the connection is established, any data coming in on this port is discarded. The discard service is also provided for UDP. The server listens for data on UDP port 9. Upon receiving the data, the datagram is discarded.

Finger

Finger is a very simple protocol used to obtain information about users logged on to a machine. The information given to an inquiring user depends entirely on the specific implementation of the finger. Typically, when the client sends a command, a list of users currently logged on to that host is provided in response. Be aware, however, that the implementation of finger varies as does the information provided in the retrieval. Typical information retrieved with the use of finger is the name of the user, the job title of the job running on the machine, the interface to the user (that is, the terminal being used), the location of the workstation, etc.

Finger is now published as RFC 1196, which has clarified some ambiguities about the protocol.

The Bootstrap Protocol

Earlier in this book, we learned that the reverse address resolution protocol (RARP) is used to obtain an IP address from a physical address. Although widely used, RARP has some disadvantages. Because it is intended to operate at the hardware level, it is cumbersome to obtain and manage the routine from an applications program. It also contains limited information. Its purpose is to obtain an IP address, but not much other information is provided. It would be useful for the message reply to contain information about other protocols supported by the machine, such as the gateway address, server host names, etc. Because of these problems with RARP, the Internet now supports the bootstrap protocol, also known as BOOTP.

BOOTP uses an IP datagram to obtain an IP address. This approach seems somewhat circuitous at first glance, but the destination address in the IP datagram is a limited broadcast value (all ones, yielding 255.255.255.255). A machine that chooses to use BOOTP sends out an IP limited broadcast. A designated server on the network receives the BOOTP message and sends a proper answer back to the inquirer in the form of yet another broadcast.

BOOTP utilizes UDP at the transport layer. Consequently, the operation is connectionless. The UDP uses a checksum to check for data corruption. BOOTP performs some transport layer functions by sending a request to the server. Then a timer is started, and, if no reply is received within a defined period, BOOTP attempts a retransmission.

The format for BOOTP is illustrated in Figure 10.4. All fields are of fixed length, and the replies and requests both have the same format. The field labeled *operation* is set to 1 to denote a request and 2 to denote a reply. The next two fields are identical to the ARP protocol, with *hardware type* and *hardware length* identifying the type of hardware and the length of

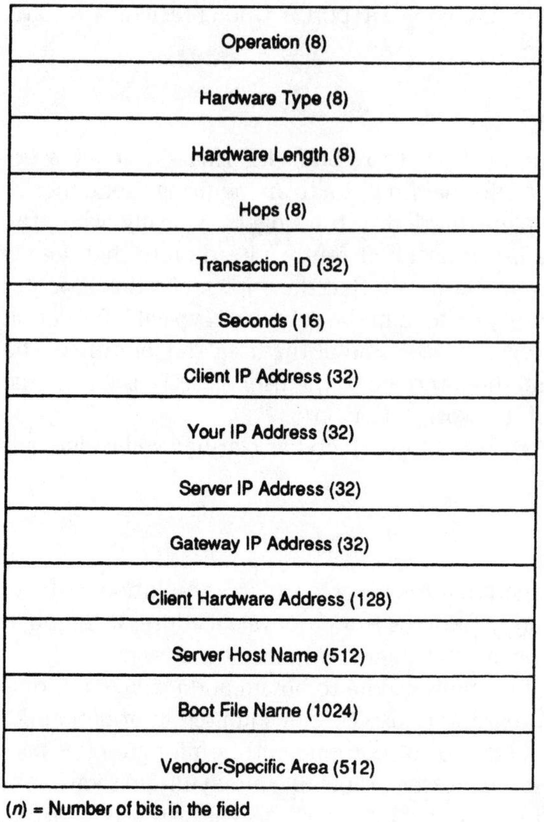

Operation (8)
Hardware Type (8)
Hardware Length (8)
Hops (8)
Transaction ID (32)
Seconds (16)
Client IP Address (32)
Your IP Address (32)
Server IP Address (32)
Gateway IP Address (32)
Client Hardware Address (128)
Server Host Name (512)
Boot File Name (1024)
Vendor-Specific Area (512)

(n) = Number of bits in the field

Figure 10.4 BOOTP Message Format.

the hardware address. The *hops* field must be set to 0 for a request message. The server is allowed to pass a BOOTP message to another machine, perhaps in another network. If so, it must increment the hop count by one. The *transaction ID* field coordinates requests and response messages. The *seconds* field determines (in seconds) the time since the machine started to establish the BOOTP procedure. The next four fields contain the *client IP address,* as well as the *requester's IP address, server IP address,* and *gateway IP address.* The *client hardware address* is also available. Next are the *client server* and the *boot file* names, and finally the *vendor specific area,* which is not defined in the standard.

Network Time Protocol

Chapter 6 discussed the use of an Internet control message protocol (ICMP) time-stamp option in which communicating machines such as gateways and hosts coordinate their clocks. The question that remains is, how do these machines obtain their timing information? After all, who can say that one gateway has a more accurate clock than another? The answer to this question is provided in this section, which discusses the network time protocol (NTP), published in RFC 1119. In addition to RFC 1119, you might wish to refer to RFCs 956 and 957. Reading RFC 1119 is highly recommended if you need detailed information on clocking protocols, algorithms for smoothing the clock, how to develop clock offsets, and how to estimate round-trip delays for synchronizing clocking values.

The NTP operation is depicted in Figure 10.5. Clocking information for a network is provided through the primary time server designated as a root. The time server obtains its clocking information from master sources. In the United States, this is usually one of four sources:

- *Fort Collins, Colorado*:   Station WWV operated by the National Institutes of Standards and Technology (NIST) using high-frequency (HF) transmissions.

- *Kauai, Hawaii*:   Station WWVH operated by NIST, also operating with HF transmissions.

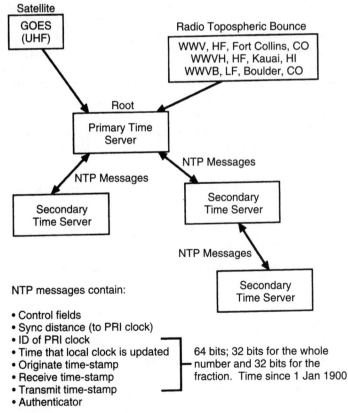

Figure 10.5 Network Time Protocol.

- *Boulder, Colorado*:   Station WWVB, operating with low-frequency (LF) transmissions.

- *Geosynchronous Orbiting Environmental Satellite (GOES)*:   Operated by NIST in the ultra-high frequency (UHF) range

These master clocking sources are used by the primary time server to derive accurate clocks. Other countries might have their own clocks used to provide clocking over large areas. Most of these clocks provide very accurate clocking synchronization on the order of less than 1 millisecond. Local clocks are even more accurate. Part of the problem with obtaining absolutely accurate clock information stems from variable propagation delays resulting from different atmospheric conditions, interrupt latencies at the machines, and small oscillator drifts in the clocks.

The primary time server, upon receiving clocking information from a master clocking source, uses the NTP protocol to coordinate clocks at the secondary time servers. Secondary time servers can in turn provide clocking for other secondary time servers. The accuracy of the clocking decreases as NTP messages are propagated through the clocking hierarchy. Although Figure 10.5 shows one primary time server servicing an internet, this need not be the case. Multiple primary time servers can service clocking within the network.

The NTP messages contain, as you might expect, *time-stamps* that are used by the primary and secondary time servers to calculate clock offsets and correct clocking inaccuracies. (Several *control fields* are contained in the NTP message; they are not discussed here because they are beyond the scope of this discussion.) The *sync distance* is an estimate of the round-trip propagation delay to the primary clock, as seen by the originator of the NTP message. The *ID of the primary* clock contains the unique identifier of the primary time server. The next four fields contain the following time-stamp information:

Time local clock updated: time that the originator of this message has had its local clock updated.

Originate time-stamp: time that this message was originated.

Receive time-stamp: time that this message was received.

Transmit time-stamp: time that this message was transmitted after receiving it.

All time-stamps are 64 bits in length, with 32 bits reserved for a whole number and 32 bits for the fraction. Time-stamps are benchmarked from January 1, 1900. Does the 32-bit field provide enough space for growth? Most definitely. The value 2^{32} provides magnitudes well beyond what we foresee as needed in the future.

The last field is *Authenticator*. It is an optional field used for authentication purposes.

NTP uses port 37 and can operate above UDP or the TCP. Be aware that the information retrieved and displayed to the user on a terminal is not very readable. For example, the value gives the number of seconds since January 1, 1900, midnight GMT. Consequently, the date of January 1, 1980 GMT at midnight would be retrieved and displayed as 2,524,521,600. Of course, a simple program can be written to translate this notation into a user-friendly format.

Daytime

Daytime is similar to the time protocol, except that it returns times that are easier to read. The returned string is ASCII text. The information returned from the daytime protocol is usually displayed as weekday, month day, year, time zone. This protocol is used quite often in Internet standards when machine-readable protocol is not required (as in the time protocol discussed above).

The Point-to-Point Protocol (PPP)

The point-to-point protocol (PPP) was implemented to solve a problem that has evolved in the industry during the last decade. With the rapid growth of internetworking, several vendors and standards organizations developed a number of network layer protocols.

IP is the most widely used of these protocols. Machines such as routers, however, typically run more than one network layer protocol. While IP is a given on most machines, routers also load network layer protocols developed by companies such as Xerox, Apple Computer, and SUN. Thus, machines communicating with each other did not readily know which network-layer protocols were available during a session.

In addition, until the advent of PPP, the industry did not have a standard means to define a serial link, point-to-point encapsulation protocol, such as the capability that exists on a LAN with an Ethernet Ethertype field or link service access points (LSAPs). The encapsulation protocol carries or encapsulates a network layer PDU in its information (I) field and uses another field in the frame to identify which network layer PDU resides in the I field. The PPP standard solves these two problems.

PPP encapsulates network layer datagrams over a serial communications link. The protocol allows two machines on a point-to-point communications channel to negotiate the particular types of network layer protocols (such as IP) to be used during a session. After this negotiation occurs, PPP is used to carry the network-layer PDUs in the I field of an HDLC-type frame. This protocol supports either bit-oriented synchronous transmission or asynchronous (start/stop) transmission. It can be used on switched or dial-up links, but requires full-duplex capability.

PPP is divided into three major components. The first component deals with the HDLC frame and how it is used for encapsulating datagrams in the I-field of the frame. The second major component of PPP is the link control protocol (LCP), which is used to establish the link, test the link for various quality-of-service features, configure it, and release the link. The third major component is a generic family of network control protocols (NCPs) for establishing which network-layer protocols are to be used for the connection.

PPP supports the simultaneous use of network protocols. For example, the protocol allows two users to negotiate the simultaneous use of IP, Digital's DECnet IV network layer, IPX, and XNS.

The PPP PDU uses the HDLC frame as stipulated in ISO 3309-1979 (and amended by ISO 3309-1984/PDAD1). Figure 10.6 shows this format. The flag sequence is the standard HDLC flag of 01111110 (Hex 7e). The address field is set to all 1s (Hex ff), which signifies an all-stations address. PPP does not use individual station addresses because it is a point-to-point protocol. The control field is set to identify an HDLC unnumbered information (UI) command. Its value is 00000011 (Hex 03). The I field contains the user data (the datagram) for the protocol identified in the protocol field.

Once negotiations have occurred between two stations and these stations agree as to which network layer protocols will be used, the information field actually contains the datagram. For negotiations, the protocol value is set to a leading 8, a 0 or a C (as discussed in the next paragraph). The I field contains the control values used to perform the various negotiations. The maximum default length for the I field is 1500 octets. Other values can be used if the PPP implementors so agree. The frame-check sequence (FCS) field is used for error detection. As with most HDLC FCS checks, the calculations are performed on the address, control, protocol, and I fields.

The protocol field is used to identify the PDU encapsulated into the I field of the frame. The values in this field are assigned through RFC 1060. On a more general note, the field values are assigned initially in accordance with the values in this figure. As suggested in the figure, the values beginning with a 0 identify the network protocol that resided in the I field. Values beginning

Flag	Address	Control	Protocol	Information (I field)	FCS	Flag

```
       Flag = 01111110
    Address = 11111111
    Control = 00000011
   Protocol = See RFC 1060
Information = Network layer PDU
        FCS = 16 bits
```

Figure 10.6 PPP Frame Format.

with 8 identify a control protocol used to negotiate the protocols that will actually be used. The leading value of C identifies the protocol as LCP.

LCP supports the establishment of the connection and allows for certain configuration options to be negotiated. The protocol also maintains the connection and provides procedures for termination. To perform these functions, LCP is organized into four phases:

Phase 1: link establishment and configuration negotiation

Phase 2: link quality determination

Phase 3: network-layer protocol configuration negotiation

Phase 4: link termination

PPP requires that LCP be executed to open the connection between two stations before any network-layer traffic is exchanged, which consists of a series of message exchanges called *configure packets*. After these packets have been exchanged and a configure-acknowledge packet has been sent and received between the stations, the connection is considered to be in an open state and the exchange of datagrams can begin. LCP confines itself only to link operations. It does not understand how to negotiate the implementation of network-layer protocols. Indeed, it does not care about the upper-layer negotiations relating to network protocols.

The PPP frame I field is used to carry the link control protocol packet. The protocol field in the frame must contain hex C021 to indicate the I field carries link control protocol information. The format for the field is shown in this figure. The *code* field must be coded to identify the type of LCP packet encapsulated into the frame. As examples, the code would indicate if the frame contains a configure request, which would likely be followed by a configure ACK or NAK. Additionally, the code could indicate (for example) an echo request data unit. Naturally, the next frame would probably identify the echo reply.

Summary

The TCP/IP protocol suite contains a wealth of protocols beyond that of TCP and IP. The major applications protocols were examined in Chapter 9. This chapter has summarized other popular protocols. The RPC and NFS systems are some of the most widely used upper-layer protocols today. The Internet has chosen to standardize these systems on Sun Microsystems products. X Windows is gaining in popularity for the use of bitmapped, display-oriented protocol. Clocking protocols have been in existence for a number of years, and the network time protocol represents the culmination of many of the earlier efforts. PPP is now being deployed in both public and private internets.

11

Internet Network Management Systems

An internet is of limited long-term value if it cannot be managed properly. One can imagine the difficulty of trying to interconnect and communicate among different computers, routers, etc., if the conventions differ for managing alarms, performance indicators, traffic statistics, logs, accounting statistics, and other vital elements.

In recognition of this fact, in the early 1990s, the IAB assumed the lead in setting standards for TCP/IP-based internets and sponsored two network management protocols. One protocol is intended to address short-term solutions and is called the *simple network management protocol (SNMP)*. The other protocol proposes to address long-range solutions and is called *common management information services and protocol over TCP/IP (CMOT)*.

This chapter examines these Internet network management protocols with the emphasis on SNMP. Emphasis is also placed on the Internet Management Information Base (IMIB, or MIB) and the Structure for Management Information (SMI). The CMOT protocol is discussed in more general terms because it is not used much today. The abstract syntax notation one (ASN.1) language is used in this chapter, but the examples are kept simple.

A more thorough explanation is available in *Network Management Standards*, by Uyless Black (McGraw-Hill, 1992).

Summary of the Internet Network Management Standards

Table 11.1 lists and describes the titles of the major requests for comments (RFCs) pertinent to the Internet network management standards.

TABLE 11.1   Common Internet RFCs for Network Management

1052	IAB recommendations for the development of internet network management standards
1155	Structure and identification of management information for TCP/IP-based internets
1213	Management information base for network management of TCP/IP-based internets: MIB II
1157	A simple network management protocol (SNMP)
1441	Introduction to SNMPv2
1142	SNMPv2 SMI
1095	CMIP over TCP/IP (CMOT)
1085	ISO presentation services over TCP/IP-based internets or the lightweight presentation protocol (LLP)

RFC 1052 provides useful information on the background of the development of these standards. The standards themselves are contained in three documents. *RFC 1155* contains common definitions and identifies information used on TCP/IP-based networks. It is similar in intent to the OSI Network Management Standard IS 7498-4 and IS 10040. *RFC 1213* contains information dealing with IMIB. This document is the second release of the MIB, and is known as MIB II.

The other important document is *RFC 1157*, which describes the SNMP. Although subsequent RFCs contain additional information for the use of SNMP, *RFC 1215* (how to define traps for use with SNMP) and *RFC 1187* (bulk table retrieval with SNMP) are useful documents for ancillary information. Additionally, *RFC 1212* (concise MIB definitions) is a very useful document that provides information on producing MIB modules.

RFC 1095 and 1085 deal with CMOT and the lightweight presentation protocol (LPP). As stated earlier, the CMOT approach has not proven to be successful; it is listed in this table if you want to analyze it for historical reasons.

Table 11.1 also lists two RFCs that pertain to version 2 of SNMP (SNMPv2). Be aware that several other RFCs are published on SNMPv2, but you should read RFC 1121 and 1142 before the others. All RFCs can be obtained from many sources (your Internet host or access node, for example) using anonymous file transfer protocol (FTP) or E-mail.

Layer Architecture for Internet Network Management

Figure 11.1 depicts the internet layers for network management standards. Note that the SNMP forms the foundation for the management architecture. The network management applications found at the top are not defined in the Internet specifications. These applications consist of vendor-specific network management modules such as fault management, log control, security and audit trails. As illustrated in the figure, SNMP rests over the user datagram protocol (UDP). UDP in turn rests on top of IP, which then rests on the lower layers (the data link layer and the physical layer).

The Internet Naming Hierarchy

The network elements within an internet have many common characteristics across subnetworks, vendor products, and individual components. It would be quite wasteful for each organization to spend precious resources and time using ASN.1 (and modified ASN.1) to describe these resources. Therefore, the Internet provides a registration scheme wherein resources can be categorized and identified within a registration hierarchy. This concept is founded on the ISO/ITU-T naming convention, which identifies objects and entities within a system.

Figure 11.2 shows the ISO and Internet registration tree for the Internet MIB. At the root level, three branches identify the registration hierarchy as ITU-T (0), ISO (1), or joint ITU-T/ISO (2). As we are concerned with the Internet activities, Figure 11.2 shows the ISO branch in more detail. Notice branch 3, labeled IE-ORG. The next branch identifies the Department of Defense (DOD) with the value 6. Under this hierarchical tree, Internet is found with a value of 1. Within the Internet hierarchy are four nodes. One is labeled management (Mgmt) with a value of 2. Finally, the leaf to this node is labeled MIB (1).

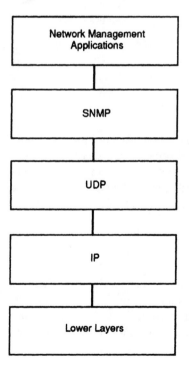

Figure 11.1 Internet Network Management Layers.

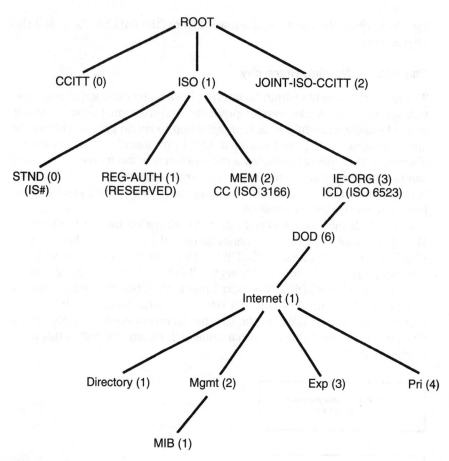

Figure 11.2   Internet Registration Hierarchy.

The registration hierarchy permits the assignment of unique identifiers to objects (also called variables). (*Managed object* is a general term used to identify any internet-managed resource, such as a router, TCP connection, or an IP address table.) The identifier is derived by concatenating the numbers associated with each node in the tree. In Figure 11.2, the Internet MIB is identified by 1.3.6.1.2.1.

Structure of Management Information

Structure of management information (SMI) describes the identification scheme and structure for the managed objects in the Internet. The SMI document deals principally with organizational and administrative matters. It leaves the task of object definitions to the other network management RFCs.

SMI describes the names used to identify the managed objects (that is, the network resources). These names are ASN.1 OBJECT IDENTIFIERS and use the naming convention depicted in Figure 11.2. Referring to Figure 11.2, the *Directory (1)* subtree is currently reserved. It is anticipated that this subtree will be used to determine how the emerging OSI Directory services (X.500) will interface with an internet.

Mgmt (2) is used to identify the managed objects in the network. This subtree is managed by IAB, and the numbering is delegated by the IAB to other managed objects. Each definition in the tree is named as an OBJECT IDENTIFIER, which is a unique identifier of a managed object.

Exp (3) identifies objects used in experimental endeavors. Again, the authority for naming through this subtree rests with the IAB.

Finally, the *Pri (4)* tree permits private enterprises to register their own managed objects. The tree is still administered by IAB, but the private enterprise, upon receiving a node of the tree, can define new MIB objects within the hierarchy. The IAB recommends, however, that all private names be registered under one authority.

Parts of the SMI standard are written in ASN.1-type coding, but the syntax for SMI is simpler than the ASN.1 syntax. The objective of this approach is to provide a less rigorous convention for describing managed objects in the Internet. Shortly, we examine the syntax rules for defining SMI objects. For the present, we need only concern ourselves with the types of managed objects defined in these standards.

SMI syntax and types

The Internet standards use ASN.1 constructs to describe the syntax of the object types, but the full ASN.1 set is not allowed. The primitive types permitted are INTEGER, OCTET STRING, OBJECT IDENTIFIER, and NULL. In addition to the primitive types, the constructor types SEQUENCE and SEQUENCE OF are also allowed.

The SMI standard defines other object types. Listed below are some examples, but the list is not all-inclusive of the types allowed:

Network Address: This type allows a choice of the Internet family of protocols. The type is defined in the modified ASN.1 notation as CHOICE and allows a developer to choose the protocol within the family. Presently, only the Internet family is identified.

IP Address: This address is used to define the Internet 32-bit address. The ASN.1 notation is OCTET STRING.

TimeTicks: This type represents a non-negative integer used to record events such as the last change to a managed object, the last update to a database, etc. The SMI standard requires that it represent a time increment in hundredths of a second.

Gauge: The SMI definition for this type is a non-negative integer that can range from 0 to 2^{31-1}. The gauge definition does not permit counter-wraparound, although its value can increase or decrease.

Counter: This defined type is described as a non-negative integer, again ranging from 0 to 2^{31-1}. This type differs from gauge in that the values can be wrapped around and its value can only increase.

Opaque: This defined type allows a managed object to pass anything as an OCTET STRING. It is so named because the encodings are passed transparently.

The Management Information Base

The Internet network management structure is organized around object groups, of which 10 have been defined. Figure 11.3 depicts the composition of these object groups. Note that several of the object groups are discussed in this book, notably, IP, ICMP, TCP, UDP, and EGP. Each of these object classes is defined further in the Internet MIB. RFC 1213 provides a detailed description with the modified ASN.1 notation for each of these groups.

An organization is not required to implement all the MIB object groups. Certainly, if one is using exterior gateways, the external gateway protocol (EGP) group is mandatory. If an organization implements UDP at the transport layer, however, it might not need to implement the TCP group. The decision to deploy MIBs depends on the type and nature of the network and the applications supported by the network. These standards do require that if an object group is supported, all elements in that group also must be supported.

The object groups consist of objects, also called variables. An *object* is anything deemed important enough to manage in the network (e.g., a packet switch, PBX, modem). For the Internet MIB, each object must have a name, syntax, and encoding.

The name is an OBJECT IDENTIFIER, which must be identified through the Internet registration hierarchy naming conventions, described earlier in

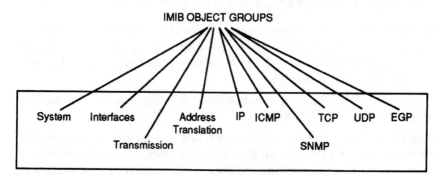

Figure 11.3 MIB Object Groups.

this chapter. Using OSI terms, an object is also defined by a type and an instance. The object type and the object instance (in conformance with OSI conventions) serve to identify unambiguously an object. The Internet network management standards do not use all the OSI terms, but they are still relevant. The syntax for each object uses ASN.1 for its description. As stated earlier, not all ASN.1 constructs are permitted. We describe those that are used later in this chapter.

The third aspect of an object is its encoding. This term describes how the object type is represented through the object type's syntax. In addition, encoding deals with how the object type is coded (represented) while being transmitted on the network communications channel. The encoding is done in conformance with the basic encoding rules (BER) of ASN.1.

Overview of the object groups

Each object group of Figure 11.3 is described briefly in this section. Be aware that this general explanation is to give you an idea of the major operations of the groups. RFC 1213 should be studied carefully to appreciate the full functions supported by the MIB definitions.

The *system* object group describes

- the name and version of the hardware, operating system, and networking software of the entity
- the hierarchical name of the group
- when the management portion of the system was reinitialized (in time)

The *interfaces* object group describes the

- number of network interfaces supported
- type of interface operating below IP (e.g., LAPB, Ethernet, etc.)
- size of datagram acceptable to the interface
- speed of the interface (bit/s)
- address of the interface
- operational state of the interface (up, down, etc.)
- amount of traffic received, delivered (unicast or broadcast), or discarded, and the reasons

The *address translation* group describes the address translation tables for network-to-physical address translation. This group will eventually become obsolete, as its functions now reside in the IP group.

The *IP* group describes

- if the machine forwards datagrams
- the time-to-live value for datagrams originated at this site

- the amount of traffic received, delivered, or discarded, and the reasons
- information on fragmentation operations
- address tables, including subnet masks
- routing tables, including destination address, distance metrics, age of route, next hop, and protocol from which route was learned (RIP, EGP, etc.)

The *ICMP* group describes

- number of the various Internet control message protocol (ICMP) messages received and transmitted
- statistics on problems encountered

The *TCP* group describes

- retransmission algorithm and maximum/minimum retransmission values
- number of TCP connections the entity can support
- information on state transition operations
- information on traffic received and sent
- port and IP numbers for each connection

The *UDP* group describes

- information on traffic received and sent
- information on problems encountered

The *EGP* group describes

- information on traffic sent and received and problems encountered
- the EGP neighbor table
- addresses to neighbors
- the EGP state with each neighbor

The *transmission* group was added to the second release of the MIB (MIB II). This group contains MIBs, object groups, and objects that pertain to unique transmission systems. For example, a transmission group has been defined for the cell-based technology, asynchronous transfer mode (ATM).

The *SNMP* group was also added to MIB II. It contains 30 objects used with simple network management protocol (SNMP). Most of the objects deal with error-reporting capabilities and are explained later in this chapter.

Table 11.2 lists and briefly describes the objects for the system group. Similar tables could be created for each group, but this level of detail is beyond the scope of this book. This table is included to give you an idea of the

TABLE 11.2 System Group

Function: The system group provides general information about managed objects. This group must be implemented for all objects.

sysDescr	An octet string to describe the object, such as hardware, operating system, etc.
sysObjectID	An OBJECT IDENTIFIER to identify the object uniquely (with naming hierarchy values) within the naming subtree
sysUpTime	In TimeTicks, the time since the object was declared up and running (reinitialized)
sysContact	An octet string to identify the person/organization to contact for information about the object
sysLocation	An octet string containing the location of the object
sysServices	An integer value that describes the service(s) offered by the object, based on the location of the service within a layer

MIB definitions. (All Internet objects are described in my book *Network Management Standards*.)

All Internet objects are described further with certain *key words* (reserved words). Five notations are used to describe the format of a managed object:

Object descriptor: As the name implies, this describes the object in ASCII text.

Syntax: The syntax describes the bit-stream representation of the object.

Definition: This notation describes the managed object in text to aid the human reader in understanding the notation.

Access: This notation describes whether the managed object is read-only, write-only, read-write, or not accessible.

Status: This notation describes whether the version is mandatory, or optional and if the object is obsolete.

Templates to describe objects

All object definitions are defined with templates as well as ASN.1 code. The template format is shown in Figure 11.4. (The fields in the figure were listed and described in the previous section.)

Each of the 10 object groups in Figure 11.3 is defined in RFC 1213 with the standard template format. It is of little value to repeat these templates here—they consume almost 50 pages in the standard. Each group was described briefly in an earlier section to give you an idea of the principal functions of each group. The remainder of this section shows one example of the templates taken from the interfaces object group.

Figure 11.5 shows the template for a leaf entry of a registration tree for the TCP/IP interfaces. (Be aware that several intermediate nodes are not

OBJECT:
A name for the object type, with its
corresponding OBJECT IDENTIFIER

Syntax:
The ASN.1 coding to describe the syntax
of the object type

Definition:
Textual description of the object type

Access:
  Access options
Status:
  Status of object type

Figure 11.4 Template for IMIB
Object Type Definitions.

OBJECT:
  ifType {if Entry 3}
Syntax:
  INTEGER {
  other (1),   –none of the following
  regular1822 (2),
  hdh1822 (3),
  ddn-x25 (4),
  rfc877-x25 (5),
  ethernet-csmacd (6),
  iso88023-csmacd (7),
  iso88024-tokenBus (8),
  iso88025-tokenRing (9),
  iso88026-man (10),
  starLan (11),
  proteon-10Mbit (12),
  proteon-80Mbit (13),
  hyperchannel (14),
  fddi (15),
  lapb (16),
  sdic (17),
  t1-carrier (18),
  cept (19),   –european equivalent of T-1
  basiclsdn (20),
  primarylsdn (21),
                      –proprietary serial
–... and others not shown,
  }

Definition:
  The type of interface...immediately "below"
  the IP in the protocol stack.
Access:
  read-only
Status:
  mandatory
Note: ...means some of the material of RFC is omitted.

Figure 11.5 Interface Type (ifType)
Template.

included in this example.) The notation of ifType {IfEntry 3} means the
IfType belongs to parent IfEntry 3 in the tree.

The syntax clause describes the abstract syntax (in ASN.1) of the object
type. As the entry shows, the physical, data link, and subnetwork interfaces

that exist below IP are described and assigned an integer value. Thus, two machines that exchange information about the interface supported below the IP layer are required to use these values. For example, ifType = 6 must be used to identify an Ethernet interface.

Definition of high-level MIB

Figure 11.6 depicts the RFC 1213 ASN.1 notation for the MIB groups. The code can be understood in the context of the objects illustrated in Figure 11.3 and the naming hierarchy tree in Figure 11.2.

The IMPORTS statement designates that a number of definitions are imported from RFC 1155. All objects are tagged as OBJECT IDENTIFIERS and defined with yet another name within the naming tree ({mgmt1}, {mib 1}, etc.).

The SNMP

SNMP owes its origin to decisions made by the IAB in early 1988. At that time, the IAB met to discuss methods to develop network management protocols to operate on TCP/IP-based networks. The result of that meeting was the decision to develop two parallel management systems, SNMP and CMOT.

SNMP is designed to be a simple, short-range solution to network management on the Internet. It is based on an earlier protocol called the simple gateway monitoring protocol (SGMP). Refer to RFC 1028 for a description of this earlier protocol.

```
RFC1213-MIB ::= BEGIN

IMPORTS
    mgmt, NetworkAddress, IpAddress, Counter, Gauge, TimeTicks
    FROM RFC1155-SMI;
    OBJECT-TYPE
    From RFC-1212;

mib-2      OBJECT IDENTIFIER ::= {mgmt 1}

    system        OBJECT IDENTIFIER ::= {mib-2 1}
    interfaces    OBJECT IDENTIFIER ::= {mib-2 2}
    at            OBJECT IDENTIFIER ::= {mib-2 3}
    Ip            OBJECT IDENTIFIER ::= {mib-2 4}
    icmp          OBJECT IDENTIFIER ::= {mib-2 5}
    tcp           OBJECT IDENTIFIER ::= {mib-2 6}
    udp           OBJECT IDENTIFIER ::= {mib-2 7}
    egp           OBJECT IDENTIFIER ::= {mib-2 8}
-- cmot           OBJECT IDENTIFIER ::= {mib-2 9}
    transmission  OBJECT IDENTIFIER ::= {mib-2 10}
    snmp          OBJECT IDENTIFIER ::= {mib-2 11}
    END
```

Figure 11.6 High-Level MIB Definition.

SNMP products began to appear on the marketplace in late 1988 and early 1989. In 1988, the MIB to support SNMP was also published. In September of 1988 at Interop '88, several announcements were made regarding implementations of SNMP. As the standard matured, other RFCs were released to define its operation further. In early 1989, RFC 1098 titled *SNMP over Ethernet* was published. Today, SNMP is widely implemented over many networks and vendor products.

SNMP administrative relationships

The SNMP (SNMP, version 1) architecture uses a variety of terms that were explained earlier. Using Figure 11.7 as a discussion point, entities residing at management network stations and network elements that communicate with each other using the SNMP standard are called SNMP *application entities*. The pairing of application entities with SNMP agents (explained shortly) is called an *SNMP community*. Each community is identified by an Internet hierarchical name.

SNMP messages are originated by SNMP application entities. They belong to the SNMP community that contains the application entity. These messages are termed *authentic SNMP messages*. Authentication schemes are used to identify the message and verify its authenticity. This process is called an *authentication service*.

Figure 11.8 provides a view of other administrative relationships for SNMP. An SNMP *network element* uses objects from the Internet MIB. The *subset of objects* pertaining to this element is called an SNMP MIB view. In turn, an SNMP access mode represents an element of the set (for example, read-only elements, write-only elements). Pairing the SNMP access mode with the MIB view is called the SNMP *community profile*. In essence, the profile is used to specify access privileges for an MIB view. These relationships are determined by the SNMP community pairing by developing pro-

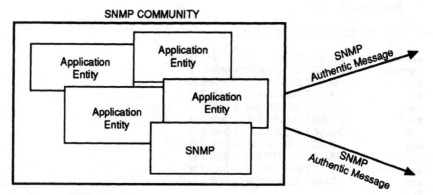

Figure 11.7 SNMP Community.

COMMUNITY PROFILE

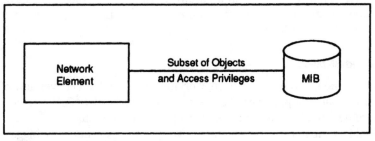

Figure 11.8 SNMP Community Profile.

files called SNMP *access privileges*. These access privileges then provide directions on how SNMP agents and network elements can use the MIB.

Example of an SNMP operation

Figure 11.9 shows an example of how the operations of SNMP work. In this illustration, a network control center (which could be a host computer, gateway, or any other machine) communicates with an IP gateway that contains an IP *agent*. An agent performs the SNMP operations and accesses the MIB residing at the gateway. In turn, the IP agent uses SNMP messages to communicate with the network control. These messages (explained in a later section) support operations such as obtaining information regarding operations, changing information, issuing unsolicited messages in the event of alarms, etc.

The data operated on by these messages are defined by the MIB, also illustrated in the figure. In a typical environment, network control contains the MIB for all its managed resources (objects). It is not necessary for each agent to store the full MIB; rather, each agent stores that portion of the MIB relevant to its own operation. In this example, the IP gateway agent would have the MIB entries pertaining to IP routing tables, address translation, ICMP operations, and other tasks with which a gateway becomes involved. The gateway would not need to store the TCP MIB object group, however,

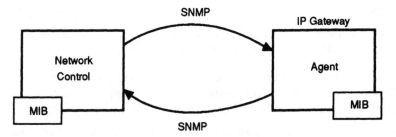

Figure 11.9 SNMP Operations between Agent and Network Control.

because TCP might not reside in a gateway. (Actually, in most gateways, TCP is used because these gateways utilize the network applications layer protocols, such as TELNET.)

SNMPv1 and SNMPv2

The Internet task forces have been working on an enhanced version of SNMP for the past couple years. As of the summer of 1993, SNMP version 2 was entering its final changes and is now a published standard.

SNMPv2 is a substantial improvement over SNMP 1. Perhaps the biggest change has been the improvement of the security mechanism deficiencies that existed in SNMP 1. For example, SNMPv2 provides authentication and integrity services that allow the receiver of a message to authenticate the originator of the message. This approach utilizes a private encryption key concept and will be implemented in the U.S. by the Data Encryption Standards (DES).

SNMPv2 also has improved access controls. As examples, reads, writes, and specific MIB views have been improved over SNMP 1. Moreover, a security and privacy feature was added to SNMPv2 that guarantees that the message has not been tampered with. Encryption options are available for each SNMPv2 message, but all these features need not be implemented in one package. Vendors and implementors can implement any of the three major parts of security: authentication and integrity, access controls, security and privacy.

SNMPv2 also provides mechanisms for coordinating the activities of multiple SNMPv2 managers. For example, locking mechanisms are now available to prevent managers from writing to the same agent. Gateways are also provided that allow SNMPv2 traffic to move to intermediate points between managers. Traps now have confirmation options. So, an agent can issue an alarm and receive confirmation that the alarm was received correctly. Another major improvement was the addition of a *get bulk* operation that allows one SNMPv2 message to access multiple objects in an MIB, and an *inform request* operation, which permits SNMP managers to communicate with each other.

SNMP PDUs

SNMP uses simple operations and a limited number of PDUs to perform its functions. Seven PDUs have been defined in the standard:

Get request: This PDU is used to access the agent and obtain values from a list. It contains identifiers to distinguish multiple requests, as well as values to provide information about the status of the network element.

Get next request: This PDU is similar to the get request, except it permits retrieval of the next variable in an MIB tree.

Get response: This PDU responds to the get request, get next request, and the set request data units. It contains an identifier that associates it with the previous PDU. It also contains identifiers to provide information about the status of the response (error codes, error status, and a list of additional information).

Set request: This PDU describes an action to be performed on a managed element. Typically, it is used to change the value sof a variable or table.

Trap: Trap allows the network object to report on an event at a network element or change the status of a network element.

Get bulk: This operation allows an agent to access table column and rows with only one get request from the user.

Inform request: This operation allows managers to communicate with each other.

All the SNMP PDUs have a common coding format based on ASN.1 and shown in Figure 11.10. The figure has been greatly simplified, assuming you are not familiar with ASN.1. I have replaced some of the ASN.1 code with ASN.1 comments, which are preceded by a double dash (- -).

The *request-ID* field is used to distinguish between the different requests in the PDUs. The *ErrorStatus* coding provides a list that describes the type

```
PDUs =
   CHOICE {
   --Allows a choice of the various SNMP PDUs
   --followed by a tag to identify each PDU on the channel
   }

PDU =
   SEQUENCE {
      request-ID
      Integer 32,

      error-status          --sometimes ignored
         INTEGER {
            noError(0)
            tooBig(1)
            --and 17 other errors
         },

      error-index           --sometimes ignored
         INTEGER (0..max-bindings),

      variable-bindings     --values are sometimes ignored
         VarBindList
   }
   --variable binding
   VarBind =
      SEQUENCE {
         name
```

Figure 11.10 SNMP PDUs.

of error being recorded. This list is accessed through the *Error-Index* field, which is listed below the *error-status* field. The *error-status* field provides values for reporting problems.

The *VarBind* sequence identifies the name of the managed element and any associated value. The *VarBindList* is a list of values that sets the variable bindings. Be aware that SNMP uses the term *variable* to describe an instance of a managed object; the term *VarBind* simply describes the pairing of a variable to the variable's value. The VarBindList contains a list of the variable names and their corresponding values.

The SNMP MIB managed objects

MIB II contains managed objects pertaining to the SNMP group, summarized in Table 11.3.

TABLE 11.3 SNMP Group

Function: The SNMP group provides information about SNMP objects, principally statistics relating to traffic and problems/error conditions. All these objects have a syntax of Counter, with the exception of the entry snmpEnableAuthTraps, which is an integer.

snmpInPkts	An indication of the number of packets received from the layer below SNMP.
snmpOutPkts	Identifies the number of packets delivered from SNMP to the layer below.
snmpInBadVersions	Indicates the number of PDUs received with an erroneous version.
snmpInBadCommunityNames	Indicates the number of PDUs received with unidentifiable or unauthenticated community names.
snmpInASNParseErrs	Indicates the number of PDUs that could not be parsed to ASN.1 objects and vice versa.
snmpInBadTypes	Indicates the number of PDUs received that were indecipherable types.
snmpInTooBigs	Indicates the number of PDUs received with the tooBig error status field.
snmpInNoSuchNames	Indicates the number of PDUs received with an error status in the NoSuchName field.
snmpInBadValues	Indicates the number of PDUs received with an error status in the badValue field.
snmpInReadOnlys	Indicates the number of PDUs received with an error status in the readOnly field.
snmpInGenErrs	Indicates the number of PDUs received with an error status in the genErr field.
snmpInTotalReqVars	Indicates the number of MIB objects that have been retrieved.
snmpInTotalSetVars	Indicates the number of MIB objects that have been changed/altered.
snmpInGetRequests	Indicate the number of respective PDUs that were received.

snmpInGetNexts
snmpInSetRequests
snmpInGet Responses
snmpInTraps

snmpOutTooBigs	Indicates the number of PDUs sent with the tooBig field.
snmpOutNoSuchNames	Indicates the number of PDUs sent with the nosuchName field.
snmpOutBadValues	Indicates the number of PDUs sent with the badValue field.
snmpOutReadOnlys	Indicates the number of PDUs sent with the readOnly field.
snmpOutGenErrs	Indicates the number of PDUs sent with the genErr field.
snmpEnableAuthTraps	Describes if traps are enabled or disabled. This value can be read or written.
snmpOutGetRequests	Indicate the number of respective PDUs that were sent.

snmpOutGetNexts
snmpOutSetRequests
snmpOutGetResponses
snmpOutTraps

CMOT

CMOT was also designed by the Internet Engineering Task Force (IETF). It was based on the ISO network management standards and can be used to run on a connection-oriented transport layer (such as TCP) or connection-less layer (such as UDP).

The CMOT layers

The CMOT architecture is depicted in Figure 11.11. If you are familiar with OSI, you should be quite at ease with this illustration. Notice that the OSI association control service element (ACSE) is used in the application layer to provide services to the network management ASEs. The remote operations service element (ROSE) is also used.

The figure shows an additional layer called the lightweight presentation protocol (LPP). Because TCP and UDP were not developed with OSI service definitions, LPP interfaces the OSI application service elements to the TCP/UDP modules. In the spirit of OSI, the next lower level, which is the IP, is transparent to the CMOT applications in the upper layers.

The lightweight presentation protocol

RFC 1085 contains the specifications of the LPP. The formal title is "ISO Presentation Services on top of TCP/IP-based Internets." LPP is needed in the CMOT protocol stack because of the presence of ACSE and ROSE,

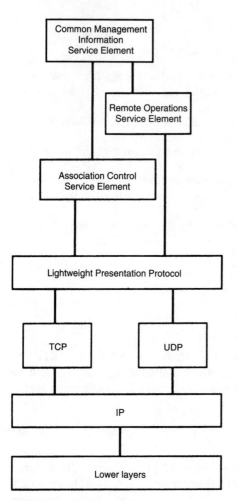

Figure 11.11 CMOT Layers.

which need certain services of the OSI presentation layer.

LPP provides these services using the following OSI presentation layer service definitions:

P-CONNECT

P-RELEASE

P-U-ABORT

P-P-ABORT

P-DATA

The following well-known port numbers are used between LPP and TCP/UDP:

163/tcp: CMOT Manager

163/udp: CMOT Manager

164/tcp: CMOT Agent

164/udp: CMOT Agent

CMOT has had a difficult time in the Internet and in most internets. Most implementors are not interested in becoming involved in object-oriented systems. Additionally, SNMP is easier to implement on a request. In contrast, CMIP requires a very "intelligent" agent because of its many features. I think a CMOT-type solution will gain favor, however, if for no other reason than the realization of the value of a more powerful network management protocol. The use of CMIP is growing, but is usually found in large, complex network (such as, BellCore's SMDS networks and a number of commercial SONETS). These implementations run CMIP over a full OSI stack, not TCP/IP.

Summary

The Internet network management standards are widely used in both local and wide area networks. The Internet MIB defines the Internet managed objects and how they can be manipulated. SNMP is the most prevalent network management standard in the industry. CMOT has received very little support thus far in the industry.

12

Stacking TCP/IP or TP4/CLNP with Other Protocols

This chapter provides several examples of how TCP/IP can be stacked with other protocols. The initial focus of this discussion is on LAN stacks, but subsequent discussions examine WANs, the integrated services digital network (ISDN), and the emerging synchronous digital hierarchy (SDH).[1] In these later examples, the TCP/IP stacks are replaced by the OSI transport protocol class 4 (TP4) and connectionless network protocol (CLNP).

The first examples show the encapsulation and decapsulation process of the PDUs on the left and right sides of the figures. For simplicity, later examples eliminate these notations. Each stack of protocols represents the protocols operating in each machine. For example, in Figure 12.1, the left stack is in one machine and the right stack is in another.

At first glance, it might seem that placing TCP/IP with other protocols is relatively simple. The concept is made somewhat more complex by the following three requirements:

- What services are needed in each layer?
- Are these services available?
- Do the layers perform redundant services?

---

[1] SDH is known in North America as the synchronous optical network (SONET).

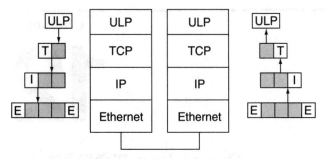

Figure 12.1 Minimum TCP/IP LAN Stack.

In some vendor products, stacking is rather lazy and haphazard, resulting in degraded throughput and response time and considerable function redundancy.

Several of the protocol stackings covered in this chapter are described in Internet RFCs. Others are not published in standards but implemented through specific vendor products. Still others have been used by me with my clients.

A Minimum TCP/IP and LAN Stack

Figure 12.1 shows the familiar TCP/IP stack. It is a simple and efficient implementation using *Ethernet* at the lower layer to connect two stations on a LAN.

The upper-layer protocols (ULPs) consist of vendor software and the end-user applications. It is a good idea to check the vendor's products in considerable detail to determine their functions, ease of use, and overhead in relation to the functions provided by the TCP and IP operations.

A Word About Operating System Dependency

Figure 12.2 adds the *operating system* notation to emphasize that how these protocols communicate with each other depends on how the operating system manages the interfaces between the layers in each machine. For example, a UNIX operating system provides different interfaces than DOS. Notwithstanding, the two machines' ability to communicate with each other (as shown in Figure 12.2) does not require the operating systems to be compatible. The essential requirement is that the PDUs exchanged between the machines in the peer layers are understandable and invoke complementary functions in each machine.

TCP/IP over LLC

Figure 12.3 shows a common LAN stack (discussed in Chapters 2 and 3) in which *logical link control (LLC)* and *media access control (MAC)* have been placed between *IP* and the *physical layer.* Typically, this approach uses *LLC type 1 (LLC1),* which is a connectionless data link protocol. The use of the LLC header is valuable because it provides destination and source service access points (SAPs) that identify the users of the layer above LLC. Of course, in this simple example, the user layer above LLC is IP. A common approach for the IP/802 configuration is to use the address resolution protocol (ARP) to perform mapping of the 32-bit Internet address to a 16- or 48-bit IEEE 802 address.

A few implementations, especially IBM token rings, support the full repertoire of the LLC standard by using LLC type 2 (LLC2) in the stack. Unnumbered information (UI) commands, exchange identification (XID) commands and responses, and test (TEST) commands and responses are all supported. Additionally, when an XID or TEST command is received with a response flag, the destination/source SAP addresses must be swapped and the relationship of the P and F bits must be preserved. That is, a P bit solicits an F bit in all cases.

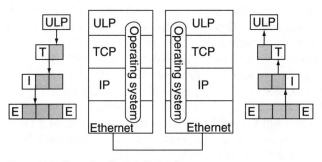

Figure 12.2 Operating System Dependency.

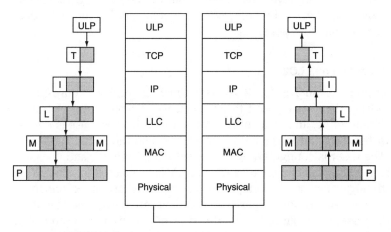

Figure 12.3 IEEE 802 Stack.

IP need not run over LLC2 in a LAN, and the LLC1 protocol provides useful features with UI exchange, XID, and TEST frames. Running LLC1 under TCP/IP is preferable because this "lean" LLC can rely on TCP to perform sequencing, flow control, and acknowledgment operations. Additionally, the use of the source SAPs and destination SAPs provides a very useful service for IP. For some applications, TCP might be considered overkill if the LAN operations already experience high throughput and high integrity. The user might consider replacing TCP, which is discussed in the next section.

Replacing TCP with UDP

Figure 12.4 shows a slightly different stack in which the *user datagram protocol (UDP)* replaces the transmission control protocol (TCP). This stack can be useful because of its simplicity and because it still provides the integrity of traffic typically offered by TCP if certain changes are made.

The biggest change is to provide traffic integrity with the ULP or LLC. We discuss the use of LLC first. In effect, type 2 provides a connection-oriented link protocol, which ensures the delivery of traffic to the receiving LLC. Like TCP, LLC2 provides sequencing, flow control, and window control capabilities by establishing a set asynchronous balanced mode (SABM) link configuration, placing some of the TCP functions below IP. This approach entails risks because LLC does not have a graceful close. Some means must be taken at a ULP to take care of connection management (closing). Of course, the ULP can provide for acknowledgments, sequencing, and flow control. If the upper layer applications operate with these features, then UDP is a good choice for the transport layer.

You need to weigh the tradeoffs of achieving connection-oriented services at LLC or the ULP level. Again, check out the vendor's ULP carefully, because some LLC2 and ULP connection-oriented services might be performing overlapping functions.

A word of caution on LLC2

Link layer protocols such as LLC2 use fixed timers to resolve a nonresponse from a station that is supposed to acknowledge the reception of traffic. Upon sending traffic, an LLC2 entity starts a timer. If a response is not received within the timer value, the timer expires, and the traffic is retransmitted. The timer is configured by the network implementor and does not vary, which works well enough on a LAN or LANs connected together. This approach might not work well, however, if LANs are interconnected through WANs, which might experience wide and variable delays. The LLC2 timer is not adept enough to handle this type of operation. Consequently, LLC1 is a better choice for LAN-WAN-LAN internetworking. It has no timer;

it lets TCP handle the timeout operations. As we learned in Chapter 7, TCP's adjustable timers provide a better approach.

NetBIOS over TCP or UDP

Figure 12.5 shows a typical stack for personal computer-based networks that use IBM's NetBIOS. The illustration shows *NetBIOS* used above *TCP* or *UDP*. NetBIOS is designed principally to interconnect PC applications. It is used to locate application resources, establish connection between these

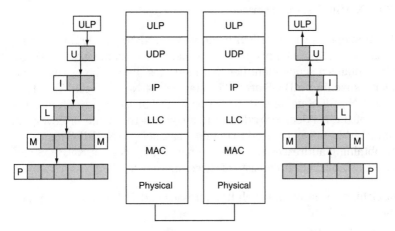

Figure 12.4 Using UDP in Place of TCP.

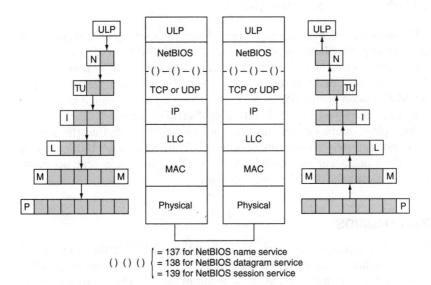

$$() \ () \ () \ \begin{cases} = 137 \text{ for NetBIOS name service} \\ = 138 \text{ for NetBIOS datagram service} \\ = 139 \text{ for NetBIOS session service} \end{cases}$$

Figure 12.5 Personal Computer Network Layers.

applications, receive data between the applications, and then terminate the connections. NetBIOS provides both connection-oriented and connectionless modes. All the resources managed by NetBIOS are referenced by a 16-character name, and applications are registered through this name.

The NetBIOS is reached through internet well-known port numbers (described in Chapter 7) as follows:

Port 137 = NetBIOS name service

Port 138 = NetBIOS datagram service

Port 139 = NetBIOS session service

NetBIOS supports the NetBIOS name server (NBNS) node. In some installations, the NBNS is mapped to the internet domain name system (DNS). NetBIOS contains a scope identifier that identifies the machines that operate under a specific NetBIOS area. The stacking of NetBIOS and TCP typically uses a NetBIOS name with its scope identifier to map to an internet DNS. One of the services provided in this stack is the name discovery, in which an IP address can be used to obtain an associated NetBIOS name.

After obtaining addresses through the naming services, a NetBIOS session can be established. It consists of three phases:

1. Establishing a session in which IP addresses and TCP ports are mapped to the remote entity.

2. Exchanging NetBIOS messages.

3. Closing the session by the other entity.

To establish a session, an entity must listen on a well-known service port for incoming NetBIOS session requests. The NetBIOS session server accepts requests for the end-user application. It is important to note that the TCP connection must be open before NetBIOS services can occur. The NetBIOS session occurs with a request packet containing called and calling IP addresses, as well as called and calling NetBIOS names.

For a close operation, an end user requests to NetBIOS that the session be closed. Typically, the system obtains a TCP graceful close. If the graceful close does not occur successfully and the TCP connection remains open, NetBIOS closes the NetBIOS session itself.

IP over NetBIOS

Figure 12.6 shows yet another possibility with NetBIOS. In this scenario, *IP datagrams* are encapsulated in the *NetBIOS packets*. This implementation represents a minimum service stack, wherein NetBIOS is run with connectionless services.

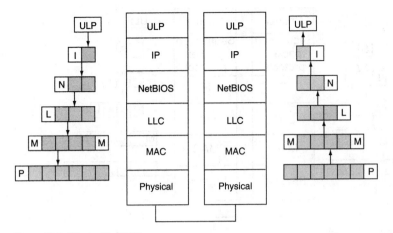

Figure 12.6 IP over NetBIOS.

The principal consideration for this stack is the address mappings between IP and NetBIOS. The NetBIOS names must reflect the IP address; part of the NetBIOS address space is coded IP.xx.xx.xx.xx. The *IP* value indicates an IP over NetBIOS operation, and the *xx.xx.xx.xx* represents the IP address. Broadcast addresses are coded as IP.FF.FF.FF.FF.

This stack provides connectionless services at IP, NetBIOS, and LLC. Consequently, any connection-oriented services for sequencing, flow control, data integrity, etc., must be addressed by the ULPs. As another option, LLC2 could be configured, which would provide a minimal level of data integrity, sequencing, and flow control. I recommend, however, that the connectionless services be provided in a ULP and LLC be kept simple and efficient.

XNS over IP

Figure 12.7 shows a simplified version of the widely used Xerox network system (XNS) stack. XNS was developed in the 1970s and 1980s by the Xerox Corporation for use in its product lines. In most instances, the protocols were designed to work with Ethernet LANs. Xerox has made the XNS software available to the public, and the stacks have found their way into many other vendors' products. The lower layers of XNS come as no surprise. XNS also uses the IP protocol. At the layer above IP, XNS uses the *Sequenced Packet Protocol,* which has some of the functions of TCP (but it is not as functionally rich).

Figure 12.7 also shows the *courier* protocol resting in the ULP layer. The courier entity provides general services associated with the OSI presentation and session layers. It also supports procedure calls in which a request for a service is made to another entity. The results are returned, signifying the success or failure of the service request.

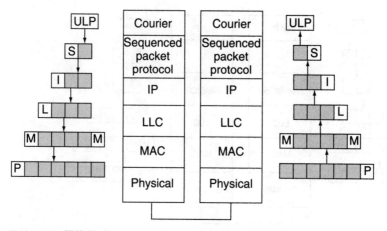

Figure 12.7 XNS Stack.

The figure also shows IP residing in the stack. The term used by XNS to define a set of complementary protocols is the *Internet transport protocols*. Note that all of these complementary protocols might not be implemented in this module. They deal with functions such as error reporting (similar to ICMP) and the error protocol (similar to the echo function of ICMP). Additionally, the XNS IP layer typically uses the routing information protocol (RIP) for exchanging routing information between routers, gateways, and host machines.

IP Router Stacks

Figure 12.8 shows the stacks of an *IP router*. In this example, the router connects two LANs: one an 802.3 CSMA/CD network and the other an 802.5 token ring network. The stacks at the router vary, depending on which port is being managed. Notwithstanding, the only difference in the stacks exists at the physical and MAC layers; LLC and IP remain the same. The operations associated with this stack are covered in more detail in Chapters 2, 3, and 5.

Relationship of IP and LAN Bridges

Figure 12.9 shows two LANs connected through a bridge. In this situation, IP does not exist at the bridge. The *MAC relay entity* is responsible for routing the traffic between the two ports (that is, the two networks). You might wonder why LLC is located at the bridge, as its principal function is to provide an interface from the upper layers into MAC. The reason is that

IEEE 802.1 MAC bridges allow the traffic to move from either the incoming MAC port across the relay entity to the outgoing MAC port or from MAC into its LLC for bridge management functions. Once at the LLC at the gateway, traffic can be passed back down to MAC or to the relay entity for operations such as bridge learning and bridge forwarding. In any event, LLC is required for all 802 MAC bridges.

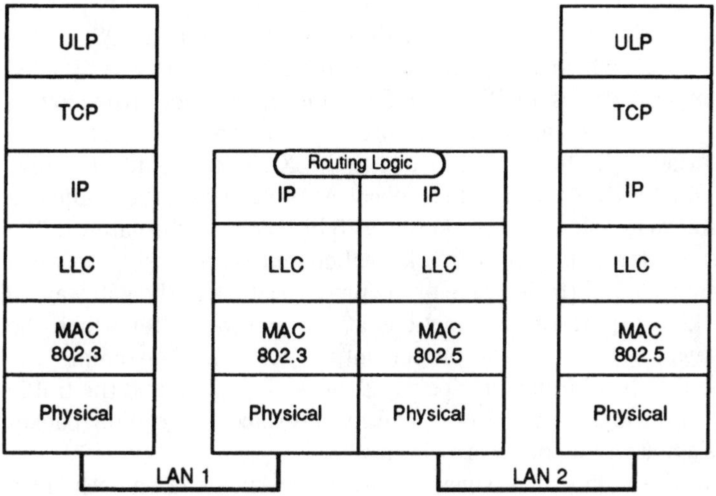

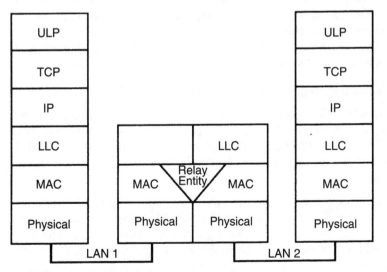

Figure 12.8 Typical LAN Router.

Figure 12.9 Typical LAN Bridge.

IP and X.25

IP and X.25 can connect in various ways:

- LANs
- public data networks
- amateur packet radio

IP, X.25, and LANs

Figure 12.10 shows the use of X.25 on a LAN. In this example, OSI TP4 is placed on top of IP, which is in turn stacked on X.25's network layer (called *packet layer procedures*, or *PLP*. The LAN station does not invoke lower-layer X.25 services, such as link access procedure balanced (LAPB) or the V-series interfaces. Rather, it encapsulates the X.25 packet into the LLC and MAC PDUs for transport to the gateway. At the gateway, the traffic traverses the stacks in reverse order. At the X.25 PLP layer in the gateway, the X.25 packet header is used to map a logical channel relationship between the user computer and the left side of the protocol stack in the gateway. IP is then invoked to perform its functions at the gateway, after which the gateway relays the traffic to the proper output port. In this example, the LAPB data link control frame encapsulates the X.25 packet, and the traffic is transmitted through EIA-232 or a V-series interface to the WAN packet switch. This stack works, but it is awkward.

Notice that the X.25 packet layer procedures are invoked on both links: (a) between the router and the LAN station, and (b) between the router and the packet switch. In effect, this operation requires that the router maintain two connections. A better implementation is for the router to accept X.25 traffic from the user device and pass it transparently to the packet switch. Therefore, the router does not participate directly in the connection between the user station and the packet switch. Of course, the router must still examine the packets and forward them to the proper machine.

IP, X.25, and public data networks

The placement of X.25 on a LAN is not very common. More typically, a user host computer connects with X.25 to the packet switch of a public data network (PDN). Figure 12.11 shows the layers for this configuration. RFC 877 has established a few simple rules for the X.25-IP and X.25-packet switch interfaces:

- A virtual circuit is handled as usual—on demand. When the host computer receives a datagram by the X.25 module, it sends a call-request packet to the switch. Upon receiving a call-connected packet, the host transmits the IP datagram in the X.25 user data field of the X.25 packet.
- The first octet of the call user data field of the call-request packet must contain hex CC to signify IP is running on X.25.

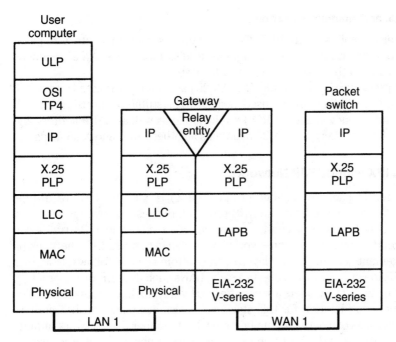

Figure 12.10 X.25 on a LAN.

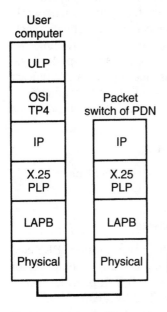

Figure 12.11 IP, X.25, and a Public Data Network.

- M-bit operations are allowed.
- Unless negotiated otherwise, the maximum size of the IP datagram is 576 octets.

IP, X.25, and amateur packet radio

Another possibility for an IP-X.25 combination is to encapsulate X.25 packets into IP datagrams. This technique is used to support the AX.25 protocol, which runs on the amateur packet radio system.

The procedure is very simple. One AX.25 packet is encapsulated into one IP datagram. LAPB flags are not used, nor is zero bit stuffing or unstuffing. LAPB cyclic redundancy checks (CRCs) are included as well as LAPB address and control fields. Otherwise, AX.25 maintains all other LAPB and X.25 fields.

Using IPX with UDP/IP Networks

The Internet packet exchange protocol (IPX) is Novell's Netware IP-type product. It is derived from the XNS protocol. Because Netware is so widely implemented, a short discussion is appropriate to show how IPX traffic can be carried through internet networks. As shown in Figure 12.12, the stacking arrangement is from the top layer to the bottom layer as follows: ULP, IPX, UDP, IP, lower-layer protocols (typically, LANs such as IEEE or Ethernets).

The IP and UDP headers are not affected by this stacking arrangement. The principal consideration for this stack is address mappings. An IPX address space consists of a network number and a host number. The network number is four octets, and the host number is six. This combined number is used by IPX to route each IPX packet to its destination. Like the IP scheme, once the network number has fulfilled its function of reaching the destination network, the host number routes the traffic to the host attached to the destination network. For the IPX UDP/IP interface, RFC 1234 requires that the first two octets of the host number be set to 0, and the last four octets represent the node's IP address. This approach provides an easy method to handle unicast transmissions by simply discarding the first two octets of the host number.

The maximum transmission unit (MTU) for IPX is 576 octets. For this stack, the resulting PDU will be 604 octets:

IPX of 576 + IP header of 20 + UDP of 8 = 604

All implementations supporting this stacking arrangement must be able to receive an IP packet of 604 octets.

Transmitting 802 LLC Traffic over IPX Networks

A different approach, depicted in Figure 12.13, is transmitting IEEE 802 LLC1 traffic over IPX networks. This is a fairly common implementation for organizations that have configured their LANs with IPX. It provides a convenient method of continuing to use IPX over an 802 LAN card.

The protocol stacking arrangement is as follows from higher layer to lower layer: ULP, TCP, IP, 802.2 LLC, IPX, and the physical layer. RFC 1132 has established two rules for this protocol stacking arrangement. First, ad-

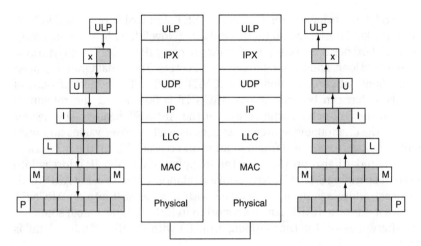

Figure 12.12 IPX over UDP/IP.

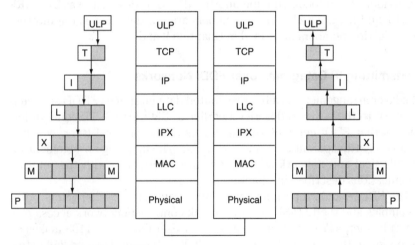

Figure 12.13 802 LLC over IPX.

dress mapping between IP addresses and IPX addresses is performed using ARP; however, the IPX physical address is 10 octets (4 bytes for IPX network address and 6 bytes for the IPX host address). Second, this protocol stacking arrangement does not use the IPX checksum.

Transmitting IP Datagrams over ARCNET Networks

ARCNET is a widely used protocol for LANs, and RFC 1201 has established a procedure for the transmission of IP datagrams over these networks. As you might expect, IP datagrams are encapsulated into ARCNET PDUs in what is known as the *client data area*.

Several vendors have agreed on an ARCNET standard as published in "AR-CNET Packet Header Definitions Standard" (Novell Inc., November, 1989). This standard permits two types of frames to carry IP traffic. The short frame is 256 octets long, and the long frame is 512 octets. The IP datagram is placed in the client data area behind the ARCNET header. The largest amount of user data that can be sent across ARCNET is 504 octets; the remaining octets of the 512-octet frame consist of the ARCNET header. The header contains destination and source addresses as well as offset values and fragmentation flags to perform fragmentation and reassembly on the network.

This standard also provides for the mapping of a 32-bit IP address into the corresponding 8-bit ARCNET address. Mapping occurs using ARP; all IP broadcast addresses must be mapped with a value of 0 into an ARCNET broadcast address. RARP is also supported in RFC 1201, although some minor differences exist in the mapping. Consult with the RFC if more detail is required.

Be aware that Datapoint Corporation uses different ARCNET protocol IDs to identify protocols running on ARCNET. IP is designated as 212, ARP as 213, and RARP as 214. These numbers are not the same as the Internet identification numbers described in Chapters 2 and 3.

Transmitting IP Datagrams over FDDI Networks

The layer arrangement for fiber distributed data interface (FDDI) service is identical to the services described earlier in Figure 12.3. The only difference is that FDDI contains two sublayers at the physical layer, which is completely transparent to IP and 802.2 LLC. The mapping arrangement for the physical and network addresses is in conformance with the Internet specifications described in Chapters 2 and 3.

The FDDI standard permits a maximum frame size of 4500 octets. After preambles and the LLC/SNAP (logical link control/subnetwork access protocol) header, 4470 octets are available for user data. RFC 1188 makes an exception in this case in that it defines 4096 octets for data and 256 octets for headers at the layers above MAC. Gateways supporting FDDI must be able to accept packets this large and, if necessary, perform fragmentation operations. Additionally, although hosts can accept large packets, it is recommended that hosts not send datagrams greater than 576 octets unless they know the receiving host can support a larger size.

Addressing schemes on FDDI networks are quite similar to those discussed earlier for the other IEEE 802 networks. The only restriction is that interworking IP and ARP over FDDI requires the use of a 48-bit physical-level address.

As you might expect, IP over FDDI requires using 802 LLC type 1 using the conventional LLC frames: UI, XID, TEST. Be aware that IEEE specifies its control values with the least significant bit first (the little-endian). The

Internet Protocols are just the opposite and document their control fields in big-endian order. This difference presents no problem as long as users working with IEEE and Internet networks understand the documentation.

IP over Switched Multimegabit Data Service

Switched multimegabit data service (SMDS) is a public network offering packet-switched connectionless service. Its purpose is to support high throughput with low delay, as well as large PDUs of up to 9188 user octets. SMDS provides no explicit flow-control mechanisms; rather, it has a subscriber-to-network and a network-to-subscriber access class enforcement mechanism that provides congestion control in the network.

IP can rest on top of an SMDS network by interfacing into the IEEE 802 LLC sublayer. In turn, LLC rests on top of the SMDS layers. This arrangement is straightforward because the interface protocol into SMDS is based on the IEEE 802.6 metropolitan area network (MAN) distributed-queue-dual-bus (DQDB) MAC protocol. This protocol has a rich MAC convergence function that allows connectionless services such as LLC1 and IP to be encapsulated into the DQDB PDU.

The concept of IP over SMDS is based on using SMDS to support multiple logical IP subnetworks (known as LIS). Each LIS is managed by separate administrative authorities but uses the common SMDS for communications. For LIS configuration, all stations within the LIS are accessed directly from one SMDS. This method requires that all LIS members have the same IP network and subnetwork numbers. Communications for stations outside LIS are performed through an IP router. An SMDS group address is used to identify all members within the LIS, which permits SMDS to deliver traffic to the LIS members.

The layering arrangements for this stack are shown in Figure 12.14. The IP interface occurs through the media convergence function (MCF), which interfaces directly into LLC. The queued-arbitrated functions (QA) define the procedures for sharing the DQDB. Resting beneath the QA are functions common to both queued-arbitrated, and prearbitrated (PA) functions. The PA functions are not relevant to this discussion but are used for isonchronous services such as voice and video. The physical layer provides the ongoing cabling and physical transmission for the dual cable bus. As you might expect, the services with this stack are quite common to other services that use LLC. The use of LLC1 frames is the same as for the protocol stacks discussed earlier in this chapter.

OSI's Transport Protocol Class 0 over TCP

Figure 12.15 shows the stacking arrangement to run OSI's TP Class 0 (TP0) over TCP. You might wonder why such a stacking arrangement would be desirable, but the principal advantage is that it provides convenient and easy

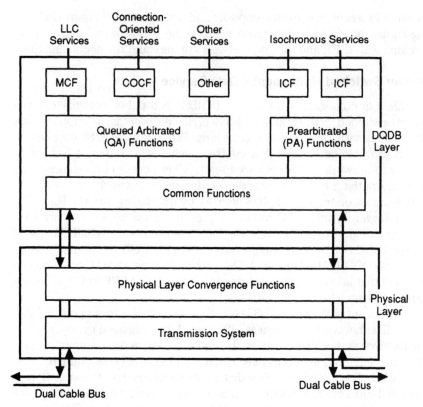

Figure 12.14   IP over SMDS with 802.6 DQDB.

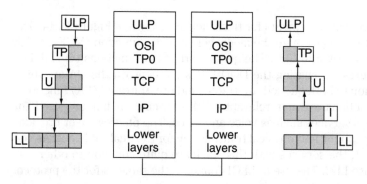

Figure 12.15   OSI Transport Class 0 over TCP.

access to the upper layers of the OSI Model and allows an organization to continue using the TCP/IP suite. Additionally, TP0 is a minimal level of service for the transport layer, so redundancy of function is not risked when implementing both OSI's transport layer and the Internet's TCP with TP0.

In the OSI Model, a connection between a transport layer user and the transport layer is achieved through service definitions known as primitives. These are defined in ITU-T's X.214 recommendation and ISO's 8072 standard. For using the stack in this scenario, RFC 1006 defines the mapping of these OSI primitives to receive TCP service. The OSI transport layer does not work with a client-server approach; therefore, an OSI indication primitive is used instead of a server listening on a well-known port. The mapping between TCP and TP0 occurs through the use of the OSI service definitions. Table 12.1 lists these mappings, as well as mappings of the parameters between the network service and TCP.

OSI Connectionless Transport Layer over UDP

This section describes a similar approach to Figure 12.15, except that connectionless services are used, both at the OSI layer and the Internet layer. The scheme is almost identical to that described in the previous section, ex-

TABLE 12.1 Mapping TP0 and TCP

TP0 ↔ Network layer definitions	TCP service
N-CONNECT.request	Open completes
N-CONNECT.indication	Passive Open (Listen) finishes
N-CONNECT.response	Listen finishes
N-CONNECT.confirmation	Open (Active) finishes
N-DATA.request	Send data
N-DATA.indication	Data ready

TP0 ↔ Network parameter	TCP parameter
Called address	Server's IP addresses
Calling address	Client's IP address
Data (NDSU)	Data
Others	Ignored

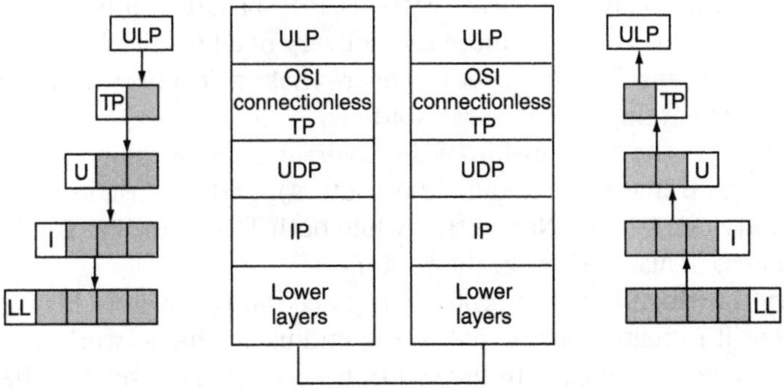

Figure 12.16 OSI Connectionless Transport Layer over UDP.

cept that no connection-oriented services are invoked. Rather, the OSI network services N-UNITDATA.request and N-UNITDATA.indication are the only ones permitted between connectionless OSI and UDP. The parameter mapping is also quite simple. The source and destination addresses in the OSI layer map to the called and calling IP addresses for UDP services. User data maps directly to the UDP user data. Any other fields that exist in the OSI Model are ignored. The stacking arrangement is also quite simple, as depicted in Figure 12.16.

TCP/IP (and Others) over ISDN

Figure 12.17 shows a typical protocol stack for interfacing a user workstation to a packet switch through an ISDN node. Notice that IP is no longer included in this stack because most vendors are implementing these options with IP's OSI counterpart, CLNP. Although nothing precludes using TCP or IP in the user computer in place of OSI TP4 and CLNP.

The traffic is transmitted from the user computer across the ISDN *R reference point* and the *terminal adapter (TA)* stack, which maps the X.25 layers according to the X.25 specifications. Operations then take place on the right side of the TA. The TA uses the ISDN layers to establish proper D and B channel operations to the *ISDN node* across the *S/T reference point*. Although not depicted in this figure, after the three layers of ISDN are operational, the terminal adapter dequeues the X.25 traffic and transports it transparently through the ISDN layers to the ISDN node. Once at the ISDN node, the traffic is passed up through the ISDN layers and then passed off to an ISDN *packet handler* (which, in the real world, is nothing more than a packet switch). The packet switch assumes the functions of X.25 and sends the packet down through the X.25 stack to communicate with the network *packet switch*.

TCP/IP over Frame Relay

The placement of TCP/IP over frame relay is an effective approach for internetworking frame relay networks with TCP/IP-based workstations. Because frame relay does not guarantee the delivery of all traffic, TCP acts as the last "line of defense" for the user to ensure that critical user traffic is accounted for between the two end-user stations.

Figure 12.18 shows the relationship of the layers located at the end-user host machines, the frame relay nodes (the routers), and the frame relay switches (the network nodes). Notice that while both TCP and IP reside in the host machines, IP also resides in the routers.

Vendors vary on which network protocol is placed in the switch. Figure 12.18 shows that it remains transparent to the end user. The network protocol can also remain transparent to the router because it is considered the network's responsibility.

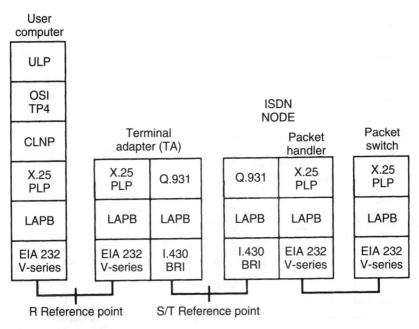

Figure 12.17 ISDN Connections.

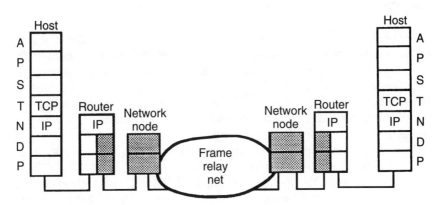

Figure 12.18 TCP/IP and Frame Relay Layers.

Stacks for the 1990s

Figure 12.19 shows one of several possibilities for a set of protocol stacks using emerging technologies. The user machine could consist of the layers discussed in the previous examples, as well as voice images such as telephone calls, and video images such as high-definition television. The lower layers are labeled *user network communication layers* and could be ISDN, LAN, TCP/IP, or whatever layers are needed to transmit the traffic

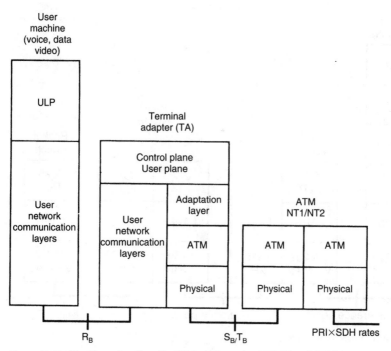

Figure 12.19 The Emerging Signaling Digital Hierarchy, BISDN, and ATM.

from the user device onto a network or communications channel. The *terminal adapter* is a much more sophisticated device than the present ISDN terminal adapters. On the left side, it has the layers used to accommodate the user layers. It also has a set of protocols (or a layer) called the *control plane* and the *user plane*. This software accommodates the traffic coming out of and into the user layers. The plane acts as an intermediary between the user layers and the *adaptation layer.*

The adaptation layer is application-specific, so it is highly variable. It passes the traffic to the *asynchronous transfer mode (ATM)*. The ATM is the key component in emerging communications network technology for the 1990s. It forms the foundation for broadband ISDN (BISDN) and performs switching and multiplexing functions for traffic it has received. Its physical connection might be to another ATM machine, labeled in this figure as *ATM NT1/NT2*. This configuration is not required, and all the multiplexing and switching functions could be performed within the terminal adapter (although that probably will not be the case because of the expense involved). Therefore, in this example, the ATM NT1/NT2 is responsible for receiving traffic from other devices and terminal adapters and multiplexing the traffic into multiples of primary rates, which are labeled in this figure as *PRI×SDH* (synchronous digital hierarchy) *rates*. SDH is the cornerstone of the merging of BISDN, MANs, and integrated voice/data (IVD) applications.

Summary

TCP/IP exists in a wide variety of standards and vendor products. Most implementations are based on the layered protocol approach, in which TCP/IP is encapsulated into other PDUs, or other protocols are encapsulated into TCP segments and IP datagrams.

Chapter

13

TCP/IP and Operating Systems

This chapter provides an overview of the relationship between computer operating systems and the TCP/IP suite of protocols. The focus in this chapter is on the UNIX and IBM PC operating systems, due to their prevalence in the industry. Keep in mind that many other interfaces are also available. For example, C function calls and Fortran subroutine calls could be used as shown in Figure 13.1. The UNIX examples included in this chapter illustrate the implementation using the System V UNIX release from AT&T. The PC explanation focuses on higher-level calls to obtain services for an application layer or a PC keyboard user.

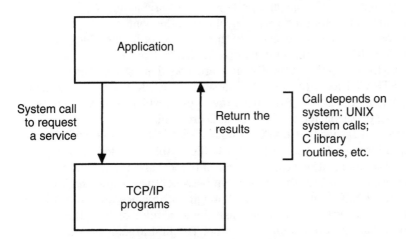

Figure 13.1 Accessing TCP/IP through UNIX Calls.

UNIX and TCP/IP

This section provides several examples of the UNIX operating system and its interface with TCP. I cite the BSD 4.3 UNIX interfaces in this section because of their prevalence in the industry. UNIX was developed at Bell Labs in the late 1960s. It was designed originally for single processor computers and includes many features that make it quite popular among software developers. Principal among those features are timesharing capabilities and its system calls, which provide the programmer with easy operations.

Connection-oriented services

The concept of a *socket,* which is discussed several times in this book, is very much a part of the BSD UNIX input/output (I/O) concept. A socket is really nothing more than an end point in the communications process. Unlike some socket concepts with I/O files, the TCP/IP BSD UNIX concept allows a socket to be created without providing a destination address. A destination address in a later system call is used to create a final binding between the sending and receiving addresses.

Figure 13.2 shows the system call that creates a socket. It is identified as *socket* and consists of three arguments. The *domain* field describes the protocol family (a domain) associated with the socket. It could include, for example, the Internet family, PUP family, DEC family, or Appletalk family. The *type* argument stipulates the type of communications desired with this connection. The programmer can establish values to specify datagram service, reliable delivery service, or a raw socket. The third argument allows the programmer to code the type of service provided by each of the *protocols* within the protocol family. This argument is required because protocol families usually consist of more than one protocol. It is the task of the programmer to supply the specific protocol in this argument. If left at 0, the system selects the appropriate protocol within the domain.

The domain values are available in the <sys/socket.h> file. The UNIX domain is AFUNIX; the Internet domain is AF_INET. The socket types are also found in the <sys/socket.h> file and are coded in the systems call as SOCK_STREAM for a reliable, stream service; SOCK_DGRAM for a datagram service; and SOCK_RAW for a raw socket, which provides access to underlying protocols for communications programmers.

We learned earlier that UNIX allows a socket to be created without furnishing addresses for the socket (in UNIX V, this is called *naming* the socket). Communications cannot occur until local and foreign internet addresses are declared for the association between the communicating entities. In the UNIX domain, local and foreign path names are used. Figure 13.3 shows the system call to establish the local address with the socket. The *bind* call sets up half an association. The first argument in the list is called *s* and contains the integer number value of the socket. The local *name* argument can vary, but usually consists of three values: the protocol family, the port number, and an internet address. The *namelen* argument contains the length of the second argument.

Figure 13.4 shows the next step in mapping the TCP/IP connection between two machines. The *connect* system call allows the programmer to connect a socket to a destination address. As the figure illustrates, the *s* (socket number), the *name* (destination ID), and *namelen* (name length) are included as arguments. The name parameter in the system call identifies the remote socket for the binding.

The asymmetric nature of port bindings allows easy implementation of a client-server relationship. The server issues a bind to establish a socket for a well-known service, such as the file transfer protocol (FTP). It then passively listens for a client to send a connect request to the server's passive socket. If a connection is unsuccessful, an error is returned to the requester. Over 20 error codes are available with the connect call, such as ECONNREFUSE, which signifies the host refusal of the connection because

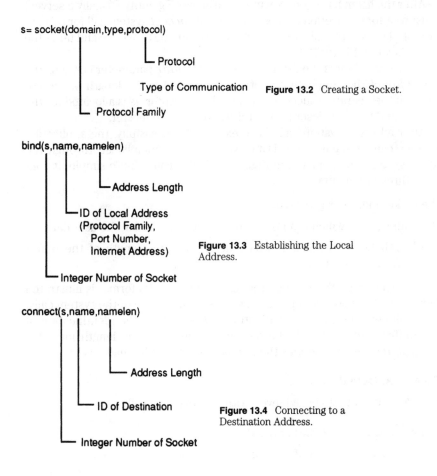

s= socket(domain,type,protocol)

└─ Protocol

Type of Communication   **Figure 13.2** Creating a Socket.

└─ Protocol Family

bind(s,name,namelen)

└─ Address Length

└─ ID of Local Address
(Protocol Family,
Port Number,
Internet Address)   **Figure 13.3** Establishing the Local Address.

└─ Integer Number of Socket

connect(s,name,namelen)

└─ Address Length

└─ ID of Destination   **Figure 13.4** Connecting to a Destination Address.

└─ Integer Number of Socket

the server process cannot be found given the name furnished, and ETIME-OUT, which means the connection attempt took too long.

After a server has set up a passive socket, it listens for requested incoming connections (this function is only supported on reliable stream delivery). This operation is performed with the *listen* system call, which takes the form shown in Figure 13.5.

The parameter *s* is the socket on which connections occur; the *backlog* parameter establishes the maximum queue size for holding incoming connection requests. If the queue is full, an incoming connection request is refused with an indication of ECONNREFUSED. Other error codes associated with listen are

EBADF = s is invalid

ENOISOCK = s is not a socket

EONOTSUPP = socket does not support a listen operation

After the listen has been executed, the accepting entity (usually a server) must wait for connection requests. It uses the *accept* system call for this operation. The accept pulls the first entity in the queue to service and takes the form shown in Figure 13.6.

The *s* parameter is the listening socket, the *addr* parameter contains the *sockaddr* of the connecting entity, and *addrlen* is the length of the address. If the operation succeeds, a new file descriptor *ns* is allocated for the socket, and the new descriptor is returned to the requester.

After all these system calls have executed successfully, the application entities can exchange data. Data exchange is accomplished through the *write* system call, depicted in Figure 13.7. The call is quite simple. It contains three arguments.

the socket identifier (*descriptor*)

the buffer (*buf*), which is a pointer in memory containing the user data

the length field (*sizeofbuf*), which determines the length of the buffer search for the user data

To receive data, the *read* system call is invoked. Its format is illustrated in Figure 13.8. Note the repetitive aspects of the design of the system calls. This call contains the socket identifier (*descriptor*), the identification of the buffer (*buf*) in which the data will reside, and the length indicator (*sizeofbuf*), which describes the number of bytes to be read.

Other input/output calls

Input/output can also be achieved with the following calls:

```
send(S,buf,sizeofbuf,flags)
recv(S,buf,sizeofbuf,flags)
```

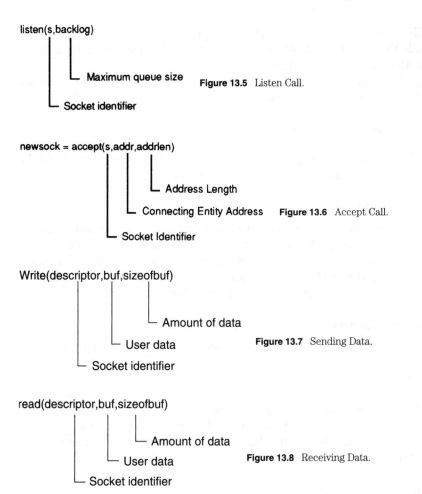

Figure 13.5 Listen Call.

Figure 13.6 Accept Call.

Figure 13.7 Sending Data.

Figure 13.8 Receiving Data.

The only difference between these calls and the write and read calls is the extra *flags* parameter. It allows the programmer to use other options in receiving or sending data to or from a connected socket. The flags field (established in the <sys/socket.h> file) can be set to signify the following:

MSG_PEEK: examine the next message without reading it.

MSG_OOB: receive out-of-band (urgent) data.

MSG_DONTROUTE: send data but do not actually route it (for diagnostic/maintenance purposes).

Two other input calls are available. The *recvfrom* call is used to request input on a socket either in a connected or unconnected state. Its form is

```
recvfrom(s,buf,len,flags,from,fromlen)
```

Two other parameters are present with this call. The *from* parameter holds the message sender's address. The *fromlen* parameter returns the length of the sender's address.

The *recvmsg* call can also be used to receive input on an unconnected socket. It has fewer parameters than recvfrom and takes the form

```
recvmsg (s, msg, flags)
```

The *msg* parameter defines a structure that includes the address and the size of the incoming message, as well as authentication entities.

Datagram services

Two other calls similar to *recvfrom* and *recvmsg* are *send to* and *sendmsg*, respectively, except they send data rather than receive it. The *send to* and *recvfrom* calls are used with UDP datagram services. In addition, a connect call is permitted with UDP operations to map a socket to a destination address. Accept and listen are not used with UDP.

Closing a connection

A socket can be closed if it is no longer needed with the following system call:

```
close(s)
```

Data can, however, continue to be sent or delivered even after the close is issued (check with your vendor for this feature). After some period of time, the data are discarded. If the user does not wish to send or receive any more data, it can issue

```
shutdown(s, how)
```

where parameters for *how* are

0 = not interested in receiving data

1 = no more data will be sent

2 = no more data will be sent or received

Other system calls

We have reviewed the most commonly used UNIX systems calls for invoking TCP/IP services. Several others are available and warrant an explanation (the parameters for these calls are not included in this general explanation):

select: multiplex input/output operations on more than one socket

gethostbyname: obtain host name (usually its domain name) *sethostbyname*: set host name

getpeername: obtain the name of a peer connected to a socket

gethostbyaddr: obtain internet address of the host

getsockname: obtain a socket and its associated local address

getnetbyname: obtain network name

getnetbyaddr: obtain network address

getprotobyname: obtain protocol name

getprotobynumber: obtain protocol number

All the UNIX calls are not included; several others are available for domain sources, mapping and swapping network numbers, and obtaining information on servers and clients.

Example of programs to invoke UNIX-based TCP/IP services

Figure 13.9 shows an example of a program using UNIX calls to open a socket, read it, and close. Figures 13.10 and 13.11 show examples of reading and sending datagrams. These examples are from *UNIX SYSTEM V, Release 4, Programmers Guide: Network Interfaces* (Prentice Hall, 1990) and are reprinted with the permission of Prentice-Hall.

PC Interface Program

PC vendors offer a number of interface programs to invoke TCP/IP services and internet applications services. This section highlights several user commands available in the IBM Interface Program. Further information is available in IBM manual number SC23-0812-0.

While studying this section, note how easily the user commands work with this interface program. Granted, the parameters associated with the commands require a user to have a firm grasp of how the TCP/IP protocols operate. In this context, a "user" of this interface is a systems/communications programmer. An *end-user* interface (with friendly screen menus and blinking color lights) is beyond this discussion. Note that IBM uses the syntax diagram shown in Figure 13.12 to document many of its products, including the material in this section.

Sending mail through SMTP

The *netmail* command supports transmitting user mail through simple mail transfer protocol (SMTP) to another user or users. Figure 13.13 shows the syntax of the command. The *mail_file* parameter identifies the file to be sent. The *rcpt* parameters use the Internet naming convention for the user host. The *repeat arrow* signifies that more than one user can be identified.

```
#include <sys/types.h>
#include <sys/socket.h>
#include <netinet/in.h>
#include <netdb.h>
#include <stdio.h>
#define TRUE 1
/*
    *This program creates a socket and then begins an infinite loop. Each time
    *through the loop it accepts a connection and prints out messages from it.
    *When the connection breaks, or a termination message comes through, the
    *program accepts a new connection.
    */
main()
{
    int sock, length;
    struct sockaddr_in server;
    int msgsock;
    char buf[1024];
    int rval;
    /*Create socket.*/
    sock = socket (AF_INET,SOCK_STREAM,0);
    if (sock < 0){
                    perror (''opening stream socket'');
                    exit (1);
    }
    /*Name socket using wildcards.*/
    server.sin_family = AF_INET;
    server.sin_addr.s_addr = INADDR_ANY;
    server.sin_port = 0;
    if(bind(sock,(struct sockaddr*)&server, sizeof server)<0){
                    perror(''binding stream socket'');
                    exit(1);
    }
    /*Find out assigned port number and print it out.*/
    length = sizeof server;
    if (getsockname (sock, (struct sockaddr*)&server,
      &length) < 0){
                    perror (''getting socket name:);
                    exit(1);
    }
    printf(''Socket port#%d\n'', ntohs (server.sin_port));
    /*Start accepting connections. */
    listen(sock, 5);
do{
            msgsock = accept(sock, (struct sockaddr*)0,(int*)0);
```

Figure 13.9 Accepting an Internet Domain Stream Connection.

```
            if (msgsock = -1)
                    perror (''accept'');
            else do {
                    memset(buf, 0, sizeof buf);
                    if ((rval = read(msgsock, buf, 1024)) < 0)
                            perror(''reading stream message'');
                    if (rval = 0)
                            printf(Ending connection\n'');
                    else
                            printf(''-- > %s \n'', buf);
            } while (rval! = 0);
            close(msgsock);
} while (TRUE);
/*
    *Since this program has an infinite loop, the socket ''sock'' is
    *never explicitly closed. However, all sockets will be closed
    *automatically when a process is killed or terminates normally.
    */
    exit (0);
```

Figure 13.9 *(Continued)*

```
#include <sys/types.h>
#include <sys/socket.h>
#include <netinet/in.h>
#include <stdio.h>
/*
    *The include file <netinet/in.h> defines sockaddr_in as follows:
    *struct sockaddr_in(
    *       short sin_family;
    *       u_short sin_port;
    *       struct in_addr sin_addr;
    *       char sin_zero [8];
    *);
    *
    *This program creates a datagram socket, binds a name to it, then
      reads
    *from the socket.
    */
main()
{
            int sock, length;
            struct sockaddr_in name;
            char buf[1024];

            /*Create a socket from which to read.*/
            sock = socket (AF_INET, SOCK_DGRAM,0);
            if (sock < 0){
                    perror (''opening datagram socket'');
                    exit (1);
```

Figure 13.10 Reading Internet Domain Datagrams.

```
        }
        /*Create name with wildcards.*/
        name.sin_family = AF_INET;
        name.sin_addr.s_addr = INADDR_ANY;
        name.sin_port = 0;
        if (bind (sock,(struct sockaddr*)&name,
          sizeof name) < 0){
                        perror(''binding datagram socket'');
                        exit (1);
        }
        /*Find assigned port value and print it out. */
        length = sizeof (name);
        if (getsockname (sock, (struct sockaddr*)&name,
          &length) < 0(
                        perror(''getting socket name'');
                        exit(1);
        )
        printf(''Socket port #%d\n'', ntohs(name, sin_port));
        /*Read from the socket. */
        if (read(sock, buf, 1024)<0)
                        perror(''receiving datagram packet'');
        printf(''-- > %s\n'', buf);
        close(sock);
        exit(0);
```

Figure 13.10 *(Continued)*

```
#include <sys/types.h>
#include <sys/socket.h>
#include <netinet/in.h>
#include <netdb.h>
#include <stdio.h>

#define DATA ''The sea is calm, the tide is full...''

/*
    *Here I send a datagram to a receiver whose name I get from the command
    *line arguments. The form of the command line is:
    *dgramsend hostname portnumber
    */
main(argc, argv)
        int argc;
        char*argv[];
{
        int sock;
        struct sockaddr_in name;
        struct hostend *hp, *gethostbyname();

        /*Create socket on which to send. */
        sock = socket(AF_INET, SOCK_DGRAM,0);
        if(sock<0){
                        perror(''opening datagram socket'');
                        exit(1);
        }
        /*
            *Construct name, with no wildcards, of the socket to send to.
            *gethostbyname returns a structure including the network
            address
```

Figure 13.11   Sending an Internet Domain Datagram.

```
*of the specified host. The port number is taken from the
 command
*line.
*/
hp = gethostbyname (argv[1]);
if (hp == 0){
            fprintf(stdarr, ''%s: unknown host\n'', argv[1]);
            exit(2);
}
memcpy( (char*)&name,sin_addr,(char*)hp- > h_addr,
  hp- > h_length);
name.sin_family = AF_INET;
name.sin_port = htons(atoi(argv[2]));
/*Send message.*/
if (sendto (sock, DATA, sizeof DATA, 0,
  (struct sockaddr*)&name, sizeof name)<0)
            perror(''sending datagram message'');
close(sock);
exit(0);
```

Figure 13.11 *(Continued)*

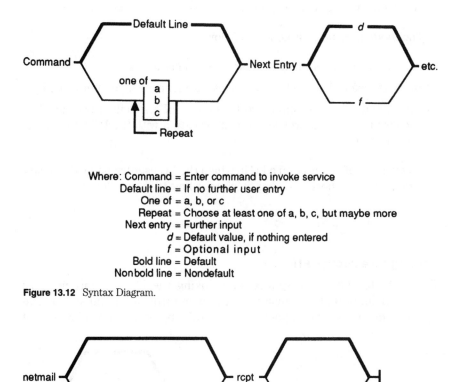

Where: Command = Enter command to invoke service
        Default line = If no further user entry
            One of = a, b, or c
            Repeat = Choose at least one of a, b, c, but maybe more
        Next entry = Further input
                d = Default value, if nothing entered
                f = Optional input
            Bold line = Default
        Nonbold line = Nondefault

Figure 13.12   Syntax Diagram.

Figure 13.13   netmail Command for SMPT Services.

An example of an entry on a PC in which the PC user wishes to send mail in the file called *sales memo* to *UBlack* at *ACME.COM.* would appear as

```
$ netmail sales memo UBlack@ACME.COM.
```

Sending a file through TFTP

Figure 13.14 shows the syntax for a user command to transfer files between hosts with the trivial file transfer protocol (TFTP). The *action* parameter is coded as

wrp: write the file designated as *localname* into the file system of the foreign host designated as *foreignname*

rrg: read the file designated as *foreignname* from the foreign host into the local file designated as *localname*

o: override or supersede ongoing local files

The *mode* parameter is coded as follows:

netascii: file transfer using standard ASCII characters

image: transfer files and binary images with no conversion performed

mail: append the files stipulated to the end of a specified user mailbox (afterward the user can retrieve this information with the PC/UNIX (AIX) mail command)

An example of an entry on a PC in which the PC user transfers the binary file /receipts from host4 to /tempreceipts at host10 is as follows:

```
$ tftp -w /receipts host4 /tempreceipts image
```

Sending a file through FTP

Figure 13.15 shows the syntax for invoking the FTP operations. This command supports the transfer of files to and from a foreign server. The *xftp* command assumes a packet size of 1576 bytes and a window size of

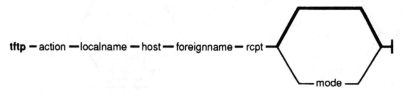

tftp — action — localname — host — foreignname — rcpt

mode

Figure 13.14   tftp Command for TFTP Operations.

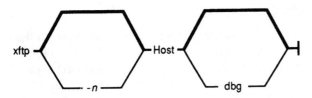

Figure 13.15 xftp Command for FTP Operations.

6K bytes. Files are transferred in the standard ASCII format, although other commands are available to request binary transfer. The -*n* parameter provides the user with automatic login, which precludes the user from entering an ID and password. The *host* parameter is the name of the client host. The *dbg* parameter is coded into one of four values to request the following services:

0: obtain trace service messages

1: obtain error messages

2: show all receipt packets

4: show all sent packets

Upon being executed, the xftp command can be followed by several subcommands, which are provided to the user with the following prompt on the screen: xftp>. The user can then enter the subcommands. Several examples of subcommands are the following:

acct: provide accounting information

append: append a file to another file

binary: data transferred is binary

dir: display a listing of the directory

get: retrieve a foreign file and stores it at the local host

pass: provide password information

put: send a local file on a foreign host

Here is an example of the xftp operation:

```
$ xftp host 4
login operations (e.g., TELNET)
xftp> binary
xftp> put/receipts/tempreceipts
status messages of file transfer
xftp> quit
user is logged off
```

Using tn to invoke TELNET login services

Figure 13.16 shows the syntax for logging onto a foreign host through the TELNET interface. The tn command is used to access a TELNET protocol. Note that several subcommands can be used as part of tn by keying in control-T and single character subcommands. These subcommands allow the user to obtain many of the services of TELNET described in earlier chapters, such as are-you-theres, breaks, keying in data, establishing echo modes, and displaying status.

The *host* parameter identifies the TELNET connection to the specific host. If this parameter is not supplied, the user is prompted to provide a host name. The *-d* indicates that the debugging option is on, and the *-p port* identifies the foreign port number for this connection; otherwise, the system defaults to the TELNET port.

A typical example of a TELNET login is as follows:

```
$ tn host 4
login occurs
user can enter subcommands
```

Retrieving network statistics

The *netstat* command allows an end user to obtain information about the state of the network and the state of connections. The netstat command is depicted in Figure 13.17. Four options are available to obtain these services:

-a: displays the state of all connections.

-i: displays the state of configurations that are automatically configured (connections that are loaded into the system).

-r: displays the routing table.

-v: displays statistics about the LAN device driver on this internet interface.

The following example is of a user keying in the netstat command to obtain the local IP routing table:

```
$ netstat -r
routing table is displayed on the screen
```

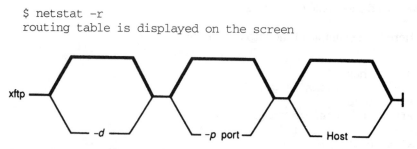

Figure 13.16 tn Command for a TELNET Login.

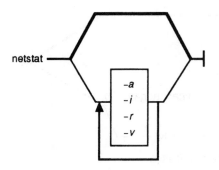

Figure 13.17 netstat Command to Obtain Network Statistics.

Using PING to obtain echo services

Figure 13.18 shows the syntax for the PING service. After entering the command PING, the user chooses one of four parameters to obtain the PING service:

-*g*: a GGP echo request message is sent to a specified *host*.

-*i*: an ICMP echo request is sent to a specified host.

-*m*: a submask is returned for a specified host.

-*t*: an ICMP-type time-stamp request is returned for a specified host.

The following is an example of how a user executes PING to obtain the ICMP time-stamp service:

```
$ ping -t host 4
Information on screen contains the three ICMP time-stamp
values: originated, received, transmitted
```

Using route to manipulate the IP routing table

Figure 13.19 depicts the syntax for adding or removing routes from the IP routing table. The commands *add* and *delete* add and remove a route, respectively. The -*f* command clears the host gateway table. The *destination* parameter is an IP address identifying a host or network where the route is

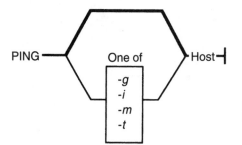

Figure 13.18 PING Command to Obtain Echo Services.

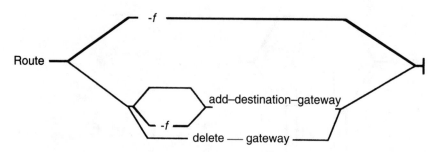

Figure 13.19 ROUTE Command to Add and Remove IP Routes.

directed. The *gateway* parameter is an IP address that identifies the next gateway to process the datagram.

The following is an example of the route command in which gateway 14.3.2.1 is established as a default gateway:

```
$ route add 0 14.3.2.1.
```

Summary

Through the use of operating system calls, such as those in UNIX, a communications programmer can manipulate TCP/IP open and close sockets, transfer data, obtain name server support, and perform other services. On a higher level, programs such as the IBM Interface Program allow a user to obtain the upper internet application-layer services such as file transfer, mail exchange, and remote terminal login without needing to understand the more complex operating system calls.

14

Management Considerations

The discussion in this chapter on OSI classifies several of the ITU-T and International Standards Organization (ISO) protocols as OSI, which is not actually correct, although it is common in the industry to do so. These protocols instead use the OSI Model as a foundation for their design. Strictly speaking, the number of defined OSI protocols are very few, because the intent of OSI is to provide a model first, and define protocols second.

I should also like to state (I am sure I am one of the few people in the industry that has this opinion) that, as a Model, OSI has been very successful. Its major problem is that the OSI architects made the mistake of embedding actual protocols into the Model. Unfortunately, most people do not distinguish between the OSI protocols and the OSI Model.

Vendor Strategies with Internet-Based Products

By 1990, enterprises such as commercial banks, insurance companies, and government departments had either written a plan to migrate to the OSI standards or were planning to write such a plan. Indeed, the U.S. government, which was the chief architect and sponsor of the Internet, issued a directive for government agencies to migrate to GOSIP (The U.S. Government OSI Profile), which is an implementation of OSI. The use of the Internet standards has overwhelmed OSI. But OSI is hanging on, and a number of my clients are now using OSI or are planning to migrate to it. In any case, it appears that in the future a user must deal with vendor-specific protocols, Internet protocols, and OSI protocols.

Without question, every major communications vendor is planning one or both of the following scenarios:

- migrate away from vendor-specific products toward the OSI and TCP/IP suites
- maintain the vendor-specific layers and provide interfaces between these layers and the OSI/TCP/IP suites

The following scenario is *not* what the vendors and manufacturers are openly espousing: vendor-specific protocols as the best approach, and their product lines built strictly on specific customer requirements (i.e., tailored to the individual customer).

It should be emphasized that a company tasked with the design, manufacturing, and selling of computer and communications products must frequently produce a system tailored to the specific user environment. In a situation in which the environment does not fit the OSI or TCP/IP framework, what is to be done?

The answer is obvious: Build the product to meet the customer's needs, and try to design the product to have "hooks" into and out of the OSI and TCP/IP worlds. A number of manufacturers are adapting to this approach with considerable success. Moreover, it is not contradictory to the spirit of OSI. The TCP/IP standards do not address this issue. Remember, OSI does not care what the system does in its internal operations, nor does it care how the system does it. OSI only stipulates that a given and standardized input into *any* system must produce a predictable and standardized output from that system.

The vendors react to the marketplace

It might prove useful to move back in time and examine what was going on during the embryonic stages of the integration of computers and communications. During the 1970s, several manufacturers realized that they could not afford to continue operating in an unorganized and ill-structured communications environment, *even* within their own product lines. Consequently, they began to develop a more coherent approach to their own products and embarked on efforts to build a structured framework (architecture) for their communications protocols.

The implementation of vendor-specific architectures alleviated the incompatibility problem of products within the vendor's product line, but it did nothing to address the serious problem of incompatibility between the different vendors' computers, terminals, and other equipment. If anything, the development of vendor-specific systems made matters worse, because each manufacturer embarked on a separate course to invent a "better mouse trap."

At this time, several standards groups became active in these issues. The ISO began work in 1979 on the OSI, and the OSI Model was published in 1984 to serve as a standard model for computer communications.

Of course, we have learned that the Internet standards served as pioneers to some of the OSI protocols. Moreover, TCP and IP served as a valuable foundation for launching all the Internet standards. Without question, many dollars have been saved by the U.S. Government and private industry because of the Internet standards.

So what about the future? Does it make sense to maintain both OSI and TCP/IP? Is one better than the other? Should a user care? With these questions in mind, let us examine some of the activities in the computer and communications standards arena and develop some answers.

A Simplified Comparison of the TCP/IP and OSI Stacks

Figure 14.1 shows the relationship of the OSI (more accurately the ITU-T/ISO) stack to the TCP/IP stack. Several organizations and many people have stated that some of the layers shown in Figure 14.1 are functionally equivalent. Numerous reports and articles have been published stating that the transmission control protocol (TCP) and transport protocol class 4 (TP4), as well as the Internet Protocol (IP) and the connectionless network

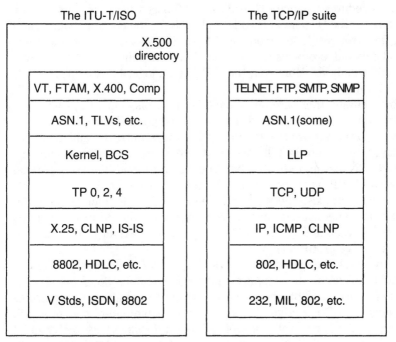

Figure 14.1   Comparison of ITU-T/IS and TCP/IP Suites.

protocol (CLNP), do the same things. It should be stated categorically: the OSI and Internet protocols perform similar functions, but there is definitely not a one-to-one mapping of their services. The following discussion focuses on a comparison of the stacks and a general analysis of mapping the functions of one stack to the other.

The lower two layers of these protocol stacks do not present any serious compatibility problems. Indeed, the top five layers can rest somewhat transparently over the bottom two. Both stacks use existing international standards. For example, at the physical layer, the ubiquitous EIA 232-E standard is used in both stacks, although the OSI stack cites the use of the V-Series Recommendations. EIA 232-E is compatible with its counterparts in the V-series (V.24 and V.28). EIA 232-E also aligns with ISO 2110 for the physical connection.

X.21 or X.21*bis* can also be applied to both stacks at the physical layer. The physical level LAN standards, as published by the IEEE 802 standards, apply to both stacks. No reason exists why the integrated services digital network (ISDN) physical layer cannot be applied to both stacks, and the ISO publishes these standards under the 8802 numbers. The emerging optical fiber standard, fiber distributed data interface (FDDI), can be used with both sets of standards.

The data link layer presents no major problems because most vendors have adapted a version of high-level data link control (HDLC), such as link access procedures balanced (LAPB) in X.25-based networks, link access procedure for the D channel (LAPD) in ISDNs for the control channel, and LAPM for error-correcting modems. The LAN standards use compatible, physical data link protocols with the media access control (MAC) sublayer of the 802 standards. Moreover, the IEEE 802.2 logical link control (LLC) standard works well with both stacks.

To be accurate, there are no actual OSI protocols defined at layers one and two. None of these standards just discussed are OSI protocols.

Mapping problems occur at the upper five layers and especially the upper three layers. As Figure 14.1 illustrates, at layer three the OSI stack contains X.25 and CLNP. Admittedly, the functions of CLNP and IP closely parallel each other. CLMP, however, is more functionally rich than IP.

No correlation exists between X.25 and the TCP/IP stack. X.25 is designed as a connection-oriented network interface. Some of the functions supported in X.25 are carried in TCP and to some extent in the Internet control message protocol (ICMP).

One could ask then why can't we use X.25 as a functional equivalent to TCP and ICMP? First, the mapping would be horrendous. Some of the functions do not map, and others are contradictory to the intent of the protocols. Second, TCP is designed to be a very reliable end-to-end protocol. X.25 is designed to be a reliable protocol, but it does not have the graceful close features of TCP; X.25 gives the network the option of discarding packets in certain situations (reset, restart). Third, ICMP carries a number of diagnostic and status messages, but it does not support the number and type of diagnostic packets that X.25 supports.

So a question arises: what is to be done with X.25 in relation to TCP/IP? The answer is that nothing prevents the network manager from mapping TCP/IP over an X.25 network, as we learned in Chapter 12. Moreover, it is technically feasible to use CLNP in place of IP and place it between TP and X.25. The long-range goal of OSI is to migrate from TCP to TP4. TP4 is overkill for the X.25-based network, and TP2 is a more likely candidate at the transport layer for the X.25/CLNP stack.

TCP/IP does not have any comparable protocols to OSI in the session and presentation layers. Abstract Syntax Notation One (ASN.1) is finding its way into the Internet network management standards (for example, in the simple network management protocol, or SNMP), but it is not used to the extent it is used in OSI. TCP/IP does not have the OSI transfer syntax protocol (shown in Figure 14.1 as TLV, for type, length, and value notation). Nothing precludes a user from employing TLV with the Internet protocols, as long as each end of the communications channel knows how to use it. Some Internet implementations use the external data representation (XDR) protocol, which is quite similar to but incompatible with TLV.

The session layer presents vexing problems. Its services are required by almost all the OSI application-layer protocols. Therefore, it is not easy to bypass if a user is accessing an OSI application layer protocol. TCP/IP does not have a session layer, although several of the TCP/IP application-layer protocols perform session services.

Other mapping problems occur in the applications layer, where the TCP/IP protocol stack is best known for the file transfer protocol (FTP), SMTP, and TELNET. The OSI stack contains very elaborate protocols with file transfer and access management (FTAM), X.400 message handling system (MHS), and the virtual terminal (VT). To say that these map to each other would be a disservice. Certain functions can be mapped on a limited scale, but the TCP/IP application layer protocols simply do not perform the many services of their counterparts in the OSI stack and vice versa.

For example, FTP permits third-party transfers; FTAM does not. On the other hand, FTAM allows considerable manipulation of objects within a file. FTP does not have this level of granularity. FTP permits two logical connections between two FTP clients and control servers: a control connection and a data connection. This concept does not exist in FTAM.

The future OSI environment will rely heavily on the ISO OSI network management standards and the ITU-T X.500 directory services. The Internet has made great progress in this arena with SNMP. Presently, the concept of X.500 does not exist in the TCP/IP suite, although the domain name system (DNS) is an ideal application for placing into an X.500 directory.

IP and CLNP

I have made the point a number of times that CLNP and IP are quite similar. I have also made the point that they are not compatible. Figure 14.2 shows the protocol data units of CLNP and IP; obviously, the formats are quite different.

TP4 and TCP

TCP is similar to many of the ISO/ITU-T transport-layer operations. Many of their support functions, such as port/TSAP multiplexing, end-to-end acknowledgment, and timer operations, are designed to achieve the same goals. The two protocols do, however, differ in many of their features, and in several instances the capabilities in one protocol do not exist in the other. Figure 14.3 compares the formats of the two data units.

TP4 does not use port identifiers. Its identifiers are the destination and source reference fields and transport service access points (TSAPs, located in the variable part of the transport protocol data unit [TPDU]).

Both protocols support the sliding window concepts, TP4 with the credit (CDT) field and TCP with the window field. The variable part field of TP4 can be coded to negotiate many services, such as throughput, delay, etc. This capability does not exist in TCP. The OSI transport protocol is organized around five classes of protocols—each providing a specific set of services. One of these classes is TP4. TCP has no such capability.

ISO CLNP PDU	IP DATAGRAM	
Protocol identifier	Version	Header length
Length indicator	Type of service	
Version/protocol ID extension	Total length	
Lifetime	Identifier	
Segment/more/error report/type code	Flags	Fragment offset
Segment length	Time to live	
Checksum	Protocol	
Destination address length	Header checksum	
Destination address	Source address	
Source address length	Destination address	
Source address	Option and padding	
Data unit identifier	Data	
Segmentation offset		
Total PDU length		
Options		
Data		

Figure 14.2 ISO CLNP PDU and IP Datagram.

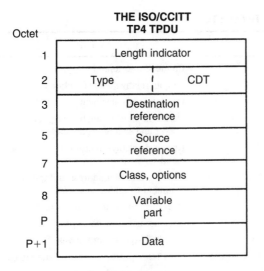

**THE ISO/CCITT
TP4 TPDU**

Octet

1	Length indicator
2	Type ¦ CDT
3	Destination reference
5	Source reference
7	Class, options
8 / P	Variable part
P+1	Data

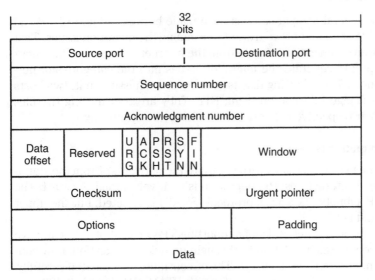

**THE TCP
SEGMENT**

32 bits

Source port ¦ Destination port
Sequence number
Acknowledgment number

Data offset	Reserved	U R G	A C K	P S H	R S T	S Y N	F I N	Window

Checksum	Urgent pointer
Options	Padding
Data	

Figure 14.3 Comparison of TP4 TPDU and TCP TPDU.

A number of articles I have read state that TCP is more efficient than TP4. This finding is not surprising. TP4 provides more services, but function rarely comes without cost. Several options now exist that allow a user to run TP0 and TCP (see Chapter 12). The principal differences between TP4 and TCP are summarized in Table 14.1.

TABLE 14.1 Comparison of TP4 and TCP

TP class 4	TCP
Connection-oriented	Connection-oriented
Complex, with many functions	Simple, relatively few functions
Complex and varied TPDU	One format for segment
Data placed in specific SDUs from upper layer and sent as TPDUs	Data sent on a stream basis from upper layer and sent as segments
Expedited data can arrive out of sequence with earlier data	Urgent data stays in order within the stream and segment
Uses OSI service access point (SAP)	Uses the IP 32-bit address and the port number to achieve a socket
Push function nonexistent	Uses push function to force transfer
Supports multiple classes (0–4)	Does not use class concept
Uses OSI-based service definitions	Uses TCP-specific primitives
Uses TP-specific timers and state diagrams	Uses TCP-specific timers and state diagrams
No graceful close	Supports a graceful close

Migration Issues

Now that a general comparison has been made between IP and CLNP and TCP and TP4, it should prove fruitful to examine the migration issues. That is, how can an organization migrate from the Internet stack to the OSI stack?

It is helpful to separate the migration issues into the categories of network and host. The following discussions cover each issue. In it, two hosts wish to exchange information using FTP. They are transmitting the files through their respective networks and an intervening gateway.

Network migration issues

What are the migration issues with regard to the networks? From the standpoint of layer interactions, the migration is relatively straightforward. The CLNP or IP subnetwork access protocol (SNAP) is affected, but the upper layers should not be.

The effects on the networks of supporting TP4 instead of TCP can have major consequences in relation to throughput, delay, congestion, flow control, timeouts, retransmissions, etc. The effects must be evaluated carefully. Additionally, the replacements of FTP with FTAM, SMTP with X.400, and TELNET with VT will affect traffic conditions within the networks. These effects must also be evaluated carefully.

Host migration issues

Equally important is an assessment of migration issues in the host machines. Resolution between all layers is required because a host runs all internet layers. The only protocols that might not exist in a host are the route discovery protocols, such as the external gateway protocol (EGP) and the open shortest path first (OSPF) protocol.

Migration of Internet to OSI Network Architectures

Whatever one's thoughts are about defense expenditures, it remains a fact that in the computer and communications industry, many standards are established (developed, nurtured, and published) by the U.S. Department of Defense (DOD). Therefore, it is important to follow the activities of the DOD, because its decisions affect the marketplace.

Previous discussions in this book have examined how the DOD-developed TCP, ICMP, and IP are used throughout the world. We have also learned about the need to interconnect separate networks, some using DOD protocols and some using other schemes.

Internetworking DOD and non-DOD architectures

When an OSI or Internet network architecture is employed, a gateway is used to connect the separate networks. Obviously, an internetwork gateway must have the facilities to support each network that attaches to it.

An IP/CLNP gateway has been designed by the DOD to provide the transition between the DOD and the OSI protocol suites at the internetwork level. Basically, this gateway discriminates between the different protocol suites employed during the transition period. When a packet arrives at a gateway interface, a module checks a network-layer protocol identification field and then passes this data unit up to the appropriate internetwork module, either the Internet's IP or OSI's CLNP. Thereafter, when the appropriate internetwork module has received the packet, the standard IP or OSI functions are performed.

The DOD has identified two ways of achieving DOD/OSI interoperability: dual DOD/OSI protocol hosts and DOD/OSI application-layer gateways.

Dual DOD/OSI protocol hosts

This approach is simply a host machine that has complete protocol suites available as part of its capability. For example, the host machine can have a standard vendor-specific or DOD protocol stack, or it can have the pure OSI stack. Indeed, as the movement to OSI progresses, a host machine could have both stacks and select the protocols necessary for a particular configuration. If a machine has only DOD protocols, a file transfer could be achieved by the following:

- using FTP on the originating DOD protocol host machine to transfer to a dual protocol host machine

- using TELNET on the originating machine to remotely log into the dual host

- using FTAM on the dual host machine to transfer the file to the destination OSI protocol host.

With this scenario, a host provides gateway services between two other host machines.

Application-layer gateways

The DOD also intends to develop application-layer gateways that allow the two protocol suites to communicate with each other. Basically, the application-layer gateway acts as a protocol converter by performing a staging or conversion operation. It then invokes a corresponding application process using the other suite. The Defense Communications Agency will provide application-layer gateways for file transfer (FTAM/FTP) and electronic mail (X.400/SMTP) gateways.

Activities of Vendors

A number of vendors have announced or are planning to announce products based on the OSI network and transport layer protocols. Most companies, organizations, and standards groups recognize, however, that it is impossible to migrate immediately from a vendor-specific or mixed stack to a pure OSI stack. Invariably, the movement to OSI will require what are known in the industry as *transition aids*. Essentially, these transition aids act as converters between the different layers in the stacks. It is also recognized that a movement to OSI requires an extended period where different protocols exist and interoperate with each other. This coexistence is usually planned for an extended period of time because of cost considerations of the migration.

Several standards groups, private companies, and government agencies are well into their planning and implementation stages for OSI. Because of the complexity and cost of this transition, some of the organizations have adapted several levels for achieving OSI functionality. For example, the DOD has specified three levels of OSI implementation and functionality: limited, OSI equivalent, and advanced. Most forward-thinking companies are planning a migration strategy based on these ideas.

Limited OSI capability

With this approach, the users in an organization can specify and use OSI protocols in addition to or in place of the protocols attached to their networks. The full OSI Model is not implemented; rather, the most important protocols are acquired or developed.

In most organizations, this immediate use of OSI entails the use of X.25. It also entails the use of standard network service access point (NSAP) address formats. Other products that allow the immediate use of OSI deal with the X.400 message handling system and the National Bureau of Standards phase 1 implementor agreements for FTAM.

Equivalent OSI capability

The second stage of implementation involves a more advanced implementation of OSI. For example, the DOD has established the next phase as bringing phase 2 of the National Bureau of Standards FTAM functions, as well as virtual terminal protocols based on the ISO standards.

Advanced OSI capability

The last stage provides advanced OSI capabilities, entailing the implementation of many of the 1988 Blue Book specifications. The 1988 X.400 recommendation is substantially different from the 1984 recommendation. The final stage would bring the 1988 X.400 recommendation into the DOD protocol suite.

In addition, the ISO X.500 directory services will be part of the advanced phase. The OSI management protocols will also be included here (although they are still in various stages of development). It is also anticipated that the international standards, for security services, will be brought into the last stage.

Activity in the Internet Task Forces

The Internet authorities have been working on the problems discussed in this chapter and have developed a number of proposals, which are summarized in this section.

The Address problem

This section builds on the section titled "Possible Replacements to IP" in Chapter 6, so be familiar with it before reading this section.

How to migrate to a larger network address is one of the more difficult problems. We examined the IP address in Chapter 3. We examine its OSI counterpart here, as shown in Figure 14.4. The OSI address is modeled on the OSI NSAP, which is defined in ISO 8348 and ITU-I X.213, Annex A. A brief explanation of the OSI NSAP follows.

The ISO and ITU-I describe a hierarchical structure for the NSAP address, and the structure for the NSAP address. It consists of four parts:

1. The *initial domain part (IDP)*, which contains the authority format identifier (AFI) and the initial domain identifier (IDI).

2. The *authority format identifier (AFI)*, which contains a one octet field to identify the domain specific part (DSP).

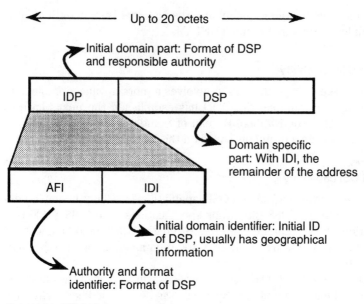

Figure 14.4 OSI Address

3. The *initial domain identifier (IDI)*, which specifies the addressing domain and the network addressing authority for the DSP values. It is interpreted according to the AFI.

4. The *domain specific part (DSP)*, which contains the address determined by the network authority. The contents vary, depending on value of the AFI.

TUBA

The Internet has been examining ways to either enhance IP to accommodate larger addresses or replace IP. Several ideas are under consideration, and one of these is called TUBA, for TCP & UDP with bigger addresses. The approach is fairly simple. The Internet applications and transport layers run on top of CLNP instead of IP. Thus, an internet avails itself of the use of the OSI addressing conventions, yet can still use TCP or UDP at the transport layer and (of more importance) can continue to use the Internet application-layer protocols. Figure 14.5 shows the protocol arrangement for TUBA. The OSI network layer protocols are substituted for the Internet layer protocols: CLNP for IP, and IS-IS for OSPF. Additionally, OSI's ES-IS is substituted for ARP.

It is a reasonable guess that computers (workstations, personal computers, mainframe hosts) will evolve into multiprotocol stack machines, such as those in the router industry, with the ability to support the Internet family, the OSI family, hybrids, and other vendor-specific protocols. Lurking in the background of TUBA is a body of users migrating to some of the OSI upper-layer protocols—especially at the application layer (X.400, X.500, CMIP, etc.). While embryonic, it could mean yet another stack, also depicted in Figure 14.5.

As of this writing, the Internet protocols are much more effective and persuasive than the so-called OSI protocols. It is likely that the two protocol suites will merge. Some people (including myself) believe both TCP/IP and TP4/CLNP are already obsolete and will be dramatically revamped in the near future.

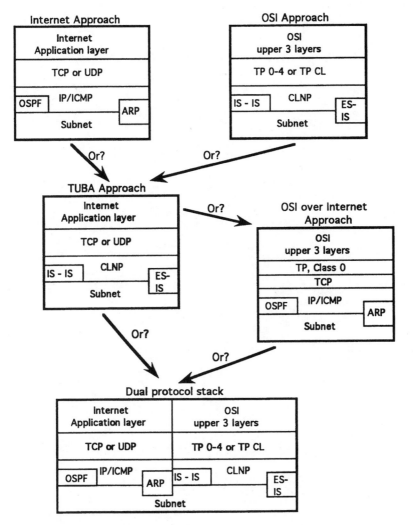

Figure 14.5 Protocol Arrangement for TUBA.

Summary

The TCP/IP and OSI standards are garnering the most support for use as international data communications network standards. They are rich in function, and they offer many options to the user. They are also incompatible. Fortunately, migration and transition strategies are ongoing, and in the future we will see increased use of dual stacks and protocol converters.

Index

Illustrations are in **boldface**.

ABOUT THE AUTHOR

Uyless Black is president of Information Engineering Incorporated, a Virginia-based telecommunications consulting firm. He has designed and programmed many data communications systems and voice and data networks. As a former senior officer for the Federal Reserve, he managed numerous large-scale data communications systems. He has advised many companies, including Bell Labs, AT&T, Bell Northern Research, and BellCore, on the effective use of computer communications technology. He is the author of 14 books and numerous articles, including *The X Series Recommendations*, *The V Series Recommendations*, and *Network Management Standards*, all published by McGraw-Hill. He is also a series advisor for the *McGraw-Hill Series on Computer Communications*.